DATE DUE

ALSO BY THE AUTHORS

Discipline Without Shouting or Spanking

*How to Discipline Your Six-to-Twelve-Year-Old . . .
Without Losing Your Mind*

20 Teachable Virtues

The 8 Seasons *of* Parenthood

THE 8 Seasons *of* Parenthood

HOW THE STAGES OF PARENTING CONSTANTLY RESHAPE OUR ADULT IDENTITIES

Barbara C. Unell and
Jerry L. Wyckoff, Ph.D.

TIMES BOOKS

RANDOM HOUSE

All rights reserved under International and Pan-American Copyright Conventions. Published in the United States by Times Books, a division of Random House, Inc., New York, and simultaneously in Canada by Random House of Canada Limited, Toronto.

Library of Congress Cataloging-in-Publication Data

Unell, Barbara C.
   The 8 seasons of parenthood : how the stages of parenting constantly reshape our adult identities/ Barbara C. Unell and Jerry L. Wyckoff.—1st ed.
       p.   cm.
   Includes bibliographical references and index.
   ISBN 0-8129-3085-1
       1. Parenthood.   2. Parents—Psychology.   3. Parent and child.
4. Parent and adult child.   5. Developmental psychology.   I. Title: Eight seasons of parenthood.   II. Wyckoff, Jerry.   III. Title.

HQ755.8.U55 2000
306.874—dc21
99-048600

Random House website address: www.randomhouse.com

Printed in the United States of America on acid-free paper

98765432

First Edition

To our children—Amy Elizabeth Unell,
Justin Alex Unell, Allison Leigh Wyckoff,
and Christopher Britton Wyckoff

The 8 Seasons of Parenthood

SEASONS OF PARENTHOOD	CHILD'S PRIMARY DEVELOPMENTAL MILESTONES	CHILD'S AGE (approximate)
FIRST CIRCLE: Parenting young children		
CELEBRITY	Pregnancy: Prenatal growth to birth	0 to 9 months gestation
SPONGE	Infancy: From birth up to walking	Birth to about 1 year
FAMILY MANAGER	Toddlerhood/Preschool: From walking through preschool	1 to 5 years
TRAVEL AGENT	Middle years: From elementary school up to puberty	6 to 12 years
VOLCANO DWELLER	Adolescence: From puberty to leaving home	13 to 17 years
SECOND CIRCLE: Parenting adult children		
FAMILY REMODELER	Leaving home to becoming independent	18 to 24+ years
PLATEAU PARENT	Being independent to parenting grandchildren and/or caring for a parent	25 to 49+ years
THIRD CIRCLE: Being parented by children		
REBOUNDER	Caring for a parent/ parenting adults to needing care by our adult children	50+

Acknowledgments

Life's most persistent and urgent question is:
What are you doing for others?
—MARTIN LUTHER KING, JR.

WE ACKNOWLEDGE the following people for their steadfast support during the years of researching and writing this book: To Robert Unell and Millie Wyckoff for their interminable and limitless understanding about sharing their spouses with this literary partner for so many months and months and months. Our appreciation and a deep debt of gratitude is respectfully extended to our two sage and sensitive advisors and mentors, Theresa Park and Elizabeth Rapoport, whose heartfelt passion for this project gently nurtured us through its birthing process, and whose understanding of its significance helped to educate it, refine it, and give it moral guidance and wings to fly. The dutiful attention and illuminating suggestions of Amy Stuber gave us invaluable inspiration, insights, and the world's best truffles, for which we are truly grateful. Through the magical power of our e-mail age, Jane Warren was our confidante extraordinaire, offering daily doses of priceless encouragement. We would be remiss if we didn't express our appreciation to Barbara Stuber for the priceless historical pictures that she is gifted in painting, the re-creation of the lazy, hazy, crazy days of her childhood spent as Barbara's bosom buddy. Members of our personal health and welfare club who deserve a round of applause: Marty Thomas, M.D.; Amie Jew, M.D.; Carol Fabian, M.D.; James Coster, M.D.; Jean Hammond, R.N.; Jennifer Bingham, R.N.; Rose Robertson, R.N.; Aaron Armstrong; Nicole Owen; Donald Julian; Sandy Julian; Bob Vacinek; and Janice Barrett. Finally, it was our good

ix

fortune to have Mary Shaw Branton as the fairy godmother of *The 8 Seasons of Parenthood*. She helped us believe that miracles do happen and watched over us during this project from the time it was only a twinkle in our eyes.

A special thanks goes to Gail Sheehy, who has illuminated the psychological and physical journey of aging with her pioneer work in late adult development.

Opening their hearts to our questions about their experiences as parents and professionals through the different seasons were mothers and fathers in these cities across the country: Los Angeles, Colorado Springs, Saint Louis, Minneapolis, Birmingham, Chicago, Boston, Salt Lake City, Kansas City, Greensboro, New York City, San Francisco, Aptos, Washington, D.C., Naples, and Fort Myers. Those who lent us their time, talents, and tears included Carey Winfrey, Eileen Pearlman, Ph.D., Elaine Macon, Susan Kennedy, David Saferstein, Avis Leader, Bonnie Tilson, Barbara Gordon, Peggy Saferstein, Patti Demoff, Marsha Biel, Ph.D., Debbie Montgomery, Ellen Hamilton, Alice Vollmar, Jon Levine, Lauren Levine, Larry Kaplan, Gail Kaplan, Cindy Wetmore, Donna Zeigenhorn, Susan Kennedy, Larry Brenner, Holly Brenner, Marvin Brenner, Marilyn Brenner, Daniel Brenner, Jack Stuber, M.D., Jean Cerne, Cindy Himmelberg, Daryl Lynch, M.D., Kelly Lynch, Richard Siebs, Ed.D., Vicky Siebs, Jack Hayhow, Paul Silbersher, Nicole Wise, Elaine Nelson, Fran Brozman, Jeannie Sumner, Ken Schifman, Lisa Schifman, Rhonda Swade, Debbie Simon, Lili Shank, Mary Ann Hale, Steve Thomas, Cathy Alpert, Bob Faw, Bob Regnier, Ann Regnier, Sadie Kaufman, Peter Brown, Stephanie Newkirk, Eleanor Hensley, Page Reed, Patty Prater, Kate Katz, Dan Katz, Ann Levine, Bobbie Roth, Shirley Rose, Noreen Bridgham, Steve Hayes, Steve Kirschbaum, Polly Runke, Katie Nelson, Joe Nelson, Jill Nelson, Lynn Kaufman, Andy Kaufman, M.D., Jay Barrish, Ph.D., Adele Hall, Teri Cohn, Steve Cohn, M.D., Bunni Glasberg, Florine Lieberman, Lori Canfield, Andrea Krakow, Caren Nelson, Teresa Christensen, Ethel Takeguchi, Staci Barger, Marcie Steinberg, Terri Engle, Renee Brandenburger, Christine Shouse, Staci Wokutch, Pegeen Barr Blank, Tammy Kennedy, Rachelle Accurso, Pam Linquist, Jana Gates, Suzi Rice, Marque Ann Barton, Elaine Kain, Anita Kingsolver-Ballard, Rebecca Mason, Carol Traul, Nancy Niles-Lusk, Janet Dunklau, Colleen Leh, Jeanne Plowman, Susan Atkins, Bertha Newman, Shirley Seigel, Janet Long, Sharon Eckert, Connie Kiblen Watkins, Margaret Martin, Kay Korte, Freda Unell, Tinka McCray, Jane Havens, Eulalie Zimmer, Ronnie Rosewicz, Mary Felling, Darla Fisher, Jodi Graverson, Kathy Wenstrup, Betsy Montolio, Stephanie Stinson, Lori Johnson, Cathy Foster, Brenda Walden, Debi Combs, Larry Mallin, Beverly Mallin, James Conrad, Charlene Conrad, Kay Schmidt, Fathe DeVries, Penny Hershman, and all those who gave so much to the development of this book, but who preferred to remain anonymous.

A special thank-you to the following individuals who have publicly acknowledged the truth that is the foundation of *The 8 Seasons of Parenthood* through their media interviews in which they related how their children redefine their lives: Robin Williams, Rob Reiner, Tom Hanks, George Lucas, Paul McCartney, Jane Seymour, Madonna, Kirk Douglas, Barbra Streisand, Connie Smith, Anne Lamott, Meryl Streep, Keely Shaye Smith, Rosie O'Donnell, Gillian Anderson, Leeza Gibbons, Jaclyn Smith, Meredith Viera, Deborah Norville, Elle Macpherson, Lisa Kudrow, Catherine Hicks, Sara Ferguson, Ben Stein, Tim McGraw, Faith Hill, Andrea Thompson, Walt Weiss, Meg Ryan, Rene Russo, Randy Quaid, Deborah Pryce, T. Berry Brazelton, M.D., Mel Gibson, Joan Rivers, Steven Spielberg, Cokie Roberts, Jodie Foster, Steve Kroft, Jennifer Louden, Kathie Lee Gifford, Juli Inkster, Phil Mickelson, and the late Benjamin Spock, M.D.

Finally, to the mothers and fathers of the world who, knowingly and unknowingly, contributed to this labor of love by sharing their lives with us.

AUTHORS' NOTE: In creating this book, we've drawn upon dozens of Circles groups and hundreds of personal and group interviews that we've conducted, as well as actual case studies from Dr. Wyckoff's practice as a family therapist. We've tried to capture the widest possible cross section of parental experience. To protect the privacy of the people we interviewed, we have changed the names and defining details of their personal lives, yet have described as accurately as possible their parenthood experiences. We've discovered that their stories are everyone's stories.

Contents

The 8 Seasons *of* Parenthood

Introduction

All the time a person is a child, he is both a child and learning to be a parent. After he becomes a parent, he becomes predominantly a parent reliving his childhood.—BENJAMIN SPOCK, M.D.

"WHAT DO YOU WANT to be when you grow up?" asked your parents' friends and family when you were a child. You may have proudly answered: rock star, professional ball player, fireman, teacher, lawyer, computer programmer. Or, more hesitant to commit, you may have just blurted out, "I don't know." Regardless of your reply, you could be sure of one truth: Your parents watched with hope and apprehension as the child you were matured into adulthood and who you were as a "grown-up" became defined by what you did in life—your job, your career, your vocation.

But during your own childhood, two future grown-ups were actually in the process of being formed—you, "the adult," as well as you, the "parent-to-be." The "parent-to-be" is a silent figure that everyone, even your parents, ignores...until a great miracle happens: Your baby is born.

Because of your child's birth, everything in your life is altered. People even comment on the fact that you no longer seem to be the same person. The truth is, they're right. You aren't the same person. You are now not only committed to being a successful banker, lawyer, teacher, or graphic designer, but also have a new path to walk that directs your decisions in life because you have a new name: parent.

Your work schedule, your next car (one with extra safety features, now), your interest in your spouse, and your relationship with your family and friends, are all set on their ear because you have a new identity. Your choices of where to live, when to work, how much time to spend with friends, how you relate to your parents, how you dress, how much money you save and spend, and what you eat and drink—just to name a few aspects of your life—change according to each season of parenthood you experience. In becoming a parent, you embark on a series of transformations. From the moment your child is born to beyond the season when he or she becomes a parent, the influence of parenthood on you—your choices, your priorities, your fears, your sacrifices—never ends until your life ends.

Yet your story is only part of a larger circle. No other experience in your parents' lives determined their adult developmental path as parenthood did. For them, as for every man and woman who embarks on the journey of parenthood, being a parent becomes, for better or for worse, the single most powerful driving force for the rest of adult life.

The 8 Seasons of Parenthood introduces the revolutionary idea that parenthood is truly not about how we raise our kids. Quite the opposite: Parenthood, this book suggests, is about the impact that our children make on us, an impact that gives definition and meaning to our entire adult life cycle. In fact, it is precisely the stages of our children's lives that *determine* our spiritual, intellectual, emotional, and physical states of being, from the moment of conception on. Many books tell us how we can shape our kids' lives as they move through the defining stages of infancy, "terrible two's," school years, adolescence, and so forth. We're certainly shaping our children's lives, but they are simultaneously re-creating us season by season, in effect causing us to redefine ourselves through this shared experience.

This book probes the life cycles of parenthood—of mom and dad being "born," when our children are conceived and born, being needed, then rejected, and back and forth again. It describes how each of these well-defined, predictable seasons of parenthood produces profound and specific reactions in us, sometimes even triggering identity crises that reverberate throughout diverse aspects of our lives. Work and marital issues, historic grievances with our own parents, friendships, practical living arrangements—all of these and more are affected by the roller coaster of emotions unleashed by that most primordial of experiences—parenthood. In each chapter, this book examines the most common, and most critical, issues that accompany a parent's development at each stage of his or her child's life.

Everyone recognizes that there is a bond of common understanding experienced by parents who are passing through the same seasons of parenthood. With this book we're providing a language to explain why this is so. Once you have a child, you instantly and intuitively recognize the chasm between adults who are parents and adults who are not. We address how deeply connected you as a parent become to the fellowship of parenthood and how parenthood is bonded to the rest of the adult human experience. This is not a "how to" book that gives instructions to alleviate parental concerns (when should my child eat, talk, walk, and so on). Rather it resonates with familiar issues of adult life: morality, family ties, the prioritizing of life goals, and reconciliation with our own parents. It is a work designed to strike a chord in all of us who are parents already, as well as those thinking of becoming parents and those wanting to better understand their parents.

It is our intention that readers will discover themselves in the stories of scores of parents in every season of the parenthood life cycle systematically woven throughout this book. Drawing on hundreds of interviews, which we'll describe shortly, we include a wide variety of perspectives: those of parents who experience parenthood through a single child to those of parents raising a young child and grown children at the same time—and everywhere in between. Their stories are everyone's stories.

Through this combination of narrative and commentary, we've tried to bring an intensely personal, as well as professional, dimension to the key issues of each season of a parent's development. For each season, we use individuals' stories to illustrate what is common knowledge to experienced parents but has never been fully articulated—that the most precious and formative relationship humans have is that of parent to child, child to parent. This book is about the heart of the family experience.

As the stories of parenthood in this book unfold, we offer you a fresh understanding of how parents' growth and change—brought about by their children's growth and change—shape who we are as human beings, as families, and as a society. CBS News correspondent Steve Kroft reflected on this truth in *Father and Son:* "I became a father well into my forties, having no idea how much it would change my life and the way I look at things: my job, my time, my future, even my politics. . . .

"I am amazed at how much he knows even at eighteen months, how much of his personality is already developed, how much he is already a boy. . . . He will lead me off on long walks with the dog, looking for deer and squirrels. We explore a world that changes for him every week in size and wonder. Trying to look at things through his eyes has given me a second childhood."

The intergenerational experiences we share in each of our journeys make up the circles of our soul. You will recognize yourself in these universal stories, realizing ultimately that you are never alone—we are all part of the circle.

THE BIRTH OF THIS BOOK

Child development information answers our questions about what to expect from our children, what forces drive their changes as they develop from infancy through adolescence. But over the past twenty years, other nagging questions haunted the two of us about the life changes *we* experienced as we accompanied our children on their way toward adulthood. We asked ourselves: If we were privy to the twists and turns our children's journey would predictably take, why couldn't there be a "companion guide" for parents that would contain information about what *our* lives would be like as we grew by their side? And what about all of the years after our children were adults? What would parenthood be like then? Children stop being children, but parents never stop being parents!

We wrestled with these questions during every one of our children's stages of childhood. As we journeyed through parenthood, we realized that we were changing, actually passing through stages of development— seasons of parenthood—ourselves, according to where our children were along their development growth chart. At the same time, we were also reliving those stages of our own childhood years. But these changes still seemed to catch us off guard, surprising us with feelings of being unprepared to make the necessary adjustments in order to "let go" of our children's old stage (and ours) to make room for a new stage in their lives (and ours).

Particularly life altering were those points of passage when our children and, therefore, we were moving from one stage of development to another in a momentous period of transition. The shift to the next season of parenthood had a domino effect, precipitating a whole new set of emotional, physical, intellectual, and spiritual adjustments.

Moreover, we learned that the traveling compounds interest as we age. For example, the growth that we experienced during the first season of parenthood, pregnancy (what we call the "Celebrity" season), does not altogether fade into black; we use those lessons during all subsequent seasons. Just as our children accumulate skills as they grow, we grow right alongside them through the seasons of our lives.

THAT FIRST SEASON of parenthood—the Celebrity season—could not have been more riveting for coauthor Barbara Unell. From the momentous day in 1980 when she gave birth to her twins, Justin and Amy, they became the defining miracles of her life. Feeling as if she had been catapulted to another planet as she lay holding one baby under each arm in her hospital bed, she realized that her view of life as she knew it was changed forever.

Knowing that she couldn't possibly be alone in feeling this way, Barbara became inspired, personally and professionally, by the desire to research this transformation, this metamorphosis, that she herself had experienced. Four years later she and her husband, Robert, launched the first national magazine ever created for parents of multiples, *TWINS*, in recognition of the need to help families of multiples (twins, triplets, and more) receive research-based multiple-birth information on a convenient, timely basis. Other educational and supportive publications they created included the monthly city parenting magazine, *Kansas City Parent,* and the syndicated parenting information newspaper page, *Parent Life.* Barbara also wrote the book *Anorexia Nervosa: Finding the Lifeline,* coauthored with Patricia Stein, R.D., in response to the need that she identified for a practical resource to guide families in understanding how to support each other through recovery from this disease.

Barbara has always been a committed activist and spokesperson on numerous issues related to children and caregivers. Because of her desire to motivate children to learn skills of kindness, respect, and compassion within a society that too often glorifies models of violence, Barbara launched the grass-roots, school-based program "Kindness Is Contagious . . . Catch it!" in 1990. Today the program is in place in over four hundred schools in the Kansas City area and in thirty-seven states across the country. In 1999 she also piloted a school-based character education celebration for the Blue Valley Educational Foundation in Overland Park, Kansas, honoring staff and student ambassadors who practice behaviors of virtue to help build their schools and community. Entrepreneurs at heart, in 1999, Barbara and Robert launched the first collaborative work-life program of its kind in the nation by partnering with the Kansas City Chamber of Commerce and Ceridian Performance Partners to offer Chamber members the new benfits program, LifeWorks.

Ultimately it was the heart-wrenching experiences of simultaneously caring for her mother after she suffered a series of debilitating strokes, beginning in 1993, and adjusting to her twins' transition into adolescence that same year that taught Barbara volumes about parenthood being a cycle of "holding on" and "letting go." These lessons were reinforced in her research for this book as she shared her experiences with families of teenagers and aging parents who expressed their need for support while adjusting to the same losses, separations, growth patterns, and spiritual renewals that she had been forced to confront in her own life.

Coauthor Jerry Wyckoff, Ph.D., has been Barbara's good friend, personally and professionally, since their serendipitous first meeting in 1982 at a Mothers of Twins Club workshop in Kansas City. As a child psychologist, Jerry quickly understood that he and Barbara shared a common vision of providing parents with the tools needed to become positive role models as they helped children grow into emotionally healthy individuals. They have teamed up on numerous parent education projects: coauthoring *Discipline Without Shouting or Spanking,* published in 1984; writing the daily radio feature *Kid's Stuff,* hosted by Barbara on the Associated Press Radio Network from 1985 to 1990; and coauthoring two additional books, *How to Discipline Your Six-to-Twelve-Year-Old . . . Without Losing Your Mind,* published in 1991, and *20 Teachable Virtues,* published in 1995.

Jerry credits his first position in 1962 as a psychologist in a state institution for children with severe mental handicaps with helping to shape the direction of the three decades of his career. For seventeen years he was a psychologist in a large suburban school district, where he worked with children with a variety of handicaps and disabilities. His efforts with these children and their families broadened his knowledge and experience in helping parents solve problems with children.

During his tenure with the school district, Jerry became a first-time father, an event that brought the years of experience with other people's children into clear focus. When his son, Christopher, was a toddler and his daughter, Allison, was still an infant, a request to meet with a group of parents of preschoolers to help them with parenting issues gave rise to a support group for parents, an activity that taught participants the problem-solving techniques that are still the core of his practice. The group met from 1972 to 1992, providing weekly access to parenting help for thousands of Kansas City families.

THE FIRST CIRCLES GROUPS

After nearly fifteen years of working together, we became engaged by the discovery that parents who have lived to a ripe old age and have witnessed their children's growth through *their* own old age often have the richest perspective on how children's stages build their parents, season by season, generation by generation. And they loved to talk about it.

So in 1995 we started to listen to them with this focus in mind, conducting interviews individually with these veteran parents whose children were in the sixty to seventy-plus range. These Rebounders, as we've called them in this book, reinforced what we've learned from thousands of discussions with parents of children of different ages over the years: All of the angst and joys that parents experience as they "let go" of their respective children's stages are totally predictable. Rebounders' own development as parents was, and would continue to be, defined by their children's developmental stages, regardless of how old they were. With their children as their compass, parents are bound to visit particular ports, ports that would be familiar to other parents. Those experiences literally determine their adulthood path. Our interviewees confirmed that no matter who we are, once we get on the road with children, our route is inevitable.

This truth was the underlying theme of our research for this book, which included hundreds of conversations and interviews with parents individually from across the country and dozens of discussion groups held between 1995 and 1998 in the greater Kansas City area with parents whose children were in the same developmental stage in each group. Members of these groups, which we dubbed "Circles groups," in recognition of the life cycle of parenting, ranged from those who were pregnant to those whose adult children were now taking care of them.

We recruited our Circles groups through a variety of resources: friends, colleagues, hospitals, day care providers, schools, and nursing homes. Once people knew the focus of the discussion—how children define their parents' lives—they eagerly signed up to participate, often asking if they could bring along friends with children who were in the same developmental stage as theirs. Participants for these two- to four-hour discussions included men and women, single parents, adoptive parents, married couples, stepparents, foster parents, and grandparents. The common denominator in all of their lives: children or grandchildren in the same developmental stage.

As a catalyst for discussion, we asked the group for responses to our prepared questions (see page 305). Soon everyone had plunged into the spirit of the session, some divulging deep and intimate, yet often humorous and touching tales about how their children had changed and were still changing their lives. Typically, not an eye was dry by the end of the discussion in each group.

Even though the emotions their conversations evoked lived deep inside of them, they were never at a loss for words when sharing their most intimate stories about their most important relationships. They needed to share; it helped them make sense of their experiences and see their universality. Whether their children were two or sixty-two, or their own parents were fifty or ninety, or everywhere in between, the parents we interviewed reaffirmed our thesis: Parenthood is a life-changing process that continues for a lifetime. Many of the participants in some Circles groups didn't know each other before meeting. But when they got up to leave, such a bond of common experience had formed that they made plans to meet again.

All loved discovering how the particular season of parenthood they were in related to their, as well as their fellow group members', own childhood. It was as if someone had finally given words to the melody that they had been humming for so long. Like striking oil, out gushed the feelings of the mother of an eight-year-old: the misery she felt when her child missed scoring soccer goals and the pride of seeing him do his schoolwork when she herself—shy and afraid of failing when she was his age—had thought those competitive days of sports and report cards were done for her. She had become eight again as she relived her own childhood through her child.

Out poured the emotions of parents of twenty-year-olds who had never told anyone that they were okay with their children being away at college because of the freedom it allowed them, just as they had loved being twenty themselves, finally free of parental servitude. They prayed to God that their own parents would not need their care just yet. They frankly admitted that they were relishing the comparative down time they were experiencing.

Parents who only had preschoolers held their breath as they heard parents who had both preschoolers and teenagers talk about what life would be like for them in the next seasons of parenthood. They listened intently to just what kind of weather to expect in a few years, concerned, as it turned out, not as much about what their children would be doing, but about what they would be feeling as parents, as adults, while they witnessed their children entering a new phase. The transition years—when their children change from one stage to another—provide the most difficult challenges for parents, everyone agreed. Just when they finally seemed to be adjusting to meeting their child's wants and needs, poof! Everything changes!

The discussions helped parents define their hopes and fears for their own lives and those of their children and parents. Taking those emotions out of their safety deposit boxes was freeing for every participant, as if they had longed for the day to display their intimate, naked, most private thoughts about being parents, about their own childhoods and about their own parents.

IN SOME CASES, the Circles group had led ninety-year-olds to reflect on their children's "senior" adulthood as they lived their own final days. And they told us what they thought and felt about witnessing the circle's completion and how it held the ultimate meaning in their lives. Their generation was ending; new circles of grandchildren and great-grandchildren were moving up to occupy their space. They talked about what their own children's lives were like now and in the past, in a particular stage, compared with what their own lives had been like at that stage.

They also talked about what their parents' experiences were during a particular season of parenthood compared with what they themselves were feeling while in that same season. Finally, they realized, with awe at the gravity of the discoveries, that what they *thought* about their lives, their parents' lives, and their children's lives all contributed to how they *felt* about and responded to the conflicts within themselves that each stage of their children's growth and development evoked. For example, if they had been nervous on their first day of kindergarten or an older child's first day, their memories about that day would influence their thoughts and feelings about their younger child's first day of kindergarten, which would impact how they approached that day, whether or not they took the day off from work and asked their spouse to accompany them to school to ease their separation anxiety.

Participants begged for more stories, asking each other: Why did you feel disappointed when your kids stopped believing in Santa? Why did you hate yourself every day that your child was in middle school? Why did you cry when your seventeen-year-old left home for high school the last day of his senior year? Why do you just want to make your children happy so that your grandchildren will call you?

It seemed as if these questions had been bottled up inside of them, just waiting for the Circles group to free them. They came pouring out as each person saw his own life in a bright new light for the very first time, saw her own growth and development in the reflection of her children's sun.

Suddenly, at a most unpredictable moment, as each group of mothers and fathers whom we interviewed shared their stories, these epiphanies would be reached. "Aha" moments would happen. It was as if everyone in the group would suddenly "get it," get how deeply these feelings about their children, themselves, and their parents are embedded in their souls.

Then the group would bond as if they had known each other since they were all in diapers, had grown up together, and had remained best friends, which in a way they were, because just through the course of their brief time together, they had stripped away all pretense, bared their souls, and dared to open up their minds to a new way of thinking about what made their hearts sing. Sharing with friends and strangers of diverse backgrounds, ages, professional experience, socioeconomic status, and lifestyle helped them to understand how we are all the same inside, each a part of a universal experience that results in membership in one big family.

THE 8 SEASONS OF PARENTHOOD

Understanding the seasons of parenthood requires that you shift your perspective from how you guide your child's growth through his or her developmental stages to how your child influences your movement through the seasons of parenthood. Our challenge was to attach a meaningful label to each season of parenthood that would evoke a positive mental image. Each label we chose was derived from our interviewees' and Circles group members' colorful descriptions of what they generally felt like during that sea-

The 8 Seasons of Parenthood

SEASONS OF PARENTHOOD	CHILD'S PRIMARY DEVELOPMENTAL MILESTONES	CHILD'S AGE (approximate)
FIRST CIRCLE: Parenting young children		
CELEBRITY	Pregnancy: Prenatal growth to birth	0 to 9 months gestation
SPONGE	Infancy: From birth up to walking	Birth to about 1 year
FAMILY MANAGER	Toddlerhood/Preschool: From walking through preschool	1 to 5 years
TRAVEL AGENT	Middle years: From elementary school up to puberty	6 to 12 years
VOLCANO DWELLER	Adolescence: From puberty to leaving home	13 to 17 years
SECOND CIRCLE: Parenting adult children		
FAMILY REMODELER	Leaving home to becoming independent	18 to 24+ years
PLATEAU PARENT	Being independent to parenting grandchildren and/or caring for a parent	25 to 49+ years
THIRD CIRCLE: Being parented by children		
REBOUNDER	Caring for a parent/ parenting adults to needing care by our adult children	50+

son. In some cases, our research participants literally named a season for us; in others, we tested names on them until we found ones that comfortably fit their self-image; their emotional, physical, intellectual, and spiritual state of being; and others' reactions to them during a particular season of parenthood.

The following is an easy reference guide to understanding the definition and underlying meaning of the particular label we've given to each season.

THE 8 SEASONS OF PARENTHOOD DICTIONARY

Ce·leb·ri·ty *n.* **1.** Someone who is admired and emulated by others. **2.** Someone who has achieved a sense of notoriety by virtue of his or her accomplishment: becoming pregnant and preparing to enter the world of parenthood. **3.** The center of attention, with family and friends who dote on her every whim "for the baby's sake." **4.** A self-absorbed, privileged sense of being special. **5.** A sense of notoriety, easily recognized, stands out in a crowd. **6.** Shift from common status to being identified as part of a select group. **7.** Someone who is expected by others to perform in a certain way (in this case, produce a baby or babies). **8.** Someone in a state of feeling ambivalent about life: being exhausted and worried about one's personal well-being, yet being exuberant about one's newfound fame. **9.** A state characterized by a lack of privacy as the public takes an interest in one's every move.

Sponge *n.* **1.** Porous plastics, rubber, cellulose, or other material (in this case, a human being) similar in absorbency to sea sponges and used for bathing, cleaning, and other purposes (in this case, bonding between parent and child). **2.** One who habitually depends on others for one's own nurturing and maintenance (in this case, depending on babies for identity, continuation of celebrity status, and loving responses). **3.** A state of being in which a parent feels expected to be responsible for absorbing the baby's essence or being. **4.** A sense of being wrung out and frequently emptied of absorbed contents by constantly needing to forgo personal needs in order to meet baby's essential needs.

Fam·i·ly Man·ag·er *n.* **1.** One who handles, controls, or directs, especially: **a.** One who directs a business or other enterprise. **b.** One who controls human resources and expenditures, as of a household. **2.** One who is in charge of the affairs of children in the family. **3.** One who is in charge of the training and performance of children within the family. **4.** A state of being in which a parent feels expected to be in charge or in control of young family members' behavior, diet, intellectual stimulation, safety, shelter, social development, physical health, and well-being. **5.** An emotional, physical, intellectual, and spiritual state of being responsible for the welfare of children. **6.** The person others turn to for information, guidance, leadership, and decision making concerning matters of the family.

Trav·el A·gent *n.* **1.** One who acts or has the power or authority to act on behalf of his or her children's social and academic schedule. **2.** One empowered to act for or represent another in home, school, and community who is seen as the family liaison in academic and social settings. **3.** One who plans, organizes, and directs the adventures of children with or without their consent or approval. **4.** A representative or official of the family in the affairs of children in school, home, and community. **5.** The guide and companion on children's journeys through the middle years. **6.** One who is responsible for the successful planning and execution of children's itineraries, resulting in their safe and productive travels through the middle years.

Vol·ca·no Dwell′er *n.* **1.** One who exists in the precarious place or state of being in which adolescent volcanic eruptions (mood swings, rantings, demands, and hormonal surges) are imminent and may occur with little or no warning. **2.** One who fears that adolescent volcanic eruptions will ruin the physical, emotional, intellectual, and spiritual health of parents. **3.** One who lives in a state of being in constant worry, fear, and dread of the potential for teenage volcanic eruptions. **4.** One responsible for the care and maintenance of the adolescent and protection of the community from the teenage volcanic eruptions.

Fam·i·ly Re·mod′el·er *n.* **1.** One who undertakes the making over, restyling, and reconstruction of a family into a downsized group of individuals in a family. **2.** One responsible for making changes in the family structure as dictated by the new adult children's decisions, life changes, and level of independence. **3.** One who lives in the upheaval and chaos of reconstruction of the family structure. **4.** One who needs to adjust to the loss of parenting a child and being apprehensive about the unknown outcome of the remodeling job on the new family structure: parenting an adult. **5.** One who must face the expectations by others of the form and direction of the remodeled family (judgment of college selection, job choice, level of independence). **6.** One who bears the physical strain of remodeling the family based on the adult child's decisions and level of independence.

Pla·teau Par·ent *n.* **1.** One who has reached the level ground between having raised children to adulthood and having to parent his or her own parents. **2.** One who lives in an emotional and physical state of being that allows a panoramic view and new perspective of the first six seasons of parenthood and a first glimpse of the future season as aged parents live through it. **3.** One who harbors the expectation of others that life on the plateau is now level, calm, and serene. **4.** One who has arrived at a sense of having accomplished a steep climb and is able to enjoy the view, given the independence of the adult children. **5.** Through grandparenthood, one who is one step physically and emotionally removed from the responsibilities of raising a new generation as adult children begin their first seasons of parenthood.

Re·bound′er *n.* **1.** Someone who springs or bounces back after hitting or colliding with something (in this case, the last stage of life's health problems, struggle to remain independent, and adjustment to the need for care). **2.** One who must recover on a repeated basis from depression, health problems, or disappointment. **3.** Athlete who retrieves and gains possession of the "ball" as it bounces off the backboard or rim (in this case, one who fights for position to get attention and recognition from adult children, grandchildren, or great-grandchildren). **4.** One who holds the position of waiting for family members to make the caregiving play as part of the family team. **5.** One who expects to be cared for by his or her adult children. **6.** One who lives with the public expectation that one's adult children will make caregiving plays. **7.** Rebounders fall into three categories: *Proud Independents,* who struggle to maintain their initial family position and seek to prove their original playing capabilities; *Humble Submissives,* who take a passive role in which they expect to be included in the family game but don't demand to be on the roster; and *Aged Sages,* who strive to maintain their independent position but ask for help when needed and are grateful for the assist.

EXIT SIGNS

How do parents know when they are leaving one season to enter another? In the chart on page 13, we've listed the child's primary developmental milestones as beginning and ending points for each season to help reinforce the underlying premise of this book: children's developmental stages define their parents' seasons of parenthood. When children pass from one developmental stage to another, so do their parents. It is a gradual process for both generations, one that occurs according to each child's developmental progress.

We have noted the child's approximate age when referring to a developmental season of parenthood. Of course, some children take longer to pass through a developmental stage than others; some move ahead to the next stage before their peers, agewise. In either case, parental development will follow suit.

For example, when children move from being horizontal, squirming infants to being upright and mobile toddlers, their parents are likewise transformed from Sponges into Family Managers who are faced with conflicts over making deals with their little ones, figuring out who's in charge of whom, and evaluating just exactly what it means to be a good parent. If their toddlers weren't naturally curious to explore their world, their parents wouldn't need to face conflicts over keeping them safe and protected during this early developmental stage. The end of the Family Manager season, just like every season, is marked by children's growth. By virtue of the fact that their kids have entered elementary school, parents face new conflicts and new opportunities for their own growth as they keep up with the changing itineraries of their offspring, thereby becoming Travel Agents.

Knowing this fact of parenthood establishes two truths: First, parenthood is a predictable journey through adulthood; and second, parents can anticipate the impact that their children's growth and development will have on them. By being able to understand the normal conflicts with which all the paths of parenthood are paved, parents can prepare themselves for the sharp curves, dangerous dips, and indescribable glee created by the emotional roller-coaster ride that is parenthood.

SEASON BY SEASON, GENERATION BY GENERATION

This comprehensive, season-by-season guidebook was born to reassure you that what you are feeling and thinking during each season of parenthood is a normal reaction to your child's normal development, although with parents, just like with children, a wide range of what is considered normal exists. After reading about a season of parenthood, if you question whether you or your child needs help in coping with a transition in childhood or parenthood, consult a health-care professional (doctor, psychiatrist, psychologist, social worker, or other mental health professional). No one "right" way to think and feel exists; we have provided examples of what to expect, universally, throughout the seasons of parenthood, using empathy and understanding about the wide range that can be considered healthy parent and child development. This is a book not on parenting styles, but on predictable parenthood passages; your path is universal, your style is your own.

Therefore we suggest that you turn first to the seasons that refer to the developmental milestones of each of your children (see page 13) and reflect on your own life now or what your parents' lives were like when you were in the process of reaching those milestones yourself. You will learn about your parents' current season of parenthood in another way by reading the season that discusses parents of children who are going through your present passage of adulthood. Then read ahead to see what your life will be like when your children are older. Read about the seasons that relate to children younger than yours to experience a paradigm shift about the past, the seasons you have already experienced. Of course, you can follow the path of parenthood from beginning to end as well, by reading this book cover to cover.

ISSUES OF AGENDA, identity, change, separation, and control are the sources of the emotional turmoil that each parent faces in each season of parenthood. We've picked them from the bone, piece by piece, by offering current psychological research threaded throughout anecdotal reports from parents in the trenches. The roots of these conflicts lie in our own childhood and earlier adulthood experiences conjured up now by witnessing our children grow.

We find an ironic sense of comfort in the familiarity of these conflicts in the stages of child development that we have literally lived through. We've wrestled with them in our own growing-up years, just as our children are doing now and our parents did before us. And so it goes . . . generation to generation. With this book we can now face and understand them as normal, universal underpinnings of human existence.

Ultimately understanding the cyclical nature of these seasons of parenthood doesn't mean we're condemned to repeat the past. In fact, it helps us rewrite the parts of our family history we don't want to pass on from generation to generation. For example, if at age six Sally felt abused and labeled as the cause of all her parents' arguments, it is likely that when her son, Alex, reaches the same age, her reactions to Alex's behavior will be colored by her own childhood experiences. So to protect him from the pain she suffered, when she and her husband argue, Sally will try to make sure that he is never within earshot. By gaining some insights into the nature of why she reacts so strongly to the issue of marital fights, Sally can also watch to make sure she doesn't overreact, shielding Alex from any and all conflict.

As we describe each season of parenthood in depth and how the experiences in each season impact parents, we demonstrate how parents' reactions to their child's normal developmental changes can turn potentially negative experiences into positive growth adventures for themselves. Children's developmental changes create many different kinds of conflicts, as we'll describe here. How frequently parents experience these conflicts as their children pass through a particular developmental stage—and what parents *think* about these conflicts—can enhance or detract from their relationships within the family, build or destroy their self-esteem, and disturb or calm their very souls.

LIVING IN MULTIPLE SEASONS

Using the chart on page 13, consider what life is like if you're simultaneously in multiple seasons because your children are in different stages of their development. As you find the developmental stage of each of your children, according to his or her developmental milestone, understand that you will be simultaneously adapting to all of the changes your children experience. Therefore if you have a four-year-old and a ten-year-old, for example, you will be addressing issues in your life in both the Family Manager and Travel Agent seasons, making your emotional turmoil greater because of your need to juggle multiple roles, shift your attention to adjust to multiple conflicts, solve multiple problems, and meet multiple expectations. Doing so can make you feel as though you are in the middle of chaos . . . for what could be the rest of your life, if you are not on friendly terms with adapting to change and being flexible.

In the stories in this book, we focus on parenthood in one particular season at a time, even if you have children in different stages and, therefore, are in multiple seasons of parenthood yourselves. We do this purposefully: we want you to understand how each stage individually impacts every aspect of your life. You cannot separate your children's developmental needs from your life. They are inevitably considered in every decision you make.

As each story in this book illustrates, parents are drawn to the child with the greatest need at the moment, which pushes parents into the "season du jour" as they struggle to resolve conflicts inside themselves that are created by their "most needy" child. At the core of sibling rivalry is the attempt to grab the most parental attention possible, thereby pulling parents away from competing siblings. The more flexibility parents are able to muster as they shift from season to season, the better they will be at meeting their children's needs as well as their own.

If you're in the Travel Agent season, for example, and you have only the one elementary school-age child (or two, three, or four, in cases of twins, triplets, or quadruplets), being a Travel Agent becomes easier, if not easy, as you adjust to being the one who arranges the itinerary and keeps the schedule on track of your middle-years child. But if you also have a thirteen-year-old, you will also be impacted by the chaos of life as a Volcano Dweller. So you will become a master juggler, holding one child's stage in one hand, then letting go only to catch another child's stage in that same hand, constantly shifting from one season to the next.

BEEN THERE, DONE THAT

Parents who have more than one child may believe that if they are veterans of a certain season, they shouldn't have to experience the conflicts of that season with their second and third children. In fact, they'll experience these same developmentally triggered conflicts with each child, regardless of how many children they have. For example, if their son is now ten years old, and their daughter is now four years old, they will find themselves reliving the conflicts of the Family Manager season with their four-year-old, even though they passed through that season when their ten-year-old was four. Although their four- and ten-year-old may have different personalities and temperaments and be of a different sex, for example, each child will still define his or her parents' lives by making the same trip through each stage of childhood, a fact of life that resonated in all of our interviews.

Again, we advise that it may get easier for parents to pass through each season of parenthood after one, two, or more trips, but it will still not be easy. Parents' prior experiences with each season will give them only the ability to anticipate the impact that the conflicts in each season will have on them and potentially the confidence to believe that since they have "survived" them once, they will be able to do so again. Their personality and temperament, plus their childhood history, play additional roles in how they'll cope with the conflicts.

The potential problems in being a veteran of a certain season are threefold: First, it colors a parent's attitude about that season. You may decide, for example, that you loved or hated that particular time in your life, a decision that is influenced by your personality and temperament as much as by the behavior of your older child or children. Second, being experienced brings about a natural tendency to compare how easy or difficult it was to go through that season with child number one, for example, compared with living through that same season with a second or third child. You may feel frustrated if your expectations gleaned from prior experience aren't fulfilled. Finally, you are forced to live through your own childhood experiences once more as you witness each of your children passing through a particular developmental stage. This can be nostalgic, comforting, or upsetting.

For example, Monica, a parent of a six- and two-year-old, may believe that her two-year-old's tantrums in a grocery store will not create a crisis for her as they did when her six-year-old was two because she's "been there, done that" and should know how to prevent it from happening. However, she is best advised to anticipate that tantrums will still create a conflict in her life (see "Who's in Charge," page 96) during the Family Manager season because that's how two-year-olds express their need to control their world. Monica is guided in her reaction to this conflict by her own childhood history and comfort level with expressing anger, her prior experience with her older child, and her own personality and temperament, which influence her ability to cope with the emotional effects of her child's tantrums on her.

The important message that all parents need to receive is that the conflicts of each season of parenthood are unavoidable: how many children you have simply determines how many times you'll experience them. What you can control is what you think and do in response to each conflict. Whether you're a biological parent, adoptive parent, stepparent, or foster parent, keep in mind that your child will travel through his or her developmental stages in the same way regardless of how many parents may be in his or her life as a result of divorce, remarriage, or death.

For example, when her stepson, Joshua, enters puberty, Virginia, a mother of a twenty-year-old biological child, Sarah, will experience the same return of the "nightmare" of adolescents' mood swings and demands during her own life in the Volcano Dweller season because of the hormonal, neurological, physical, and emotional changes of adolescence, just as she did when Sarah entered puberty. As a biological mother and stepmother in this blended family, Virginia will not only relive her own childhood adolescent "nightmare," she will also bring her personality and temperament to the upheaval a teenager creates in the family.

In cases in which parents are raising their own biological children with second spouses after raising children from first marriages, the same ingredients—parental personality and temperament, attitude, childhood experience, and historical comparisons of life in a particular parenthood season—are used in varying proportions in the recipe for how well parents cope during each repeated season of parenthood. For example, if Mary and John both have children in their twenties from their respective first marriages and Mary gives birth to their twins, Mary and John will be forced to cope with the impact their new babies will make on their marriage, their individual identity, and new, yet familiar, sense of responsibility inherent in the Sponge season of parenthood, just as they did with their now adult children.

When parents enter the Rebounder season, it is *not* their interaction with their older children that is most often the primary influence on their thoughts and feelings. Instead it is their memories of their own parents' treatment of their grandparents. For example, when Rachael was growing up, she watched her mother's loving reaction to her grandma when she called or visited; and when her grandma was ill, Rachael's mom was always there for Grandma. That experience with her grandmother played a role in how Rachael treated her own mother when she became her mother's caretaker. Moreover, her mother's example and her own life experiences contributed to her expectations of and reaction to how her children treated her when she needed care. And so it goes . . . generation after generation.

SPECIAL CASES: GETTING STAGE-STUCK

Parents who have children who are developmentally delayed, to the extent that they cannot become independent enough to live on their own, may find themselves stuck in one season of parenthood for an extended period of time or for the remainder of their lives. A parent who has a child with Down's syndrome or a child with a pervasive developmental disorder, for example, may spend many years as a Sponge before becoming a Family Manager and finally a Travel Agent.

For parents of some special-needs kids, the Travel Agent season may be their final season of parenthood because they must orchestrate their children's lives throughout their own lives. As is true with all children, the child's stage of emotional and mental development determines his or her parent's growth through parenthood. Although developmentally delayed children physically grow into adults, their mental and emotional delays make their parents' progression through parenthood unique from that of parents whose children are not delayed. Parents of special-needs children often become advocates for others with the same needs, and their involvement with parents who are also "stage-stuck" helps define their lives.

Whether the problem is one of mental health (such as depression, schizophrenia, or attention deficit hyperactivity disorder) or physical health (such as cancer, cystic fibrosis, or muscular dystrophy), the key issue is whether or not the child will eventually be able to achieve some degree of independence. Children whose problems are generally treatable through appropriate medical or psychological interventions are capable of passing relatively normally through the developmental stages to adulthood. Thus, in most cases, parents of these children do not become "stage-stuck."

In actuality, many parents with special-needs children, including those who are developmentally delayed as well as those with physical or mental health problems, find themselves living in different seasons with the same child at the same time. For example, Betsy is the forty-something mother of a twenty-three-year-old son with Down's syndrome, Dan, who resides in an independent living center and works in a sheltered workshop. Because his is a mostly independent life, she is experiencing the Family Remodeler season, although she still needs to guide him in much of his daily affairs, keeping her in the Travel Agent season as well.

GOOD NEWS/BAD NEWS: GOING BACKWARD

Some parents may find themselves regressing to a previous season of parenthood as their child regresses to an earlier stage. For example, if an eighteen-year-old goes off to college and finds the experience of being on his own and having to adjust to campus life too much to handle, he may come home and become "volcano-like," forcing his parents to move back to the Volcano Dweller season, as one of our stories in Season Six illustrates. Parents generally find their child's return home a good news/bad news event, if they enjoy having the empty nest filled again. They may also begin to resent the need to deal with Volcano Dweller issues after having worked hard to adjust to being a Family Remodeler.

More good news/bad news: Parents of adult children who divorce and move back home face the same dilemma, as they find themselves having to adjust to a "change in seasons" and move from being a Plateau Parent to being a Family Remodeler again. Parents' responses to their offspring's development can encourage or stifle both generations' growth. As discussed earlier, parents who enable their adult children to return to the nest may inadvertently encourage their children's financial dependence on them, thereby forcing them to experience all of the challenges of the previous season of parenthood once more. On the other hand, parents who—with love and with the best interest of their children in mind—help their adult children adjust to being independent and encourage them to continue their developmental progress also allow *themselves* to continue to reach their own parenthood milestones.

AND THIS TOO SHALL PASS

Adapting to constant change is stressful and creates problems for us if we focus simply on the need to adapt. By taking the long view, the daily, moment-by-moment conflicts we have to face become less intrusive. Regardless of what season of parenthood we're in, we know that "this too shall pass." The great paradox of parenthood is that of life itself: just as we swear that the "moment" will last forever—our child will go to college in diapers—he's potty trained, and the "moment" we thought would never end is history.

Our research has taught us that keeping the long view in mind as we appreciate each day of parenthood helps the seasons of parenthood pass in peace. Our relationships, just like life itself, are not static; yet we spend much of our lives demanding that things stay the same. But parenthood teaches us the necessity of flexibility, the importance of resignation of control.

As you read about each season of parenthood, ask yourself: What kind of relationships do I want with my family? How would I like *my* first, current, next, and last chapter of parenthood to be written? How do I make today special, knowing it will be gone tomorrow? What ending do I want for my book of life? What legacy do I want to leave? What do I want my children to tell their children about me?

We hope this book will help you think about parenthood as a series of beginnings and endings, the seasons of your life. The most exciting and most difficult beginnings and endings we must face along the parenthood trail are birth and death, which represent the beginning and end of a lifeline that bends to form a complete circle. Understanding the starting point of the journey of our lives, our final destination, and the adventures in between helps us better understand our life's odyssey and brings grace and gratitude to today.

Parenting Young Children

Celebrity

CHILD'S CONCEPTION TO BIRTH

If you want a place in the sun, you've got to put up with a few blisters.—ABIGAIL VAN BUREN

NO RIVETING FICTION, brilliant screenplay, or lavish Hollywood production has ever created a story line as wild and crazy as the way human beings come into the world. We thought this the first time we heard about the facts of life from those who were eager to pass them on to the uninitiated. We think it is even more breathtakingly clever having experienced this drama firsthand.

When you tell people that you're going to have a baby, you are essentially telling people that your life is about to change. And you are right. Being a parent is the only experience that totally changes your life: your self-image, others' perception of you, your identity in your family. Never again will your own agenda be your absolute, automatic top priority; that becomes evident for the mother, physically, early in the game, as her body is hijacked for the fetus's needs. You start thinking in terms of bedroom sizes, numbers of bathrooms, car seat measurements, bumper pads, changing tables, and work schedules to fit the Baby into your family. Once the authorities have confirmed that your baby is inside and growing, your own hopes and dreams will forevermore be defined by those hopes and dreams you have for someone else—the Baby.

That in itself signals a spiritual, not just physical, change, according to those we interviewed. Before these women became pregnant, their careers, spouses, and friends determined the routines and priorities of their lives. After a few months of pregnancy, however, they became more spiritual and introspective. The trivialities and perhaps selfish preoccupations dropped away, and all that mattered was having a healthy baby.

What they thought about this state of affairs determined their attitude during this first season of parenthood. Director/actress Jodie Foster said it best: "I know everybody's been through pregnancy, but it's still a big deal." Why, exactly, is it a "big deal"? In her book *Operating Instructions*, Anne Lamott pinpoints one answer that she discovered late in her own pregnancy: "I woke up with a start at four one morning and realized that I was very, very pregnant. What tipped me off was that, lying on my side and needing to turn over, I found myself unable to move. My first thought was that I had had a stroke."

Lamott dryly illustrates the steep physical cost of pregnancy for the mother-to-be, for whom the experience of being pregnant mirrors that of being a celebrity. The changes that a pregnant woman's body undergoes, in what we've dubbed the Celebrity season, transform her into a popular public figure—a pregnant woman. To onlookers, she's the rosy, blooming symbol of fertility. Invisible to her adoring fans are the back pain, morning sickness, hemorrhoids, elevated blood pressure, anemia, nosebleeds, frequent urination, leg cramps, toxemia, swollen ankles, shortness of breath, and, eventually, stretch marks. Feelings of self-doubt and worry are also natural and normal, particularly as more people start to "notice" and the mom-to-be starts "showing."

The larger she gets, the more public her life in the Celebrity season, as friends and strangers alike press advice and predictions of gender on her, as well as on the father of her baby. Fathers-to-be find themselves in the position of being their Celebrities' Roadies, much like rock band roadies, who are devoted to ensuring that everything goes well for the main act. Most Roadies can bask in the limelight of the mothers-to-be, the Celebrities. Some fathers-to-be, however, may come to resent the Celebrity because of their feelings of invisibility or helplessness as they peer in from the outside of the pregnancy and know that their role now is a very minor one compared with that of the mother-to-be.

The Celebrity's pregnancy has enabled her to achieve a sense of notoriety the Roadie shares to a lesser degree. But his identity as a father-to-be Roadie is evident only in the presence of the Celebrity, because he doesn't share the physical markers that set her apart and give her special status as an important public figure. She is the center of attention; family, friends, and her Roadie dote on her every whim "for the Baby's sake." Again, depending on the relationship between the parents-to-be, fathers-to-be are only bit players who can share the stage but are consigned to supporting the main act.

With all of this star treatment, most Celebrities become self-absorbed and feel privileged because of their special status. During the first three months of this season, however, many women also often feel ambivalent about being Celebrities. The glamour of their new fame is overshadowed by their exhaustion and worry about their own personal well-being. Yet the excitement that they see in the adoring eyes of family and friends who are so "happy for them" becomes contagious as they begin to "show," sometime in the fourth month.

We talked with pregnant women who groaned loudly about the dues they had to pay but were true troopers during this season's war against hormonal changes that sapped their energy and directed it toward great desires for ice-cream cones and bologna sandwiches. When their waistlines started expanding, between four and five months into this season, so did their negative attitudes about the battle for control over their lives.

"Did someone say 'control'?" asked one of our Circles groups members, a mother of a two-year-old in her ninth month of pregnancy with her second child. "Being pregnant clues you in on the dirty little secret of parenthood: You are controlled by this new life . . . not the other way around. I had to think of what effect everything I ate would have on the baby. If it was good for the baby, I ate it even if I didn't like it. I slept on a particular side because the baby kicked less. And when I started bleeding in my eighth month, I had to quit my job . . . not to mention go straight to bed so that I could do everything possible to protect my baby's life. It's unbelievable how I could be so full of joy and so full of fear in the same breath."

THIS FEAR DURING the last two trimesters of pregnancy stems from the subconscious awareness of a mother-to-be that she is on the brink of entering another time zone, one in which the Baby controls the clock. In the early weeks after confirming her pregnancy, however, she can be aware that she is pregnant with the same nonchalance and lack of surprise with which she goes around being aware that she has teeth, to paraphrase an unforgettable description of the first trimester by Lamott.

After she tells people the Big News, her life and that of her Roadie will never again be entirely their own private business. Then the fan mail from diaper companies, insurance brokers, and hospital marketing departments starts pouring in. The Celebrity has made it big. She's a popular draw. Friends, neighbors, relatives, and co-workers begin to bond emotionally with the Baby, as they all want to share the excitement of the upcoming arrival. It's an Event to be awaited, marked on the calendar. Then mothers-to-be, in particular, can kiss good-bye any privacy they ever thought they needed to have, any shred of personal dignity.

"I found myself in positions, compromising at best, during doctor visits each month with cold instruments poking and prodding at my private parts like I was truly a biology class specimen to be dissected," related one exasperated mother-to-be in her sixth month. "It was humiliating until I just gave up fighting it. I couldn't believe that I was allowing my shy, little-girl side to disappear because I wanted my baby to be okay. When I had to have a cervical clamp inserted because of complications, I couldn't wait for the day. I was scared to death, of course, but I was walking around worried about everything all the time already. Amniocentesis was the most frightening of all the tests. But I stepped up to the table like I was going to get an Olympic medal. It was bizarre how little my being a modest person mattered. All that mattered was taking care of my baby."

As pregnancy changes women's standards of modesty, it also changes their relationship with their bodies in another way. In our interviews, many reported feeling a peculiar mix of helplessness and freedom from watching their bellies grow. The helplessness stemmed from the basic knowledge that this was the way life would be for several months; there was no way to avoid it. Having the freedom to gain weight seemed like being released from diet prison.

"My losing control over what I looked like had to be reframed," said Arlene, a psychologist in one of our Circles groups. "Instead of looking at myself as 'fat,' I had to go with 'healthy.' It wasn't easy because none of my friends had been pregnant before. It was bizarre to think that I was free to gain a whole bunch of weight when I had struggled to lose weight all my life, it seemed. Even my mother kept asking me how much I'd gained, not lost, which was a big switch for her. Then I had to hear about how hard it was for her to lose all the pounds she had put on after having my brothers and me. That made me feel more like a true mother than almost anything else. I could suddenly see myself looking round and motherly as my mom for the rest of my life."

Adding this new identity of "parent" to those of "child" and "adult" causes Celebrities and Roadies to change their relationship with their own parents, as Arlene discovered. Pregnancy automatically enrolled her as a member of her parents' exclusive club. They began to treat her differently because she wasn't an outsider anymore.

Those we interviewed who still thought of themselves as someone's daughter or son, not yet mother or father, reported feeling "weird" about becoming a part of the legion of all parents. It was a change that caught them by surprise, this feeling of not knowing exactly who they were, a child or a parent. They saw their parents with new "parent eyes" and could appreciate for the first time the miracle and sacrifice of bringing life into the world that their parents had experienced. Yet they still felt like children, their parents' children.

WHO AM I?

Of all that is wonderful in the human being, our most glorious asset is this capacity to change ourselves.
—EKNATH EASWARAN

"Me? The mom?" Rachel, six months pregnant, exclaimed. "No way!" She explained that now that she was pregnant with their first child, it felt as though she and her husband were playing house, that this "whole baby thing" reminded her of playing with dolls, when someone would be the mom and someone else would be the dad and they would shop for all the stuff they needed. How absolutely odd it now seemed to be playing out this childhood fantasy in real life, so much so that it didn't feel right to her to be called "Mom" in front of her own mom, Leah.

Actually, Leah only made matters worse. When someone would comment on the baby's upcoming arrival, Leah would shake her head in amazement, saying, "I can't believe that *we* are having this baby! It's going to be so much fun! I can't wait to be a grandmother." It was the "we" business that was making it more difficult for Rachel to differentiate between herself, "the mother," and Leah, "the mother."

Some parents reported that the emotional roller coaster of changing their identity during pregnancy changed the balance of power in their relationships with their own parents, as in Rachel's case. For others, it set into motion new conflicts over who was controlling their lives, their baby or themselves.

"As a mother, I must take my prenatal vitamins," Nora said. "But I hate to take pills. It's so hard for me to swallow them." No matter what ailed her, Nora had always regarded "popping a pill" as a dead-last resort. Nora said that she actually wondered, Who am I—the mother who does whatever the baby-to-be needs or the girl who doesn't like to take medicine?

Of course, Nora is both. What she was really having problems swallowing was being "forced" by her baby to take pills when her agenda had always been to refuse them. Her baby's agenda, however, needed to win this battle. "Welcome to the new world, huh?" she told us. Nora wasn't in charge anymore.

Basic to this new world is the fact that the self-absorption of our entire lives to date—our childhood, our adolescence, and our early adulthood being one long exercise in developing and nurturing "me"—gives way to a new kind of thinking about the priorities in our lives when we enter this first stage of parenthood. This transformation signals the beginning of the end of youthful narcissism as we move toward a life devoted to caring about the welfare of another person. The Baby now emotionally, spiritually, and behaviorally drives mothers' and fathers' change in identity.

Research has demonstrated that Nora's identity shift to "mother" is primarily a function of the biological hard wiring of human beings. Once these biological and hormonal influences shift after the baby's birth, the social and emotional pull becomes a more psychological process for the baby's mother, as it does for the baby's father.

As Roadies for their Celebrity wives, fathers must continually work at developing and maintaining an emotional, intellectual, and physical connection to being a parent in this season in which their experience is so different from that of the mothers of their children. Generally speaking, this takes more effort for fathers to achieve than it does for mothers-to-be, since fathers-to-be are forever nine months behind in making this early physical connection.

THESE SPIRITUAL, PSYCHOLOGICAL, and behavioral changes in identity have been a part of parenthood since time immemorial. Over the past several decades, however, cultural changes have sent parents mixed messages about this transformation from "me" to parent, thereby creating deep-seated emotional conflict within them. In the workplace this can be particularly harrowing. For example, Chris, a dad-to-be whose wife was six months pregnant, worried that he would get fired from his retail sales job because he had to tell his boss that he couldn't come in on Saturdays for the next three months because that was when his childbirth education classes were held. Another parent, Rhoda, chose to quit her job as a magazine editor two months before her maternity leave was scheduled to start in order to follow her doctor's orders to go on bed rest to prevent her baby from being born prematurely, despite her best friend's protest that she was ruining her career as a journalist. Each of these parents risked hurting themselves professionally by prioritizing their identity as a mom or dad over their career.

Today, on the other hand, some large corporations advocate policies that acknowledge and respect the fact that, beginning with the Celebrity season, parenthood changes employees' priorities, multiplies their identities. This agenda sends a positive message to employees to nurture, not ignore, who they are: mothers and fathers *and* daughters and sons *and* wives and husbands who hold jobs as lawyers, bankers, salespeople, and nurses.

Before 1950, many women who were pregnant were publicly discriminated against, particularly in the teaching profession. Today, mothers-to-be can legally be classroom leaders up to the day their water breaks! Laws that provide protection for women, so that they don't have to choose between being mothers and having careers, reflect tireless and still ongoing efforts by women and men to change society's perspective on how highly the identity of a mother is valued by employers, our families, and ourselves.

Even though societal attitudes about pregnancy have changed, in some cases, those public perceptions don't alter the basic fact that for a woman who is pregnant, the spiritual and emotional changes in identity she experiences in this season are far more dramatic than at any other season and far more profound, on average, than the changes her male partner experiences. Mothers we interviewed were deeply conflicted about working outside the home, losing their svelte figure, and wanting their childhood fairy tales of motherhood to come true. Acknowledging the immense differences between the sexes in identity transformation during this season helps couples understand how much emotional and spiritual work is involved for women and for their Roadies, the men who love them, in adjusting to the changes that the Celebrity season of parenthood makes in their lives.

In the case of adoption, however, the biological element is, of course, missing. Therefore, mother and father both begin parenthood on equal ground, physically, intellectually, emotionally, and spiritually. Instead of feeling like a Celebrity and her Roadie, they may be emotionally, if not also financially, drained by the search for parenthood but grateful that their quest has come to a happy conclusion. The limelight period of Celebritydom is relatively short—perhaps not much longer than a baby shower.

HELP! I'M HAVING A BABY!

Nothing in life is to be feared. It is only to be understood.
—MARIE CURIE

Veteran parents in our Circles groups agreed: Being a Celebrity is hardest of all on women who are control freaks and introverts. Our interviews revealed that both groups had the toughest time adjusting to the changes in their lives. To maintain a sense of stable identity as they felt the ground shifting beneath them, these Celebrities struggled to figure out how to bring control back to their now public lives.

They wanted more than anything, needed more than anything, to clutch tightly to their sense that they had choices, that they could control where their lives were headed, regain their privacy, and take the Baby along their path, not the other way around. Eventually, they all discovered in the Celebrity season that they couldn't control the forces of nature; they had to surrender and ride their wave of fame no matter how turbulent.

Maggie, who was pregnant with her second child, experienced this firsthand during her last trimester: she knew she should be happy about this new baby, yet the emotional costs were life altering. She'd worked so hard to get life "back under control" after her first child was born. Now she had to do it all over again! She resented the fact that she was "stuck." She wanted to get back to her "real life," regain her energy and normal weight. What she wasn't admitting was that her life as she knew it would never be the same as it had once been, because of baby number two.

We echoed the advice to her that we gave all of the parents-to-be we interviewed: Pregnancy is the best time to understand and accept that the only control button you get to push in parenthood is the one that controls what *you* think and feel about the Baby and how you respond to your thoughts and feelings about adjusting to changing relationships, worrying about the Baby, and wanting to be in control of your life. These feelings are natural and normal; everyone experiences them in differing degrees. Thinking about pregnancy as a process, not a crisis, in which you learn how to make choices as the Baby grows, helps you bask in the limelight of the Celebrity season, despite the cost.

Being a Celebrity is an emotional roller-coaster ride no matter how many times you go through it. If this is the second, third, fourth baby, or more, the sentimental journey of this season takes on the rhythm of someone fitting a big Tupperware container into an already crowded fridge. You're more confident; you know that it will fit; it's just going to take some creativity to make it work. Issues of control (controlling yourself, your body, your baby, your other children, your relationships) are so powerful, however, that rearranging the contents of your life creates inner turmoil.

RESEARCHERS HAVE LONG BEEN addressing the distinct differences in how these issues around change and control affect fathers and mothers differently. Women, by the very nature of the biology of pregnancy, are intimately involved with the baby-to-be, writes Therese Benedek in *Parenthood, Its Psychology and Psychobiology*. They can, she suggests, "override the biological process if they focus only on themselves and their needs rather than respond to the signals from the new person growing inside them."

In some of our interviews, mothers-to-be told us that they had waited their whole lives, it seemed, for this miracle; they almost immediately became devoted solely to the Baby from the moment they knew they were pregnant. It would have been impossible for them to "focus only on themselves." Then there were those women who wanted to continue their dangerous habits—drugs, poor diet, smoking, little rest—in spite of the risks they posed to the health of the Baby. Caught up in their own narcissism to the exclusion of the needs of the delicate new life growing inside them, they denied the inevitable life changes demanded by the Baby. Though Celebrities may be caught between loving and hating the idea of the Baby taking over their lives, it is their emotional and spiritual bonds they form with their baby that will become the driving force of their future relationship.

Benedek notes about fathers: ". . . men must force themselves into a commitment to the future with a child, to shift their identity more to the role of provider as well as partner to the baby's mother. Without the strength of the provider role, men may have a hard time making an emotional commitment to this new person who is about to come into their world."

We asked the men in our Circles groups to tell us what else a father—the Celebrity's Roadie—can do to bond to his new baby and commit to his new family besides embracing this role of being the "provider." The men who became involved with the Baby by attending their pregnant wives' doctor's visits, joining them in prenatal classes, and coaching them in the delivery room felt that they'd set the stage to become devoted players throughout the life of the child-to-be.

Research over the past several decades supports what these men report, proving that dads-to-be need a specific part to play in the very beginning of their children's lives in order to begin the bonding that is so necessary in the drama of parenthood. As a result, since the late 1960s fathers have been encouraged to attend ultrasound screenings, feel their baby move, and hold their newborns as soon as possible after they come into the world. This relatively new push for the Roadie father to become as involved with the Baby as the Celebrity mother has been demonstrated to strengthen the emotional and spiritual bonding needed for men to embrace their new identity as Dad.

A NEW LOOK AT RELATIONSHIPS

The giving of love is an education in itself.
—ELEANOR ROOSEVELT

Alex's parents had long been dreaming of having a grandchild, so life couldn't be more perfect for them, at the age of sixty, as they gratefully awaited the birth of Alex's first baby. Instead of separating further from their son, as they'd been doing since he'd stormed out of their house at the age of eighteen, they saw this baby as their chance to reconnect with him, even though he was now a thirty-year-old accountant working for his father-in-law's computer company.

SARA, A THIRTY-THREE-YEAR-OLD veteran stay-at-home mother, also felt a special bond with her own mother, Diane, when Sara was pregnant with her third daughter. Sara had grown up with two sisters, so she felt as though her life had come full circle. Becoming a grandma of three had likewise made the life of her fifty-five-year-old mother feel complete, Diane had told Sara. Pleasing her mother gave Sara a feeling of satisfaction, too; it had always been her top agenda.

THE PROFOUND CHANGES that a baby brings to a couple's relationships can heal or strengthen them, as Alex and Sara found with their parents. But a baby can also stress or fracture important relationships, as was true in the case of forty-three-year-old Debbie, whose third pregnancy was clearly a "surprise." Living in a two-bedroom house in which her three- and four-year-old daughters shared one room, this former bank teller and her forty-five-year-old mechanic husband, Don, needed a baby like "a hole in the head," as Debbie put it. She wasn't bringing home a paycheck, and the kids' preschool tuition kept increasing, as did the cost to feed and clothe them.

But the baby's impact on Debbie's and her husband's lives did more than just put them in stressful financial straits. It also ruined Debbie's friendship with her best friend, Alice, a banking attorney who had been her soulmate since they had met in first grade. They had been inseparable—even working at the same bank—before Debbie got pregnant for the third time.

Alice looked on the two children Debbie and Don already had as "their choice," as she put it. But having a third baby was forcing Don and Debbie to move out of Alice's neighborhood and would permanently put her out of the workforce, according to Debbie. She had told Alice that she was going to have to figure out how to make money from home now, maybe by taking care of other people's children and her own, a concept incomprehensible to Alice, whose son was in third grade. "Who wants to take care of kids all the time?" Alice shrieked when Debbie told her. "Only people who can't find real jobs."

It was clear that Debbie and Alice were at an impasse intellectually and emotionally, an impasse that Debbie would never have predicted just months earlier. Alice made her feel as though her pregnancy were a personal attack on their friendship. She was so hurt . . . and disappointed. Friends don't turn their back on you, she told us, adding that she felt better when she didn't expose herself to Alice's ridicule.

Debbie's story illustrates the domino effect of life as a Celebrity. Of course, you expect your own life to change with pregnancy, but most of the parents in our Circles groups were stunned by how impending parenthood changed *every* current relationship: with their mom and dad, sisters and brothers, aunts and uncles, cousins, friends, neighbors, boss, and peers. All inevitably change because your identity and agenda change.

O F COURSE, NO RELATIONSHIP changes during the Celebrity season more than that between the mother and father-to-be. "Whoever knew anything about placentas?" one mother-to-be laughed in one of our Circles groups. "Now my husband and I are so into the graphic details of every aspect of this pregnancy that we talk like doctors."

If conversations change from commenting on each other's hairstyles to discussing more personal parts of their anatomy, it's not surprising that they also change couples' level of intimacy. "I never felt closer to my wife than when we would go to her monthly doctor's visits together," one father reminisced. "I miss that feeling now."

Becoming a Celebrity can just as easily drive a wedge between a mother and father-to-be. When the news is shared about becoming parents, expectations of spouses' reactions run high. "The very fact of becoming a parent scared me to death," said Sheryl, a member of one of our Circles groups. "I looked at my husband, Drew, totally differently. He was now the father of the child I was carrying, not just my spouse. *That* was scary. When I told him that I was pregnant, I wanted him to be thrilled, pick me up, and go buy me flowers. Instead he looked like he had just seen a ghost. I burst into tears. We had our first big fight of parenthood."

Because the Celebrity season is so demanding emotionally and physically, on the mother-to-be, in particular, she may not relate to her husband as the same person, as Sheryl discovered. She may act like a different person, too: go to bed before the evening news when she used to be a night owl, get sick on foods she used to devour, or cry whenever she sees babies when she never even noticed them before.

Men aren't excluded from experiencing emotional changes as well, when they've made a spiritual commitment to being Dad. Those who are the family's breadwinner may feel more pressure to bring home more bacon, making them testy and resentful that they're being forced to work harder by this new little person growing inside their partners. Or they might develop a new respect for their wives' ability to pull off the miracle of bringing a new human being into the world.

The changes in the relationship are dramatic enough if the pregnancy proceeds normally; but if something goes awry, physically, with the Baby or the mother, the crisis adds new stresses to the relationship.

"I realized how much I loved my wife," one first-time father-to-be told us, "when she started bleeding in the third month, and I was helpless to do anything for her or for the baby. I kept telling her that we would get through this okay, not even realizing that I had said, 'we.' I felt like we had grown closer in our mutual goal of bringing this new life into the world."

Actress Elizabeth Stone nicely summed up this season: "Making the decision to have a child—it's momentous. It is to decide forever to have your heart go walking around outside your body."

Brooke's Mission: Lawyer and Mother

Consider the case of Brooke, a twenty-seven-year-old, radiant blond lawyer who was pregnant with her first child. She arrived at the Circles meeting looking as if she might just give birth to her baby right there. Nonetheless she was impeccably dressed and sported a dark Florida tan, which she had gotten on a recent trip to Orlando.

We soon learned, however, that despite Brooke's advanced state of pregnancy, her recent Florida sojourn had been strictly business. An ambitious and successful attorney, she told us outright that she was so sure that she could do anything she set her mind to that she had flown to Orlando to represent one of her clients, even though she had been warned not to travel because her baby was due in five days. When we asked her why she had made this decision, which seemed rather risky, she innocently confided, "This baby would not dare be early." Of course, we were curious as to how she knew that.

"My pregnancy has been just like my mother's when she was expecting me," she explained. "I was ten days early—and all my life, my mother constantly reminded me of how I disrupted her life by being born ten days early. I simply couldn't allow my child to disrupt my life the way I disrupted my mother's. She always complained about the career opportunities she lost as a social worker by staying home with her child. I felt guilty about it all my life."

Although Brooke denied wanting to be "just like her mother," the lessons of her mother's life had always felt like a straitjacket to her, clearly affecting her feelings about her baby and what role the baby should play in her life.

Her attitude of forced nonchalance about the baby didn't always feel right, she finally admitted. In addition, it was leading her to make choices she knew were not only irresponsible, but also didn't reflect her true feelings or those of her husband, Trevor.

To make matters worse, she explained in a calm but clearly confused tone, many of her friends, who were not pregnant or who weren't interested in becoming parents, told her that she was "throwing her life away" by becoming a mother. She suddenly felt estranged from everyone and scared that everything would be even more complicated after the baby was born, she confessed as she quietly brushed away the tears welling up in her eyes.

"How could being a mother and being a lawyer fit together?" she asked us despairingly.

And what did Brooke's husband, Trevor, a twenty-nine-year-old engineer, think about all of this? we asked, attempting to assess whether she could turn to him for support. "He thinks about it as little as possible," Brooke replied quietly.

The most pressing concern that Brooke had about being pregnant was knowing how the old Brooke, the lawyer, and the new Brooke, the mother, could fit together. Like the predictable identity crisis that she had experienced when she was an adolescent—a result of the war between being a dependent little girl and being a grown woman—she suddenly wasn't sure that she wanted to give up an inch of the self-image that worked so well for her—in dollars and prestige—that she had forged as a lawyer. After all, she concluded, this "mother" thing hadn't served her own mother so well.

Her memories of her own childhood were centered on her mother being home, despite the fact that her mother never accepted motherhood as a definition of personal fulfillment. Her mother's prioritizing being a mother over her career as a social worker was clearly giving direction to Brooke's life now as she wrestled with her own identity and priorities.

Brooke realized, after much discussion, that she needed to redefine herself as a mother so she could feel good about "being" Mom, regardless of what she "did" careerwise. She didn't want to repeat her mother's mistake; if she made career sacrifices, she realized, she wanted it to be because she prioritized motherhood willingly.

We told Brooke that having friends who were supportive of the changes in her life would help her feel less isolated. In addition, she needed to refocus her relationship with her mom. Up to this point, Brooke had behaved as if she had been put on earth to please, fulfilling the role of the "good girl" who did what her mom wanted her to do. Within these constraints, their relationship had been as smooth as glass. Brooke believed that she needed to be a successful partner in the large downtown law firm in order to please her mother, who always bragged about her daughter, the attorney. Now, however, this relationship was changing, as Brooke began to consider giving up—or at least scaling back—her career in favor of parenthood.

No longer defining herself as a child controlled by her mother, Brooke began to think of herself for the first time as the parent of her child, not as a child of her parent. The effect of this change on her relationships was astounding to her! She experienced a real taste of freedom by reframing herself as a parent, and she began to relate differently to others. Her best friend at work, who was a partner in the firm, said that she never expected that she would be envious of Brooke. But she could see that all of Brooke's dreams and plans for the baby were making her happier than any legal brief or prestigious title had ever done. Now *she* was even thinking about getting pregnant, following the path toward Celebrity status that she now saw Brooke occupying.

However, as in the case of many pregnant executives, Brooke was putting the entire burden of her career decision making on herself, leaving her husband out of the discussion. Trevor's trying to think about the upcoming change in the family "as little as possible," as she put it, only angered Brooke. We helped them both see that having a baby was not just a lifestyle change for Brooke as she became a Celebrity, and for Trevor, who was denying his Roadie status, but a complete life change. By planning their future together, with actual goals and timelines, the two started to realize that becoming a family of three was not only inevitable, but was going to require both of them to face the same direction on this journey.

Dena Doubles Down: A Blended Family

We met Darryl, a thirty-five-year-old obstetrician, and his thirty-year-old wife, Dena, a community volunteer, at a parenting workshop at the preschool that Darryl and Dena's children attend. Their two toddlers, Darren and Damon, ages three and four, whose biological mother had died just a year earlier, were "handfuls," as their stepmother, Dena, described them, particularly when Darryl worked the night shift or was on call. Despite her status as a single parent most days and nights, Dena was still thrilled to learn that she was going to have to grow even bigger hands to take care of her family: she and Darryl were going to have "a second family of our own," as Darryl put it. Dena was now pregnant with twins.

Suddenly she became an instant Celebrity. No longer Dena, the step-mother of Darren and Damon, she was now Dena, about-to-be-the-mother-of-twins. Her "news" became the hot gossip of every meeting she went to as the PTA president of her children's preschool and every community event she attended. She told us that it felt as if she were going to give birth to the first set of twins on the planet. People she didn't even know would come up and congratulate her at dinner parties!

Her Celebrity status in the neighborhood and among her relatives was fun, yet it complicated her family's life. Being an extrovert at heart, Dena relished the attention and instant fame. Before her twin pregnancy, she had always believed that she was a nobody, but now she finally felt that she was important, a somebody.

However, she lay awake nights worrying: How would Darren and Damon react to their new brothers or sisters? She felt guilty that so much attention was already focused on "the twins." She knew that it would be hard for Darren and Damon to feel special when the babies actually came. The situation seemed to be snowballing out of her control. No matter how hard Dena tried to change the subject or turn the attention back to the boys or her volunteer job at a shelter for abused children, it was "the twins" that people wanted to talk about.

The bigger she got, the more "popular" the pregnancy became, and the more importance she started placing on the twins in spite of her efforts to do otherwise. She felt overshadowed by the imminent birth, as if her prepregnancy self had been erased. And she wasn't sure how to reconcile these two parts of her identity.

In the quiet of the night and early morning hours, before Damon and Darren were awake, she worried silently how her husband, Darryl, must feel now that his wife was getting so much attention. He had always been the celebrity, the important doctor. Now he was just a bit player to the adoring audience that was so enthralled with her twin pregnancy.

Darryl knew the risks of a multiple pregnancy, of course. So every time Dena's new fame came up, he would try to downplay it because of his own fears. He would throw cold water on the situation by suggesting that they "see what happens before they get too excited."

Darryl appeared to lack a spiritual connection to the babies-to-be. In Dena's opinion he was treating these new lives as impersonally as he did the many deliveries he made in his practice. He had refrained from going with her to doctor visits or to prenatal classes, claiming that he already knew everything he needed to know.

Although she was always walking in Darryl's shadow, Dena admitted that she was comfortable playing the role of a doctor's wife. She was proud that he was always the one who was sought after for advice by all of her friends who didn't want to pester their own obstetricians with questions, and it had never bothered her before. But now that she and the babies were in the spotlight, she was angered that he seemed to be taking this pregnancy so lightly, without being much support to her. She took his "wait and see" approach as a direct hit at the focus of her newfound fame. Being a Roadie was not on his agenda.

Darryl seemed to be contradicting himself, too, she told us. On one hand, he was nonchalant about the whole thing; on the other hand, she knew he was really worried about the risks of multiple births, which he had talked about before. His apparent ambivalence was making Dena feel rejected; he was so distant when she needed him to be close. We helped her see that she was interpreting his comments and his apparent distance without checking with him to see just what he was thinking and feeling.

Some of her anger stemmed from the fact that she felt so changed by this pregnancy while Darryl's life was sailing along as busily and productively as always. Now she wanted to depend on him emotionally in the same way her friends did, but he always responded with his "doctor indifference" and seemed irritated that she was concerned about the way he was acting. Things were different now, she told us. She needed him to calm her fears, but he would become so negative while quoting risk factors and the possibilities of premature birth or C-section that she hated to even ask him a question. He couldn't seem to separate his "doctor" persona from his role as father-to-be. Part of the problem was that Dena expected him to be both doctor and husband/father.

WE HELPED DENA gain some perspective on how to get the support she needed without blowing holes in her relationship with Darryl. We suggested that she talk to her own doctor about her concerns with her pregnancy and give Darryl a break from being her doctor. We encouraged her to focus on answering practical questions instead of just medical and emotional ones: How much help would she need once the babies were born? Where could she get all of the equipment she was going to need? Who could help her take care of the older boys' "travel arrangements" when she would be "tied down," as she put it, with two infants?

By helping Dena create a list of these nonmedical questions and suggesting that she share the list with Darryl, we helped her see that she could use the leadership skills she had discovered and honed while working in the preschool parents club to meet her own present agenda—taking care of her pregnant, Celebrity self. Her identity as a capable organizer and mom started to take shape. She no longer felt the need to try to stop the rising tide of fame during the rest of her pregnancy and, instead, took control of her current agenda—preparing for life with four children.

Whenever Darryl's comments turned to the subject of the riskiness of the pregnancy, Dena reinforced herself for all the things that she was doing that she could control: resting often, eating a healthy diet, and avoiding straining her back as her weight gain reached forty pounds. The results of her focusing on her own agenda, not Darryl's, gave their relationship new energy and gave Dena a sense of inner peace about doing what she needed to do to please herself and her babies as well as her two stepchildren.

Her children—all four of them—were helping her become more self-sufficient and independent, areas of her character that had, prior to this pregnancy, needed strengthening. Even though she felt stronger, she had no role models to turn to. (There were no twins anywhere in her family or among her friends for advice on multiple pregnancy.) She felt strangely alone, which had become the source of much of her resentment about Darryl not being there for her in the way that she wished he would. He had avoided being a Roadie with his first wife when she was a Celebrity, just as he was doing now, so he needed time and direction from her to learn the ropes.

We encouraged her to join a Mothers of Twins Club to meet other women who were struggling with similar issues of identity change, relationship changes, and the need for support during a time when their babies seemed to be controlling them, leaving little room for feelings of having any say-so over their lives. By talking to others who also had four children, including twins, Dena addressed her concerns over her sense of separation from her friends who knew nothing about either subject. She was reassured that, yes, she would have time to talk to her friends on the phone after the babies were born, and no, having four children would not ruin her life, as her childless friends had teased her. The new relationships she formed in the club were priceless connections to the experience of multiple pregnancy that helped Dena look at the process of change as her friend, not her enemy.

To help her handle her new Celebrity status, we advised Dena that her first job was to reconcile her guilt about believing that being a mother of twins was more special than being a stepmother to her other two children. By thinking of her pregnancy in practical as well as philosophical terms, Dena began to focus on getting the support she needed to take care of all of her children, not just the two who were now in the spotlight.

Jack's Attack: "What Happened to My Wife?"

Wearing his wife on his arm like a piece of her expensive jewelry, twenty-nine-year-old Jack seemed to be frozen in another decade. A former model for a men's health magazine, he told us that he couldn't help it that he was born into the wealthy, privileged Johnston family, where playing tennis and the stock market took up most of his father's, and now his, days and nights.

Things were changing, though, he said with a tone of despair in his voice. His twenty-five-year-old wife, a former model named Marla, was pregnant with their first child, which had thrown his life into a state of chaos. "What happened to my beautiful wife?" he asked us sheepishly. Now all she did was wear sweatpants and lie around on the couch like a beached whale!

The doctor had told her to take it easy for the first three months, but Jack questioned where she should draw the line between "easy" and "lazy bum." The delicious four-course dinners that they had enjoyed by candlelight almost every Saturday night were gone, as were the Friday night parties with their gourmet club. Marla was too sick to eat like a normal person or go anywhere, including their bridge game on Thursdays. They had just found a group of players who didn't have children . . . and liked it that way. Now, he said, they felt like outsiders. Their new "group" didn't want to talk about nursing, having sex during pregnancy, or being labor coaches. Jack wasn't too sure he did, either.

These hadn't been topics of discussion in Jack's family, least of all discussions he could imagine his father, Chase, ever participating in. Chase, a self-made millionaire, was rarely home when Jack was growing up, flying to meetings all over the world in his private jet. When Chase was home, Jack didn't talk to him about anything other than school and girls, the two subjects Jack was most interested in. Jack had seen Chase not as a "father," but more as a guest in his life, a flashy, friendly uncle.

When Marla wanted him to go to prenatal classes, Jack countered by saying that his father had never done such a thing. That kind of "family" stuff just was not in his line of work, he always told Jack. His job was to provide for his family—and that did not necessarily include providing time, Jack realized now. It was a costly venture, Jack told Marla, quoting a U.S. News & World Report story that he had recently read that stated raising a child costs $1,455,581 these days.

Marla had other concerns on her mind. She was talking about his going to the doctor with her next month when she was going to have her first ultrasound. She wanted them both to be equally involved in every aspect of parenting, including giving their children everything she had ever had, emotionally, if not materially. Her parents, Twyla and Miller, had doted on her as an only child but were never able to save much on her father's salary. Miller was never promoted at the car dealership where he worked because, he said, he was committed to being home by five every day and never working nights or Saturdays so he could participate in all of Marla's activities.

Even though it meant doing without many luxuries, Twyla hadn't wanted to work outside the home so she could become involved in the PTA at Marla's school and work there as a volunteer reading tutor up through Marla's high school years. She prided herself on the little things, such as having hot chocolate-chip cookies ready when Marla walked in the door after school, and the big things, such as visiting Marla at college, an hour from home, just to bring her surprises or take her out to lunch. Being involved parents, Twyla and Miller attended all of Marla's volleyball tournaments and soccer matches, often traveling out of town with her high school and college teams.

Jack, on the other hand, with the model of rich, uninvolved parents, panicked at just the thought that becoming a dad would change his life even half as much as it did his in-laws' lives. He worried that these were going to be the longest nine months of his life and couldn't even bear to look ahead at what might be his fate as a parent.

Pregnancy brings down the structure that was in place in a marriage and begins laying a foundation for a couple's new life. In fact, the reasons so many couples never seem to travel through the seasons of parenthood in sync is that they don't understand that in this season, they can't build a new family structure on top of the old, stable life they'd begun. They would have to accept the disintegration of that old life and begin to relate to themselves and each other differently because of their new identities as Mom and Dad.

Jack and Marla demonstrated this point in fine fashion. Their marriage was in a comfortable little rhythm, humming along as smoothly as Jack's new Mercedes, when suddenly his wife, Marla, "changed on him," as he labeled the pregnancy. We asked him what it was about Marla's behavior now that was making him feel so lost and helpless. He told us that the loss of control over "what they would be doing and when," as he put it, was making him crazy. Marla had been so much fun before. Now all of her attention was focused on doing what was best for the baby, not going out and having a good time with him. He never could predict what his life would be like because their whole lives depended on how the baby was making her feel. Jack was obviously feeling left out of the relationship that Marla was forming with their yet-to-be-born child.

"I had never realized how inflexible and how caught up in my own life I was," he said. We pointed out to Jack that his new baby was giving him new insight into himself before she or he was even born. He needed to analyze the core of his love: Was he in love with Marla, their lifestyle, or the image that they projected together? We talked him through this issue as he realized that it was Marla the person, rather than Marla the image, whom he loved. By understanding the source of his love, he could begin to anticipate the new relationship he could have with Marla and the baby instead of feeling betrayed by the changes that she was experiencing.

If their marriage and new family were to survive, Jack's neat little world, which was controlled by his purse strings, was going to have to change. Yes, during her pregnancy they might choose to continue their normal activities when Marla felt better, but they might also decide that it would be wise to cultivate friendships with people who were also expecting or had recently become parents. Jack and Marla didn't realize it quite yet, but their friendships with childless couples would be changing as their lives became focused almost totally on their baby during the next stage of parenthood, the Sponge stage.

To give him a reference point on what an involved father-to-be Roadie could do to support his Celebrity wife, we suggested that Marla continue to ask Jack to go to the doctor with her. We also suggested that they discuss their respective definitions of a "good father" and how Jack saw himself involved in their son's or daughter's life. Doing so was a big commitment for Jack because he had never thought that his concept of fatherhood could be different from his own dad's.

With our encouragement, Jack and Marla told each other their worries. Their immediate reactions were to deny that they would ever do anything to hurt each other. Jack had downplayed Marla's pregnancy, it became apparent, not because he was uninterested in the baby and their future family, but because of his own fears of being an inadequate dad. We suggested that he commit himself to an occasional meeting with a family therapist so that he could have professional support and direction.

Jack also needed to know that Marla still loved him as much as ever and to be reassured that if more of their time together revolved around the baby, he wouldn't risk letting the family down financially. She informed him that she was more interested in his becoming a good father to their baby than in his being a financial whiz kid.

Marla's self-inflicted pressure to be like her own mother was eased a bit when she realized that it might interfere with their starting a new family on their own terms. Jack reassured Marla that he would love to shower their baby with all varieties of blessings, monetarily and emotionally. He would need help, though, he admitted, on the emotional part, and Marla said that she was only too happy to oblige! We let both Jack and Marla know that the changes that happen when "baby makes three" don't transform people into overnight successes as parents. Because of the biological changes that Jack couldn't experience, he couldn't be expected to automatically be as emotionally and psychologically involved with the baby as Marla during this season of parenthood. His identity as a Roadie would evolve, we felt certain.

Although they realized that their parents were still powerful forces in their lives, and would remain so, Jack and Marla could have the best of both their worlds. By recognizing problems as they arose and seeking help for their marriage before they entered the Sponge season of parenthood, they had demonstrated the desire to lay a new, solid foundation for their emerging family.

Eleanor's Sister Act: Identity Crisis

A bundle of organized energy, Eleanor sported a worried brow as she ambled into our Circles group clutching a thick pad of paper hidden in the folds of her cheerily flowered maternity dress. A preschool teacher for over fifteen years, she'd decided in college that devoting her life to small children gave her a noble purpose that had served the other two women in her family well—her forty-eight-year-old sister, Nancy, and her mom had both been teachers. At forty-five Eleanor was breaking new ground, however, by enabling her mother to become a grandmother for the first time.

Nancy wasn't married and wouldn't even think of having children. According to her, there are enough kids with so many problems in our overcrowded, uncaring world that she couldn't bear to bring another one into the world.

"How could you even consider such a thing? Are you nuts?" Nancy had shouted when Eleanor had shared her good news. Now Nancy grabbed every opportunity to bludgeon Eleanor with news items about child abuse, examples of problem children she knew, and diatribes about population growth.

"Sure, that upsets me," Eleanor responded emphatically when we asked her how her sister's view of having children was affecting her now that she was pregnant. Having never thought of herself as a heroine, Eleanor was amazed to find herself suddenly in a new position in the family: the apple of her mother's eye and the object of Nancy's messages of doom and gloom. Consequently Eleanor's relationships with the two women who meant the world to her were changing dramatically. Eleanor could feel her "old self" slipping away. Who was this "mother" to whom they were referring? Eleanor didn't know how to act anymore around her mom and Nancy.

That wasn't the case when it came to her husband, Ronnie. He was a saint, she told us. Without him and his generous salary as a pharmacist, she wouldn't be able to afford her low-paying but rewarding teaching job. She also indicated that she wanted to go back to teaching after the baby was born and believed she could easily do that and care for a baby, too. After investing six long years and lots of tuition money in getting a master's degree in special education, she couldn't imagine quitting this dream job in the special-needs preschool located close to home.

Ronnie was all in favor of Eleanor's desire to continue her career as a teacher because his mother had been a teacher, and he knew how much she had enjoyed her job, the children, and the sense of accomplishment teaching gave her. He often wished his mother could still be here, particularly to share Eleanor's enthusiasm for teaching; but, sadly, both his parents had died ten years before he and Eleanor were married.

Ronnie loved Eleanor's family because they helped fill the void in his life since his parents' deaths. He knew it was breaking Eleanor's heart to be in conflict with Nancy over what should be a happy event. Life would be perfect, Eleanor shared, if only her sister and she would stop fighting about this new adventure in her life. More than anything else right now, Eleanor wanted the acceptance of her family.

The last thing that Eleanor expected to gain from her pregnancy was a hole in her heart where her sister's love had been. "Have you ever heard of that happening?" she asked us incredulously.

We discovered in our interviews that the number of people whose hearts became pitted with potholes during their pregnancies outweighed those whose relationships suffered no bruises from spills they took along the road. Nancy's deep-seated fears about bringing children into the world were her allies; when Eleanor became pregnant, she joined the enemy camp as far as Nancy was concerned. We explained to Eleanor that all of her efforts to convince her sister that she should be happy for her, instead of resenting her new celebrity status, would most likely be in vain because of Nancy's jealousy over all the attention Eleanor was now getting.

We suggested other ways of responding to the shifting family dynamics that would be more productive in helping her cope with Nancy's jealousy. We advised Eleanor to keep her focus on what she could control, her attitude about the changes in her own life, rather than on what she couldn't control: trying to change Nancy's mind. As a consequence, when Eleanor stopped trying to control Nancy's reactions, Nancy stopped needing to defend her position.

Being the Celebrity in the family had its dangers, Eleanor quickly found. Now that the spotlight was on her, every move she made was scrutinized in a manner befitting an official investigation by a special prosecutor. Eleanor was reminded of the family wars that erupted when she was just ten. Nancy was thirteen at the time and had been struggling intensely to create her own identity separate from the rest of the family.

Now Eleanor started to see Nancy's scorn as a continuation of a conflict that her big sister was still having over her control, or lack thereof, of her sister's life. Nancy always told Eleanor what to do, and that was when the battles would begin. Their mother would become so frustrated that she would scream at them until she was hoarse. When their father came home, she would "rat out" the girls to their dad. Then he would hole up in his workshop in the garage, and her mother would blame the girls for the fact that he never spent any time with her.

Her dad had said that being in a household of women had driven him out the door. Eleanor told us that she never understood what he meant until now. In fact, she had never forgiven her dad for "ruining her family," splitting her mom's heart in two by abandoning her, just as she believed her sister was doing to her now. Eleanor asked us: Why did Nancy have to ruin the most exciting time in her life? Would Ronnie repeat her father's abandonment if he saw that the triangle of Eleanor, Nancy, and her mother continued to create tension and tears?

We helped her realize that losing her old identity—of being a victim in childhood sibling rivalry and the designated troublemaker in the family— is part of the bargain when you enter the new baby business. Nevertheless we encouraged her to share her fears with Ronnie that they would repeat her family history in their new family. Ronnie was invested in making this family a solid one as the replacement for the one he had lost.

One big question now plagued Eleanor: Could they afford for her to go back to work? Spending her nights deeply engrossed in budgeting and expense planning helped Eleanor map out her future, along with Ronnie's support. Both knew that having her income was going to be critical to maintaining the lifestyle to which they had become quite accustomed— restaurants, their health club membership, going on rafting trips. As they considered the maternity clothes and everything they needed to buy for the baby, Ronnie and Eleanor went into sticker shock.

We suggested that they start saving for later, too, knowing that if they thought this season was expensive, they were in for more surprises when they started to price diapers and all the darling outfits that she would want to buy, not to mention college tuition eighteen years down the road. Eleanor, who was proud of bringing home a check every two weeks, started to get sick to her stomach when she considered that day care would cost her at least half of her salary. What had started out being a joyous bit of news had turned into a recipe for misery.

In discussing just what motivated Eleanor to think so negatively about parenthood, she realized that adjusting to change had always been emotionally difficult. She guessed that growing up with her controlling sister, Nancy, and the turmoil of her parents' relationship had instilled in her the desire to have things always the same. She found comfort in what others considered a boring routine. But that was part of her identity—good old-fashioned Eleanor.

Our job was to help both Eleanor and Ronnie see that they were in a fragile venture, this parenthood business. In fact, parenthood is infamous for always needing repairing, from constant change. All parents must wrestle with its rips and holes, trusting that they will stick by each other while mending the tears in the fabric of their lives. We reminded Eleanor and Ronnie that they could control only themselves: their reactions to the imprints left by their family histories; their responses to the pregnancy and upcoming birth; their mode of communicating with each other.

This helped both Eleanor and Ronnie turn down the volume of the chaos that surrounded them and focus on coping with their own feelings. We felt confident, however, that they were now aware of the most important cues in the first act of the drama of parenthood.

Maria's Tailspin: Not a "Real" Mom

The best-laid plans are no match for the serendipity of pregnancy—particularly during the trying-to-get-pregnant phase. Maria, a quiet, thirty-eight-year-old teacher of Spanish, learned this lesson the hard way. After two unsuccessful years of fertility treatments and a grueling fifteen-month adoption process, Maria and her husband, Alberto, were totally drained. Guilt, anger, hopelessness, and fear topped the list of how they felt on their worst days.

Their families didn't make life any easier. Maria's mother, Anne, and mother-in-law, Adella, were disappointed that she couldn't conceive and have a baby the "normal" way, as they put it. To Maria, they seemed to view adoption as unacceptable for their family.

In spite of their families' negative attitudes, Maria and Alberto were ec-

static when they learned about an opportunity to go to Guatemala to adopt a baby girl. But that wasn't going to make her a "real" mother, Anne had said to Maria, who worried that Anne was right.

Maria was trying to put herself into the "motherhood" frame of mind but was having problems doing that without going through a pregnancy the way her friends had. She had always dreamed of being a mom, she told us. But she worried that when they finally got their baby, she would fail at being a mother.

Although she and Alberto had accepted their fate of becoming parents through adoption, they were heartbroken over the devastation that it was bringing to their family relationships. After seven years of marriage they had grown attached to each other's in-laws, even boasting about how comfortable they all seemed to be with each other. Maria was anxious being with them now, afraid of what they would say to her that would hurt her feelings. Alberto had little patience with their narrow-mindedness regarding their approach to building a family.

We encouraged Maria to share her worries about motherhood with Alberto. He needed to understand that she was feeling a sense that she would lose out on something if their baby wasn't born from her pregnancy, which was the message that her mother and mother-in-law were sending her. Not going through the Celebrity season of parenthood made Maria feel short-changed, she admitted. No showers, no shopping for maternity clothes, no being pampered.

She told us that it felt like that time in high school when she had borrowed some homework from a friend to copy so she could get a better grade. She had always felt bad about that and knew she hadn't done the work that deserved the grade, just as she wouldn't be doing the work to earn this baby or get the glory for having done so.

Maria and Alberto needed time to adjust to the loss of their dream of experiencing the Celebrity season, just as their own mothers had. Their task was to build a new agenda for their own family and a new basis for the relationships with the grandmothers of their new offspring as well.

We discussed the kind of encouragement that Maria and Alberto would need during the time they were trying to accomplish these goals. Rejecting organized support groups as too conventional, as well as too "embarrassing," Maria wanted them to start their own "private support group"—a

Saturday night date during which they shared all of their worries and frustrations. They were becoming parents, and they needed to approach the adoption the same way they would a pregnancy.

Change was something that Maria and Alberto were familiar with; it had been their mantra all through their twenties. They had moved to take new jobs all over the country and adjusted many times, adapting to new places and making new friends. Now that their forties were looming, they decided that becoming parents would create a fresh beginning for their relationship as a couple. They began to form a "new family" with close friends made up of couples who offered to be godparents, aunts, and uncles to their addition to their family.

We encouraged them to let their circle of support widen as their own parents offered less and less encouragement for them and their plan to adopt. With supportive friends and a new attitude, their joint venture was pointed in a successful direction. Their in-laws' disapproving reaction would, we hoped, fade after Maria and Alberto had "proven themselves" as "real parents" once they had their baby.

Shelby Grows Up: Teenage Pregnancy

When we first met the spunky, raven-haired teenager Shelby, we were struck by her firm sense of determination not to let getting pregnant make her a "bad mother," as she described people who didn't take responsibility for their actions. She had seen other young mothers who had simply pretended to return to their previous lifestyles after giving birth by giving their babies over to the new grandparents to raise. Shelby was only eighteen, a senior in high school, but she had the wisdom of someone who knew how to learn from her "mistake," as she feared others would consider her baby.

Shelby was lucky. Her mother and father supported her during this tumultuous time, not approving of the whole situation, but not rejecting their only daughter, either. The pregnancy actually drew them and their daughter closer together as they started to treat Shelby as "grown-up," a real change from their overprotectiveness during her teen years.

Their rationale for how they dealt with Shelby's situation? They felt somewhat responsible, they told Shelby, for continuing to treat her like a child and not teaching her how to prevent something like this from happening. They should have known that since she was a pretty, popular, and innocent teenager, she was at risk for being taken advantage of sexually.

Shelby didn't blame them. She was willing to take full responsibility for confusing teenage lust for love. However, being pregnant gave her life a new sense of importance. In fact, she knew what she wanted to be "when she grew up"—a mother. Her new identity of "mother" gave her parents an important part to play in her life again and made her feel as if she had gained new status in their eyes.

Despite the fact that this pregnancy had a newfound benefit—support from her parents—we cautioned this mother-to-be to think again about the long-term effects of becoming a mother. Her own mother and father might be her biggest cheerleaders now, we suggested, but planning for how she was going to take care of the baby was a more important discussion to have with them than showing them the new clothes she brought home from the discount store where she worked.

Shelby told us that she hated being a statistic; she knew that teenage pregnancies often led to premature babies because the mothers got little care and less support. Although her parents had accepted her new "mother" identity, she was worried that her friends and their parents would treat her differently now that she was pregnant, which made her fear staying in high school after she started to show.

Despite her fears, she decided to try to renew her old friendships with girls who had drifted away because she had spent so much time with Mark, the baby's father and Shelby's former boyfriend, and had made little time for them. We helped her realize that these friendships might have changed as a result of her pregnancy, but she was now willing to take a risk in order to get their support.

The fact that Shelby was going to be a single parent floated through her consciousness every day. Mark wanted no part of this baby. She didn't even know how she could be in the same school with him since he no longer wanted anything to do with her and refused to talk to her about her pregnancy.

She was hurt and furious with Mark for abandoning her and their baby. We helped Shelby reconcile that anger by facing the fact that her pregnancy was as much her responsibility as his. She decided to spell out her feelings in a letter to him, hoping that he would understand that she was preparing for this new family and was expecting him to help with the responsibility of caring for their child. Although she had mustered the courage to express herself, Shelby had to remind herself that she had no control over his reaction to being a dad; all she could control was her attitude about this new life that she was about to begin with her new baby.

Self-Discoveries of Celebrities

Your pocket guide to the truths revealed in the Celebrity season of parenthood.

> ➤ **"Even though it's 2 A.M., you still need to go get the ice cream."** The difference between men and women in this season is that the mother is the Celebrity and the father is her Roadie, who offers support, encouragement, and adoration as he identifies with being the provider for the Baby through caring for her.

> ➤ **Fasten your seat belt.** The Celebrity roller coaster provides the thrill and anticipation of your parenthood journey. Your excitement is building. All of your thoughts about the ride ahead tell you that it may turn out to be really fun, but it's guaranteed to scare the hell out of you too. As they say at all theme parks: Follow all safety rules and regulations! Accept responsibility for your behavior on the ride!

> ➤ **Enjoy your fifteen minutes of fame.** During this phase of the ride, all eyes are on you. Enjoy being the center of attention; you'll never ride alone again.

> ➤ **Hold me, protect me.** Beginning the parenthood ride brings out all kinds of fears and makes you want to hang on to those people you love: parents, spouses, friends . . . Celebrities and their Roadies need each other's care and comfort, now as never before.

> ➤ **Get a good seat.** Your point of view on this parenthood ride determines how you feel on the ride. Staying positive in the midst of all of the admonitions about the risk of being a Celebrity will help Celebrities and Roadies enjoy the trip along this emotionally bumpy track.

Exit Signs

Leaving the state of Fame. Entering the swamp of Duty. The Celebrity season of parenthood with its enormous interest and attention begins to wane in the first few weeks of the Sponge season, when parents are knee deep in the swamp of diapers, little sleep, and dribbles of milk. The reality of the baby replaces the images of their dreams: it's a boy when they wanted a girl; she cries all of the time when they thought she'd sleep a lot; she doesn't smell good unless they clean her up; family and friends stop bringing food and gifts unless parents call them for help. When their fifteen minutes of fame are over, parents know it by the fact that they feel exhausted, on their own, and responsible for soaking up the new life that they alone have created. Welcome to the world of Sponges: eager to absorb, often wrung out.

Sponge

CHILD'S INFANCY

A baby overwhelms us with its lovableness; even its smell stirs us more deeply than the smell of pine or baking bread. What is overpowering is simply the fact that a baby is life. It is also a mess, but such an appealing one that we look past the mess to the jewel underneath.—BILL COSBY

FIVE O'CLOCK. RUSH-HOUR TRAFFIC. A long day of work behind her. Now, all Jodi can think about on the way home from her job is her adorable children waiting to greet her with open arms after *their* long day with their new baby-sitter.

But when she finally bursts through the door, the sounds of their screams drown out any hopes of peace and joy. Her three-month-old's diaper is soaked; her fifteen-month-old is spewing vomit into the arms of the baby-sitter; and her neighbor's nine-month-old, whom she is watching, has great gobs of mucus streaming down her cheeks.

"Fluids!" Jodi exclaimed to the sitter, taking one look at the chaotic scene. "That's what parenthood is all about in the beginning. Fluids!"

FLUIDS IT IS. And buckets of the stuff. These fluids demand one thing from parents—sponges to clean them up—which is what mothers and fathers become during this season of their lives. If mothers aren't soaking up the fluids of their baby, they're trying to absorb their own fluids: tears of joy and gratitude that flow at the birth; tears of pain brought on by postpartum depression and a healing episiotomy; streams of milk that flow from breasts that have miraculously turned into spigots; and sweat that pours from every pore due to the physical demands and bone-deep anxiety of soaking up the miracle that is their baby. Along with mothers, fathers' tears of pride and joy moisten their eyes at baby namings, first holidays, and show and tell at work. And they sweat out the long hours in shared duty as they tackle the endless needs of the Baby.

In the Sponge season, which begins at the baby's birth, parents' lives inevitably become physically, emotionally, psychologically, and spiritually controlled by their totally dependent infant's agenda: *Take good care of me. Absorb who I am. Meet my needs.* The baby's natural developmental growth from being a helpless, horizontal infant to becoming a vertical, mobile toddler grasping for independence creates this stage's boundaries, the beginning and ending markers.

Parents in our Circles groups reported that they were sure the Sponge season of parenthood would last forever! (In reality, it's a year, more or less.) Some thought it was boring and laborious; some found it terrifying and exhausting; others saw it as precious and miraculous. Some voted for "all of the above." In all cases, parents we interviewed told us that their lives revolved around whatever their baby was doing as she grew throughout her first year: smiling, staring at them, gurgling, babbling, crying, rolling over, sitting up, creeping, crawling, pulling up, and finally taking first steps. Her sights, sounds, and smells engrossed them in ways that no other experience in life had to offer. Soon after delivery or when parents hold their newly adopted baby, this great miracle happens: "It's like you grow another heart, like someone kicks down a door that was sealed shut, and then the whole world—sunshine, flowers—falls through," related talk show host Rosie O'Donnell. Journalist Keely Shaye Smith agreed when she said, "My heart has opened up in a fashion I never knew was possible. The first time I saw his little face, held him, the moment our eyes met—I've never felt so complete."

Researchers have noted that this connection—generally referred to as bonding—is innate, literally built into human beings, some to a greater degree than others. Genetics plays a role in the business of bonding—about 50 percent of who we are, psychologically, is due to heritable causes, according to Thomas Bouchard Jr., director of the Minnesota Twins Project and a University of Minnesota psychologist.

We find new research on this subject by the Louisville Twins Study at the University of Louisville revealing: In simplest terms, some infants are programmed to bond more closely to their mothers and fathers, are more naturally responsive to touch and being held, are not fussy or difficult, and appear to enjoy being soaked up by their parents' love. Other infants are born to be more resistant to their parents' care and cause parents more frustration as they try to bond to their babies.

It is understandable, therefore, that some babies seem to be high or low maintenance from day one. Still others, however, can be in such poor health that parents are catapulted into becoming medical Sponges who struggle to bond with them when they and their babies are separated by an extended hospital stay. In all cases, parents are transformed during the first few weeks of parenthood by the process of becoming 100 percent absorbent human Sponges.

Mothers we interviewed reported that the physical effects of giving birth, hormonal changes, and the fatigue resulting from childbirth and infant care are staggering during the first weeks in the soupy fog of parenthood. Even though they'd been told that they would go without a good night's sleep for a while—the baby might not sleep through the night until he's twelve weeks old at the earliest—the physical toll was exasperating and had a tumultuous effect on their emotional state. The emotional stress in turn brings about irritability, confusion, and self-doubt. Decisions that need to be made, from whether to go back to work to whether to keep the baby in bed with them at night to avoid the seemingly exhausting trip to the crib, all seemed monumental.

Parents begin playing the "what if" game in earnest during the first few weeks of this season, when every decision is a process of trial and error; this is the first realization parents have that they sorely need a road map for their parental journey. One mother voiced a common fear; a self-confident social worker, she was constantly terrified of doing the "wrong" thing for her baby and for herself. She worried: What if I can't make enough milk to satisfy my baby? What if I don't put my baby on a schedule? What if I don't use cloth diapers the way my friend did? These questions will haunt her each time she goes through the Sponge season of parenthood.

The mothers we interviewed tormented themselves with what they saw as the biggest question of all in this Sponge season: Should I go back to work or stay home with the baby? No matter what the answer, it seemed laced with guilt. The women who chose to stay home with their baby regretted not contributing to the family coffers or to their own professional or career growth. Those Sponges who worked outside the home experienced another species of guilt over someone else caring for their baby. Some parents who didn't choose to stay home with the baby felt guilty about *not* feeling guilty about their choice. Parents also felt guilty about their lives veering out of control because they were trying to fit their duties to their spouses, parents, relatives, friends, co-workers, bosses, neighbors, and themselves into their new family.

All of this guilt stems from one source: parents' belief that they're doing something wrong or aren't doing something right. Working through the conflicts of being a Sponge—changes in identity, changes in relationships, and assuming the responsibilities of parenthood—will ease their guilt and help them adjust to the fact that their lives will now and forever be a constant balancing act between meeting their child's needs and their own.

Babies can also unearth points of contention, not just in the fact of different faiths of origin, but in how the different family traditions brought to the marriage now might not be performed similarly. Decisions on who provides the christening dress, whether or not to have a bris, and whom to invite to the naming ceremony all require thought and compromise.

The stress of mobilizing for this new baby and managing their own personal lives—marriage, work, home, friends, relatives, family traditions—engulfs parents' lives. The intensity of the first month or so of being a Sponge, for even the most rational, well-organized, healthy adult, naturally puts them to a test by their need to forgo their own personal agenda in order to meet the baby's most essential needs. This test is spiritual in nature because parents become transformed from their own self-absorbed narcissism to being wholly devoted to the life of another human being who touches the depths of their souls simply by being their child—a universally wondrous experience each time it happens to a mother and a father.

A "ONE-WAY STREET": IDENTITY CRISES SQUARED

"It's pretty much a one-way street in the first weeks," new mother Rachael said, laughing as she describing her relationship with her month-old baby, Arta, to members of her Circles group. She couldn't see the long view, the big picture of how her commitment to caring for her newborn would reap rewards in love and security for her and her baby over time. She was holding tight to her old identity, still not wanting to give up her own agenda for that of her baby's.

Typically in our culture, women, more so than men, take several weeks or months of maternity leave and clear their calendar of other duties, often wondering if they can afford, financially and emotionally, not to go back to work after their leave ends, as in Rachael's case. She and her husband, Matt, both worked for the same mobile phone company, and she never missed a day on the job until she felt her first labor pains. Adjusting to the intensity of being a Sponge and being taken by surprise at the twenty-four-hour-a-day, seven-day-a-week neediness of her baby, Rachael told us that becoming a mother didn't seem like such a good bargain in terms of the time and effort to get her own life back after childbirth. She found herself distrusting Matt's ability to take care of the baby the way she thought he should, as well as resenting the quickness with which he returned to work, taking time off only until she came home from the hospital with Arta. They had never had one cross word between them before, but now their constant squabbles over who was to do what with Arta were driving her crazy.

"Kiss *me* good-bye," was how Sally, another mother in one of our Circles groups, described the change in her identity that occurred when her son, Adam, was about two months old. She resented the forces of love, anxiety, and responsibility she felt because she now had a baby who controlled her life but seemed to have little effect on her husband. Adam even controlled her weight! She couldn't believe that he weighed only eight pounds at birth and she still hadn't lost the thirty pounds she had gained during her pregnancy. Her self-image as a slim and trim, active, successful real estate agent was in conflict with her new identity: a fat, rocking, up-all-night, floor-pacing, nursing mother.

This identity crisis that begins for parents in the Celebrity season takes on a new intensity during the Sponge season. The baby's needs move to center stage through his constant demand for attention and care. He's the prima donna in every scene in the drama of his parents' lives. And all the while, the natural bonding process keeps telling them that they want to shower him with as much attention as they can. In the meantime, a couple's relationship is also demanding attention, as is being a loving son or daughter, a good friend, a responsible co-worker. All of these forces collide, creating conflict for parents who want to please each of these cast members. Many of our Circles members reported that it wasn't until they "surrendered" to the baby's needs that they felt these conflicts ease.

In *Tommy and Me*, author Ben Stein wrote: "Once I stopped resisting the responsibility of fatherhood, once I got my priorities straight about fatherhood as compared with everything else, my life was far easier, calmer, and better, not harder or more painful. It's a lot better at three in the afternoon and incomparably better at three in the morning."

Just as in the Celebrity season, mothers and fathers experience the Sponge season of parenthood from a different perspective. As Stein illustrated, fathers—the former Roadies for their Celebrity wives—are now expected to become equal partners in servitude to their new infant. For them, the repercussions of this transition to becoming a Sponge are especially dramatic because they have experienced neither the physical impact of childbirth nor the nine months of Celebrity status and glory. On this foreign ground, men may feel useless, helpless, and unsure of where they fit in the new family structure.

On the other hand, men may experience a spiritual epiphany upon the birth of their child, as did PGA golfer Phil Mickelson. "Until you actually go through it yourself, you really can't appreciate the process of birth or the cycle of life. What joy and what an amazing process that is."

After the initial rush, excitement, attention, and confusion of the first few weeks, both mothers and fathers find that they are constantly renegotiating every decision they make, from who gets up in the night to who takes the baby to day care. It is up to both spouses to reconcile the father's and the mother's place in their partnership as Sponges.

IS THE HONEYMOON OVER?

After ecstasy, the laundry.—ZEN SAYING

Given the enormous changes that even a healthy baby brings to parents' lives, it is remarkable that any relationship endures the transformation that their baby puts it through. Needing to care for a baby puts another person literally in between her mom and dad, testing the fabric of their lives, individually and as a family . . . whether this is the first, second, or fifth child they fit into their hearts.

In this season, parents need to use the virtuous behaviors that they have learned—patience, cooperation, empathy, and compassion—to continue to nurture their own relationship, while understanding the new need to focus on someone else. There never seems to be enough time, parents told us, to do everything. Regardless of how busy their lives were before their baby's birth, it is the constant emotional and physical strain of meeting the baby's emotional and physical needs that results in parents feeling overwhelmed and lost in their relationship with each other.

Talk show host Leeza Gibbons identified with this fact of parenthood in this season after her third baby. "I don't think we have been able to grow as much as a couple as we'd like to because we give so much to our children," she said.

The character of the couple's relationship before the birth of the baby, not the characteristics of the newborn, prevents these feelings about shifting priorities from becoming a fatal wound to a marriage or relationship. Just as in any other change that a couple goes through—downsizing at work, moving to a strange city, a tough bout of pneumonia—the strength of character of the relationship determines its survival.

Even in cases when the newborn faces enormous health crises, parents in healthy relationships told us that they remained determined to support each other. This spirit of perseverance and caring brought them closer together in the midst of their challenges. They committed themselves to becoming a team with the focus on cooperation in caring for the baby, regardless of the difficulties involved.

Parenthood opens up new frontiers of decision making for parents whether their baby is healthy or not. The Celebrity season most likely never included negotiating who would go to the store to get diapers in the middle of the night, who would bathe or feed the baby, who would stay home from work when he was sick or take him to play group, for example. Now the couple must prioritize those decisions in their lives. Even seemingly joyous decisions, such as choosing who the baby should be named after and who the godparents will be, can be territory that is fraught with tension.

"The hundreds of decisions that my husband and I needed to make about our baby daughter, Laura, shocked me," Beth, a Circles group mom, commented. She said that she felt as if she had turned into her mother *and* a Wicked Witch on her first day home from the hospital after her C-section. "My husband had one set of expectations for how things would work, and I had another. They were total opposites. When, where, and how everything would be done was material for putting our marriage in hot water. He didn't think I should breast-feed, and I hated for him to throw our baby up in the air while playing. Those were our two first fights. I felt that I had been cheated out of my wonderful husband. In his place, I got this weirdo, whose ideas about parenthood and baby care were totally ridiculous!"

"Was having to share control over decision making the problem?"

asked Glenda, a quiet mom with a worried brow in Beth's Circles group who was nodding her head to everything Beth said.

"Share control?" Beth questioned. "My husband never seemed to be a male chauvinist until Laura was born. Then he revealed his true colors, and they were all dark and horrid! He says that I am better at baby care than he is," she told us. "That's just because he's tired and doesn't want to deal with it. Besides, he doesn't have a clue about babies and refuses to learn."

A third member of Beth and Glenda's group, Dolly, had her own tales of postpartum marital woes: "Honey, I'm home. Where's dinner?" That's what she said her husband, Lyle, yells every night. "Like I'm supposed to go bring him his slippers, the baby, and his dinner in his easy chair so he can kick back and watch the sports channel?"

We all laughed at the honesty of these three soaking wet female Sponges. All three were obviously bothered by their need for control and their feelings of losing their familiar partners. "Am I no longer able to have a fun relationship with a man?" Dolly asked. All she did with Lyle was practical or political, never romantic or riveting, she lamented, wondering out loud whether this whole baby business was going to be a wrecking ball that would destroy her former happy home.

For Dolly, putting a new spin on the Sponge season—the honeymoon *as she knew it* was over—would help her understand that life with newborns is never the same clean, tidy lovefest it may have been before parenthood entered the scene. But it can be a lovefest just the same.

Corey, one of the few fathers who came to the Circles group for newborns, boldly brought up the subject of sex after the baby's birth. "I knew Stephanie wouldn't be in a romantic mood for a while, and we hadn't had sex during the last few weeks before Aaron's birth. So I came home early one Friday and fixed a nice dinner, took care of the baby while Stephanie took a long soak in a bubble bath, then served dinner by candlelight after Aaron was asleep. It worked!" Corey said, blushing. Corey's gentle, romantic approach to getting back into the sexual groove was to nurture his wife and to make her feel special again as his partner, even though he found himself upstaged by their newborn most of the time. On that Friday night, a new family tradition was born!

Making time to listen to each other and demonstrate that their partner is still important through kind and caring gestures of love can reestablish the romance in a marriage that a squalling baby with a full diaper regularly kills. When parents are in the Sponge season of parenthood, it's so easy to be used up by the baby's needs that devoting loving time and attention to each other seems so foreign, almost absurd. Spontaneity goes by the wayside. Forcing the time to plan special treats for themselves—making dinner dates with friends, taking the baby for long walks in the new stroller—can strengthen the new relationship as parents.

A buzzing of emotions swarms the couple during this new time of discovery about each other and their baby. They're poised to get stung by reality at any moment . . . and must work at keeping their relationship secure regardless of the swarm. What happens in this season lays the foundation for the business of parenthood—embracing change—instead of being flattened by it.

FROM ME TO PARENT

In the sheltered simplicity of the first days after a baby is born, one sees again the magical closed circle. The miraculous sense of two people existing only for each other.
—ANNE MORROW LINDBERGH

Although some parents may experience a smooth transformation from "me" to "parent" in this stage, others have told us that they found themselves asking, "When is the real Mom coming?" when they were first home with their baby. They found it disconcerting, at least, and downright overwhelming, most of the time, when they first realized, as dumb as it sounds, that *they* were their babies' parents.

In her book, *Operating Instructions*, Anne Lamott wryly described how unreal having a new baby can seem at first, particularly for first-time parents: "It feels like I'm baby-sitting in the Twilight Zone. I keep waiting for the parents to show up because we are out of chips and Diet Cokes."

To many new parents, like Lamott, their own mothers and fathers are still the "Mom" and "Dad"—not them—just as they had felt in the Celebrity season. In fact, one youthful-looking mom told us about her daily epiphanies that came when she passed her hallway mirror at home every day while carrying her baby from room to room, even six weeks after a complicated birth. Her own image would startle her, and she would shake her head in disbelief over a fact that she knew was true—the baby was *hers*. He was counting on *her* to be his mom. "It blew me away to realize that now I was responsible for the very life of this child. I was having trouble just getting my teeth brushed every day!" she said, laughing.

BECOMING SOAKED WITH PARENTHOOD in this season continues the changes in the relationships between new parents and *their* parents that began in the Celebrity season. Your own parents created a blueprint; do you follow it or rip it up and draft your own? If Dad never changed a diaper, would son never do so, either? If Mom never acted as though she cared about Dad after the baby, would daughter also ignore her husband? It's hard to change your behavior from what you were taught by your parent role models, but it can be done and, in many cases, must be done when new parents don't want to repeat old patterns of behavior that they believe are wrong or unhealthy.

Making the conscious decision to parent differently from the ways that you were parented—breast-feeding instead of bottle-feeding, for example—may be the first "official" signpost that your childhood is over now that you have a child. From this point forward, you'll begin to relive your own childhood memories through the child you're raising.

"One of the great things about having children is you get to right the wrongs of your childhood," said talk show host Rosie O'Donnell. "It's a wonderful chance to give yourself what you didn't have by giving it to your kid."

When you are a child, you are not aware, of course, of the fact that you will relive your own childhood stages during your own child's stages of childhood. Suddenly, as a new parent, you become aware of this fact; the past that you can't remember takes on new meaning. The first symptom? You now start to listen with attentive ears to your parents' old boring stories about your baby days. You even ask them: Was I breast-fed? Fussy? A "good" baby? Did I sleep through the night at three months? Eat solids before six months? Sweat at night? Take a pacifier?

As Martha questioned her mother, Claudia, about what Martha was like as a baby, another critical subject came up: How did Claudia feel during Martha's infancy? "I thought that I was supposed to be so thrilled after I became a mother, but I was absolutely miserable," Martha told us in one of our Circles groups. "I wanted to know if this happened to my mom, too, or if I was just going crazy."

Martha learned that, like her, Claudia had also suffered a bout of the "baby blues," a condition that is common in about 90 percent of new moms, according to some estimates. Often also called postpartum depression, it is most likely caused by estrogen and progesterone levels dropping after childbirth and can last for as little as a few days or as much as six weeks. Postpartum depression that lasts longer, for several months, affects fewer numbers of women and may be due to other factors, as well as hormonal fluctuations, which explains why fathers and adoptive mothers may also experience it. Several of these factors include feeling overwhelmed and helpless; disappointed if expectations about childbirth or the adoption aren't realized; exhausted by lack of sleep; guilty over feelings of rejection for the baby; and let down after the anticlimactic end of childbirth and the end of their Celebrity status or the adoption process. Mild degrees of these feelings are absolutely normal and predictable. Persistent depression is *not* normal, and it can and should be treated. (If you find yourself affected by serious depression—typical symptoms are a pervasive sense of despair, an overwhelming sense of guilt, suicidal thoughts—please seek help immediately from a health professional.)

The nonhormonal changes leading a mother to this state of misery are all about the shift from "me" to "parent." It is the "me" at war with the "parent" on the precipice, fighting over whether loving and caring for a baby will cause her to fall off a cliff and lose herself forever. Adjusting to this shift in identity demands continuous effort during the year-long season of the Sponge. Just as a baby must crawl before she can walk, a parent must transform herself into a Sponge, resolving the conflicts inherent in that transformation, before she is able to successfully transform herself again in the next season as Family Manager.

When asked whether parenthood had changed their lives, parents answering a survey in *Baby Talk,* September 1998 answered that it had— "more" or "less":

More . . .	Less . . .
➤ Stress	➤ Conversation
➤ Teamwork	➤ Free time
➤ Compromise	➤ Intimacy
➤ Flexibility	➤ Freedom
➤ Frustration	➤ Lovemaking
➤ Grown up	➤ Privacy
➤ Complicated	➤ Spontaneity
➤ Fulfilled	➤ Romance

More . . .	Less . . .
➤ Loving	➤ Time
➤ Mature	➤ Sex
➤ Patient	➤ Sleep
➤ Responsible	➤ Selfishness

As this survey confirms, parents' change in primary identity from daughter and wife to mother or son and husband to father brings about significant changes in their intimate relationships with each other. As one Circles group dad explained his dilemma: "I suddenly saw my wife, Carol, as a mother, not a wife. I even said that she seemed more like *my own* mother now that we had a baby. That thought really put a damper on our sex life. I didn't know how I was going to change my thinking about this until it suddenly occurred to me—I'm a father now. Mothers and fathers having sex is okay."

Parents need to be cognizant of the changes in how they perceive themselves, as well as each other, in this crucial identity-change passage of their lives. As they change into mothers and fathers, it is easy to forget that they are still husbands and wives. The duties of parenthood can at times seem so overwhelming that relationships outside those involving the baby may seem to be lost causes. In the Sponge season, it's a virtual guarantee that little Cody is going to wake up and want to be fed just when his parents are approaching a moment of bliss! This sort of coitus interruptus foreshadows ongoing conflicts between satisfying a couple's personal needs and meeting the demands of parenthood that must constantly be renegotiated, day and night, for the rest of their lives.

HELP! I'M RESPONSIBLE

I look at women with children and I think, Who am I kidding? Motherhood is when it gets real. Until that happens, I'm in training.—ACTRESS HELEN HUNT

A close cousin to the conflicts surrounding identity and change is their rowdy relative named responsibility, who joins the family by the truckload during this season of parenthood. Each time a couple becomes a mom and dad, whether for the first, second, third, or fourth time, or more, the truth is that their baby now prioritizes their lives, their values, their choices. Even if it seems as if a decision has nothing to do with the baby, such as buying a car or new coffee table, for example, he holds the swing vote, forcing parents to make responsible choices with his safety needs in mind: built-in infant seat, childproof locks, no sharp corners, no glass tops.

The baby's agenda is pretty basic—her whole little life is geared toward "making" you be responsible for her, learn about her, respond to her, love her, cuddle her, keep her safe, fit her into your life, and teach her to trust you. She demands that you let her sleep and eat when she wants, and for heaven's sake, keep her clean.

"I couldn't even go to the bathroom without thinking about the baby," Sharon said in one of our Circles groups. "It was as if I had to have my radar constantly on, monitoring her before I could make a move."

"We couldn't go to bed with an easy heart anymore. Part of me was always listening to every squeak and creak Kyle made," another Circles group mother said about her newborn. Even though she also had an eight-year-old and two-year-old, she "forgot that having a baby meant giving up sleeping."

"Can I find a sitter?" was the first question Margie would ask herself before saying yes to any invitation. She would dread doing the research: no sitter seemed good enough for her newborn but her parents. But she had just asked them to sit last week. Should she ask her in-laws? No, they really weren't comfortable with the baby yet. Marge decided that it was easier to stay home than to be responsible for making all of the decisions she needed to make just in the baby-sitting department before she could even get out of the house!

I F THE BABY is in trouble, physically or mentally, the need for parents to be responsible rises to a limitless level. Parents agonize in nearly "indescribable ways," as one of our Circles group interviewees labeled her emotional pain when learning how sick her premature baby really was. They also must intellectually and physically be the ultimate model of responsibility by addressing the problem, becoming an expert and advocate on their baby's behalf.

"I called my mother to rescue me after my baby was born with almost every health problem you could think of," Teresa told her Circles group. "Her response was, 'You are the mother now. You take care of that baby.' And I did. It was the best advice she ever gave me. I had to rethink everything I ever thought about special-needs kids. I wanted to pinpoint the fault. But instead I realized that it happens to people. It happened to me. I also realized that I was so upset because I wasn't thinking about my baby. I was just thinking about me. I had to let go of 'me' to be able to be responsible for her tremendous needs. Because of my daughter's problems, I never have taken for granted anything that each of my three kids has done."

A single parent is also dramatically affected by the enormous responsibilities of the Sponge season. There is no tag team, no down time; no time when she can separate herself from being both mother and father. Single parents, even more so than partners, become so saturated with the baby that it's hard to tell where the baby's life stops and theirs starts.

Adults who are irresponsible in the first place don't adapt well to the truckload of responsibility dumped on Sponges. They find justification for failing to show up for work, leaving early from their jobs, not paying their bills, not keeping appointments. Others who are highly distractible might find it difficult to remember to do the thousands of chores required to care for a child.

Serena, a member of one of our Circles groups, told us that the first month home with her baby was the most difficult experience of her life because she was so disorganized and, at the age of twenty-eight, had never needed to take responsibility for any part of her life. Her mother still made her haircut and doctor appointments, picked up groceries for her, and called her daily to remind her to take her medicine. Taking responsibility as a parent for something as enormous as caring for her baby became a truly defeating experience for her until she began to accept responsibility for taking care of herself.

The twenty-three-year-old daughter of one of our Circles group moms, Kirsten, expected her mother to take care of her baby. She used her mother to achieve her own freedom from the responsibility of parenthood, believing that she was entitled to have fun rather than be tied down to the duties of caring for her baby.

It's normal for parents to feel ambivalent about wanting to think their own private thoughts and follow their own personal agenda, while understanding deep inside their hearts that their baby needs them to be a loyal, loving servant. Albeit stressful, feeling this way is natural in this season of parenthood. The investments that are made emotionally, spiritually, intellectually, and physically in this second season of parenthood are rewarded handsomely in love and devotion between parent and child in later seasons. But it's almost impossible to foresee these dividends during this tiring and often tedious time as a Sponge.

The irony of this conflict over responsibility is that it deludes parents into thinking that they will always be as physically responsible for—and able to control—their children's well-being in future seasons as they are in this season, when their babies are totally dependent on them. Not so, of course. The adage "Parents provide the roots *and* wings for their children" is meaningful by the end of this season, when children become eager to flap their wings and explore the world, knowing that their roots are secure in their nests at home as they begin their long transition from toddlerhood to adulthood.

For those parents who learn how to thrive on being so totally needed and so wholly responsible for another human being, it will be difficult to let go of this season of parenthood. But let go they must, because at the end of this season, when their baby starts to toddle away from them, they will begin to appreciate their ultimate responsibility as a parent: helping their child grow to become an independent, self-sufficient human being who will one day be able to take care of them.

Phil's New Love: Great Expectations

Babies? Hmmm. A deep smile edged its way across Phil's lips as he sank into his favorite slatted-back rocking chair on the front porch of his fifty-year-old farmhouse, holding his daughter, Elizabeth. This was a man who had never dared believe such peace, happiness, and contentment could come into his life. But miraculously it had . . . in the form of this wiggly, cruising-the-house, ten-month-old little light in his life.

For Phil, life as a dad had become one big love affair, a love affair that he had never imagined was possible. First of all, he patiently explained to us in our interview, still smiling, he was an only child. And he did mean only. No other children had ever darkened the door of his parents' farmhouse, unless he invited them over to play and either his parents or the other child's would agree to drive the several miles to pick up and deliver. His mother and father were also "only" children, which made holiday get-togethers memorable, he reported, because they were the most boring occasions all year. Although his parents showered him with love and attention, he admitted to having had such a lonely childhood that he was determined to have a house full of children himself.

"My wife, Sally, had just the opposite experience," he told us. Having grown up in a farmhouse full of eight kids, she was right at home now in the kind of setting that she had always wanted for raising her own.

Before Elizabeth was born, both Sally and Phil agreed that she wouldn't go back to her job running the local bakery after her maternity leave, even though the perks of that job would be useful when they entertained the seed corn dealers and salesmen who came through their small Nebraska town on field days.

But now that Elizabeth was here, Sally had a change of heart about returning to her job. She admitted that she didn't want to cut out any piece of her life to make room for taking care of the baby. She wanted to do it all, just as all of her friends were doing. So Phil and Sally worked out a new plan: While Phil worked the farm and Sally spent the day at the bakery, Sally's mother would take care of Elizabeth. Sally was proud of her management position in the bakery because being one of eight children, she had never felt very special. Finally, this job gave her a sense of self-importance. Growing up with seven brothers and sisters had been mass chaos; working was a breeze compared to managing her sibling wars for all of these years.

Phil was the one who was driving her crazy, Sally told us, not Elizabeth. He wanted her to stay home and take care of the baby full-time and kept coming up with reasons for her to quit her job at the bakery. She would be too "worn out," as he put it, if she started getting up so early in the morning to go to the bakery and then had to stand on her feet all day. She wouldn't have the energy for taking care of their daughter at night.

"Worn out?" Sally exclaimed when she heard his criticism, suddenly defensive about her stamina. "Who was he to say what I would feel like!"

He then admitted that he was concerned about Sally's mother's ability to take care of Elizabeth. She was too old, he said, and he thought that she was too old-fashioned to be a good caregiver for his daughter.

Sally was furious: how dare he insult her mother, too! Her mother had always dreamed of having a grandchild, Sally thought. This is a perfect job for her *right now, not* me. *She's the one with all the expertise.*

It was clear to us that the honeymoon was definitely over for both Phil and Sally as they worked at cross-purposes. Phil's love affair with Elizabeth was headed toward breaking up his marriage as he kept up his pressure on Sally to care for his precious daughter rather than follow her dreams.

• • •

THE DIFFERENCE BETWEEN Phil's elation and Sally's irritation over caring for Elizabeth told the story of how diverse parents' attitudes about responsibility can be. If a couple's expectations about baby care don't match, these conflicting views create a strain on the relationship and eventually on the child.

Sally discovered that she was eager to get away from baby care, something that she didn't realize until the baby came. She had had enough of it growing up—with seven children, there was always someone to feed, diaper, or burp. Now that she was finally on her own, she was ready for a change, to be responsible only for herself. Giving up herself to become a parent felt nothing like the Celebrity of pregnancy. That had been fun. Everyone had made a big fuss over her, and she and her mother had grown closer as they shared a part of her mother's life that Sally hadn't been able to relate to before.

But now things were different. She kept thinking that "Mom"—her mom—would and should be the one to take care of this baby . . . just as she had with all seven of Sally's brothers and sisters. Learning to *be* the mom who is responsible for Elizabeth would take Sally some time, we reassured her. She would have to toss out the old model of motherhood that she had engraved in her head from her own childhood and define it in a different way, one that would accommodate her interest in her career.

We encouraged Phil and Sally to create a new understanding of what parenthood would be like for them. He wanted so much to have a child of his own—a brood of his own—so that he could provide the same kind of loving family that he remembered so fondly. Now, Elizabeth was his chance to relive his childhood, with all the love and none of the loneliness. Meeting this agenda meant that he expected Sally to stay home with their daughter; this was the only template he knew.

Phil and Sally had different perspectives because of their opposite upbringings. Now they needed to meld the two into a unique family. Though they agreed that "the honeymoon was over" for them, they disagreed about why. Each thought that the other one was being selfish. Instead of having to give up her passion for her bakery job forever, Sally started to look at her life as one full of opportunities, not of doors slamming shut. She admitted that she did want to care for her family as her mother had done.

We started to brainstorm ways that she could solve her problems, which were truly "family" problems. She could literally have her cake and eat it, too, she dreamed, by starting a small bakery business in her own home.

Sally could care for Elizabeth and also immerse herself in the activity she loved—kneading dough into beautiful loaves. The rewards of being home were multiplied as she thought about being there to catch Elizabeth's first steps, first words, and first milestones . . . something she knew she would have regretted if she had "shirked her responsibility as a mother by being away all day," as she put it.

Change could be a good thing, Sally and Phil decided, if they tried to appreciate each other's points of view. They could create a family business that would provide them with much needed extra income. Phil volunteered to assist her in the bakery each day after the milking was done, and Sally offered to help him do their other farm chores while Elizabeth napped.

When they stopped defending their own positions and began looking realistically at their own dreams, Phil and Sally gained new respect for each other. They could provide Elizabeth with the two things she needed most: an energetic mother who was proud of her profession and an attentive father who understood his wife's desire to feed her culinary and maternal needs.

Elena Takes a Baby Bath: Marriage in Peril

"What do they say . . . the third time's the charm?" said Elena, a vivacious member of a Circles group, laughing as she explained to us that her third baby, Victoria, would definitely be her last.

Victoria was a surprise to Elena and her husband of ten years, Felipe, particularly since they were getting marriage counseling for what seemed to be a potentially explosive relationship between Elena and her friend, Roberto. Elena and Roberto had been childhood pals, and Felipe resented the intensity of their ongoing friendship. Elena wondered if Victoria's birth would end Felipe's jealousy of Roberto's friendship with her and make him more attentive to her and their three children.

She told us that Felipe just did not act like a father. He didn't play with their two boys, Edward and Michael, who were now three and six years old, and had never helped to take care of them when they were infants, unless she begged him to. His job as a supermarket manager provided the family with a good income, he always retorted when Elena got on her "kick" of nagging him about helping out at home. "Isn't that enough?" he would snort, his arms defiantly crossed in disgust.

Not for Elena. All she asked him to do was take them to the park or out in the yard on weekends to play while she did the laundry, cooked supper, and nursed Victoria, she explained to us. "Maybe I should get him to feed the baby more often so she will catch his heart if he plays with her," she suggested to us, "like the other two took over mine, even during all those long days and nights when they were babies."

She had felt like a mother from the first moment she found out that she was pregnant with Michael, nearly seven years ago. Edward, their second son, was supposed to be a girl, she shared with a smile. But she also fell madly in love with him the second he was born, never once regretting that they had not gotten "their girl."

Now they had that girl, Elena mused. She told us that Felipe had threatened to leave if the baby was another boy. She didn't believe him, though. He was always making empty threats to leave if she didn't do what he asked, just to maintain his position as the boss in the household, she surmised. It usually upset her and started them on a path of arguing until she finally gave in, just so they wouldn't fight in front of the children.

Now Elena's goal was to keep her job as a part-time X-ray technician; if Felipe did leave her, at least she would have the good medical coverage and lots of friends at work to give her moral support. She wanted this baby to "work" for their family's sake and vowed to do everything she could to help Felipe work with her to make theirs the warm, caring, nurturing family that she'd always wanted. She knew that this baby would either make or break the chances of that ever happening. It's now or never, she told us.

Having a baby to save a marriage is almost always a recipe for disaster, as Elena and Felipe learned the hard way. Although Elena had literally saturated her life with her two boys during their infancy, a corner of her was ready to soak up one more infant. How could you ignore the tug on your heart that a baby provides? she would ask Felipe as Victoria gazed lovingly at her.

Victoria was only four months old, but wherever they went, she was the center of attention. It was funny how this Celebrity thing worked, Elena told us after we explained that she had just passed through that season of Celebrity herself during her pregnancy.

"Oh yes," she adamantly agreed. "I was the one getting all of the attention then. Now it's her."

Felipe believed that being responsible for a baby was "woman's work." He had grown up with a dad who was never home, who worked three jobs, morning, night, and weekends; he remembered that his mother had never once complained about her husband's irresponsibility in helping her care for the children.

Now that he was a father, all he heard about from Elena was what a lousy dad he was. Truth was, he just didn't know what to do with a baby, or even a toddler or preschooler, for that matter. And then there were the diapers. Felipe could imagine the teasing he would get from his buddies at the store where he worked if they heard that he changed his kid's diapers or did any of the other "woman's work" babies require.

His dad had never played with him because he was always working. He had always said that doing that stuff was not "his job." Felipe felt guilty if he took a couple of hours off to go see his son play T-ball. Somehow that made him less of a responsible father, he thought, because his own father had never done so, saying that his contribution to the family was working hard and making money for them. Felipe always feared losing his job, even though as manager he could come and go as he pleased.

Elena interpreted Felipe's behavior in another way. All she had ever dreamed of was being a mother. When she felt their first child stirring inside of her, the world suddenly seemed to make sense to her in a strange way. She believed that she now knew what her purpose on earth was. She had become the person she was meant to be.

Her own mother had felt the same way; she was totally devoted to Elena and her brother. As a speech and language specialist, her mother chose to work at an elementary school so she could have summers off and even made sure that she got off work at 2 P.M. so she could be there when Elena and her brother came home. Elena wanted to replicate her own childhood in her own children's lives.

Understanding that they couldn't control the past, only the future, Elena and Felipe continued to go to counseling in order for Felipe to become trusting of Elena's love for him. There, he was encouraged to give up questioning her feelings for him if she formed strong friendships or was so devoted to her boys that he felt there was no affection left over for him.

His empty threats about leaving were his unconscious way of saying that he felt unable to handle the responsibilities of fatherhood as well as his father, whom he idolized, did. He also felt uncomfortable with redefining what being a father meant; he almost believed that to do so would be an insult to his own father.

Elena reassured him that she was not comparing him with his dad; she also needed to learn that she shouldn't compare herself to her mother. It took intense work with their therapist before they realized they weren't bound to their parents' models of being a mother and father. Gradually they began to create new identities for themselves and to change from the patterns of behavior they had established with their older two children. Teaching Elena and Felipe not to fear change was like giving oxygen to both. They had needed the permission to give up their fears so their marriage could breathe.

Sarah's Search: Where's a Baby-sitter When You Need One?

Sarah, a computer software designer, needed only one thing to make her happy—to find a baby-sitter for her nine-month-old son, Justin, whose father had conveniently dropped off the radar screen when she had announced to him that she was pregnant. Now that she had to go it alone as a single parent, her biggest frustration was trying to find help when she needed it.

"It can't be possible that I can't find a baby-sitter!" she complained loudly to the Circles group. "This weekend is one of the most important social events of the year for me, and I can't find anybody to take care of Justin so I can go. This party at the lake is my once-a-year chance to get together with my college friends and party like we used to. Last year at the party I was pregnant with Justin, but I didn't let that slow me down. When I asked Laura, the hostess, if I could bring Justin this year, she just laughed at me. None of the others have children yet. I guess they don't want kids there spoiling their fun."

Sarah didn't know where to turn. The high school sophomore girl who often baby-sat for her was going on a band trip for the weekend and wasn't available. Sarah called several agencies, but she felt uncomfortable with the thought of leaving Justin with a stranger for a whole weekend.

"And this isn't the first time I've been caught without a baby-sitter or had to give up plans because Justin was sick and couldn't be left with anybody," she told us. "He gets that 'daycare disease,' as his pediatrician calls it; you know, with the runny nose, fever, and diarrhea. I'm slowly losing my old friends because I have to back out of a dinner party, movie, and even lunch dates because he's sick and I have to stay home, or because I can't find a baby-sitter. My old friends aren't calling anymore. They're telling me to call

them when I can get together with them, but I never know in advance whether Justin will be sick or if I can get a sitter."

Nothing was more overwhelming to Sarah than crossing the huge chasm between her carefree, prebaby life and the totally absorbing Sponge state of being a single parent. In her case, her links to her old, childless friends were now history. Many of our Circles group members told us, as they entered this season of parenthood, that being with other Sponges was more comfortable because they understood the challenges of their lives, such as finding baby-sitters and being nervous being away from their newborn. Some felt as if they had been "dropped" from the social calendar of their childless friends. Others still included them, intrigued by their babies and the paraphernalia needed for their maintenance, but the chasm between the "haves" and the "have-nots" still yawned.

In addition to losing her childless friends, Sarah was concerned that her advancement in her career was being jeopardized by not being able to attend all of the social events and convention weekends connected to her work. Taking a baby to these events was out of the question: so many of her friends and colleagues in the industry were young and childless; they didn't understand why Sarah just couldn't get somebody to take care of Justin so she could be free to do whatever she wanted.

Sarah had even toyed with trying to hire a nanny, but she just couldn't fit that expense into her already thin budget. At times she regretted the fact that she had gotten "caught with her birth control down," and the love and joy she felt when Justin was first born had worn off after all these months of having to devote so much time and energy to keeping him healthy and safe. Life with Justin was not at all what she had expected it to be. Sarah was often overwhelmed with guilt, however, when she caught herself wishing that this beautiful little boy of hers would stop wreaking havoc with her life. Her practical side kept nagging at her as she tried to find a balance between her career and parenthood, while her heartstrings kept pulling her inevitably toward taking care of Justin.

Soaking up parenthood alone, without another Sponge, is a tiring and time-consuming business. But when Sarah began to experience the prospect of losing old friends and putting her job in jeopardy, the joy and anxiety of helping a new life begin took on a whole new meaning.

Single Sponges need to focus on parenthood one day at a time, in order to avoid being overwhelmed by constantly being on call. It's also imperative to create a support network. We encouraged Sarah to seek out people at work, in her neighborhood, in her church or synagogue, who have babies, whether they are single parents or not, so that she could begin to build a new base of friends. They would understand what she was going through and even help her with names of available sitters because they were Sponges themselves.

Her old friends could still be a part of her life if she wanted them to be, of course, even if they didn't have children; but Sarah would have to make the extra effort needed to keep in touch. She would need to help them understand what she was going through and let them help her by moving a dinner party to her house, for example, if she couldn't find a sitter, or renting a movie instead of going out, so they could still spend time together. Some members of our Circles groups reported that childless friends sometimes offered to sit for them over weekends so that they could have some time alone. Sarah could approach her friends to provide child care for her convention weekends.

Her career could stay on track even if she had to move off the high-speed rails. But again, she would need to be creative to adjust to the demands of her job and parenthood. She could try to keep up with the advances in the industry, even when she couldn't attend the weekend seminars and meetings across the country, by asking her co-workers to bring home materials for her, collect business cards, and e-mail her with contacts with whom she could network. These compromises gave her a taste of one unflinching truth: Parenthood is one long lesson in flexibility.

By seeing that some of her dreams were still possible, Sarah began to look at parenthood as a part of her life that, while circumscribing, could also move her upstream in ways yet to be discovered, instead of as an impossible job that served as a constant reminder of what she was missing.

Skylar's Love Affair with Work: Why Don't I Feel Guilty?

Skylar said that she had never thought of herself as picky, fastidious, or a perfectionist. "I was never an angry person, either," she admitted, "until I had Bailey," who, we learned, was now eight months old. "When she did something like dirty her diaper right as we were leaving the house, I'd go ballistic. I didn't know what was wrong with me; but to tell you the truth, this taking-care-of-infants thing was driving me crazy! I felt guilty because I didn't feel guilty about going back to work when Bailey was six weeks old. I couldn't wait to get back to my real life as a television anchor."

We asked Skylar when she started to feel this way. She admitted that she had never adjusted to the daily drone and resented the utter exhaustion that she had felt during the first month after Bailey's birth. When she got home from the hospital, she had been terrified of doing the wrong thing: feeding Bailey formula that might upset her system and cause colic was her chief worry. Breast-feeding was "never an option" because she knew she would be going back to work at the station, and the suggestion that she use a breast pump was "out of the question." Letting Bailey sleep on her back made her fear what her mother said would happen: the back of Bailey's head would get flat if she didn't sleep on her stomach. But Skylar was determined to put Bailey on her back to sleep, in spite of her fear, because she had done a news story on the risk of sudden infant death syndrome and knew the dangers of putting babies on their tummy to sleep.

Being the center of attention during pregnancy had helped Skylar feel special, she told us. But now, she admitted quietly, she simply dreaded going through Bailey's infancy, a time of such intense servitude.

"I never feel confident when I'm around Bailey," Skylar admitted "I can't feel good because she always seems to be fussy, and I feel like I should be able to calm her down. But I rarely can. When I'm at the station, I feel so vital, so important. I'm contributing to society through my work in ways that I think are socially relevant. The station seems to be a better place for me than home because I'm happy and fulfilled there. The work at home seems so meaningless, so frustrating. How could fixing formula and changing diapers be anything but boring?"

Skylar's husband, Logan, felt just the opposite. After his own month of paternity leave, Bailey had him wrapped around her little finger. When he went back to work, he called the nanny ten times each day. "I would gladly stay home and take care of Bailey," he told Skylar. However, his company's stock options wouldn't be his for another year; and if he quit his job, they would lose tens of thousands of dollars.

No, he couldn't quit his job, Skylar and Logan decided. And she couldn't either. "I know that I should feel guilty about not wanting to stay home, but I don't. I just can't relate to this motherhood thing," Skylar told us. "But it's weird to be so sure of my career path, when all of my friends agonize over whether or not to stay home with their children until they get into school. If

I left my job now, I'd never get as good a position in five years as I have now. Plus, I'd probably look thirty years older; I already feel as if I've aged ten years just in the past eight months."

Although some new mothers and fathers quickly adjust to the water temperature when jumping into parenthood, others like Skylar have a more difficult, if not downright impossible, time feeling comfortable. So much of what happens during this season of parenthood depends upon who the swimmers were before they came to this particular swimming hole. Until her child was born, Skylar had also never pictured herself caring for a newborn, had never changed a diaper or even fed a baby a bottle. Her mother was rarely home as she was growing up because of her job as a flight attendant; even though her father had provided a stable role model for her sister and her, they were raised primarily by their housekeeper, Alice.

Skylar was so sure that her new little darling would break while on her watch that she was paralyzed with anxiety, exactly the opposite frame of mind necessary to handle the day-to-day responsibility of absorbing another human's life. She longed to have another Alice around to take care of Bailey, just as Alice had taken care of her. She and Logan had been through seven nannies in that many months, because they just couldn't find one they liked and trusted as much as Skylar's mother had relied on Alice.

But find the right nanny they must, Skylar told us, because the high visibility of her position in network television left her no options to cut back on her hours, work at home, or even change her schedule. It was a job that she had climbed the corporate ladder to get, and now that it was hers, she couldn't imagine letting it go. Her co-workers who had children complained that they felt guilty about not being with their children most of their waking hours and missing their children's important milestones. Because she was hearing so much about guilt, Skylar began to feel guilty that she didn't feel the same way they did.

Skylar's guilt stemmed from her feeling selfish because she would rather devote her time to her career than her baby. "We don't like to do the lawn maintenance or the housecleaning because those are mundane and boring jobs, so we hire people to do them for us. Taking care of Bailey is pretty mundane and boring, too, so we want to hire someone to do that job, just as my parents did," Skylar told us.

Putting the care of their infant daughter in the context of an onerous job was keeping Skylar from the most important aspect of the Sponge season of parenthood: her transformation from Skylar the daughter and wife to Skylar the daughter, wife, and mother. But being a Sponge is tricky: the longer parents wait before adjusting their own self-image to being a mother or father, the more catch-up they have to do later. It is an unwritten law of parenthood: Each season must be worked through . . . sooner or later.

Sooner or later children will demand that their parents pay attention to them by their behavior during the Family Manager or later seasons of parenthood. They will attach themselves to their parents' hearts: making them worry when they're sick, driving them to the heights of despair when they can't find a way to comfort them, making them glow when they smile.

Millions of parents today experience this attachment to their babies as they progress through the Sponge season: soaking, dripping, getting squeezed by their life with their babies. Logan and Skylar will get just as wet, simply by being a part of Bailey's life. They are just delaying their transformation into Sponges. It's not a matter of if, but when.

Lori Makes a Move: The Married Single Parent

Lori's husband, Bruce, had to travel to training seminars for his insurance company and was gone for weeks at a time during the first year after the birth of their daughter, Sasha.

"It was a living hell," Lori recounted to us, admitting that she was glad that he had the great job he did, but it just didn't seem worth it to her for him to miss everything that was happening. "I mean everything," Lori shared. "Everything happened during this first year."

When we talked with Lori, Bruce was back home for two weeks and then was scheduled to be gone again for another six weeks. Lori had spent a few years after college working as a reporter, but she had never felt that invested in her job. Her co-workers and surroundings had seemed transient, and she wanted something more stable. That's why she had been so excited about Sasha before she learned that Bruce's absences would essentially make her a single parent. With Sasha, life would have some permanence, some structure that she could count on.

"I'm not trying to be difficult," she continued. "But this isn't the way I had pictured us being parents. What happened to all of those neat times that Bruce and I dreamed of walking Sasha through the park, just like my mom

and dad said they used to walk me with their best friends, Fran and David, and their baby? Now Bruce is too tired to do anything when he comes home on weekends. I have to beg him to take care of Sasha. He makes up excuses for why he can't be in charge of her care while I run errands and have some time to myself.

"I feel like he's not even Sasha's dad. My dad did everything—changed diapers, fed my brother and me, put us to bed. I used to love to ride horsey on his back—those are some of my best memories. What memories will Sasha have of her dad? A big zero! I don't have the luxury of choosing if I want to be a parent like Bruce gets to. I don't even remember when I've had a full night's sleep or day of fun, for that matter. I didn't think I was this angry, but I guess my resentment has been building up week after week," she continued.

To avoid yelling at him and starting a big fight when he would finally come home from the road and spend all day Saturday zoned out in front of the golf channel on television, Lori started making other plans on the weekend, plans that did not include him, just as she did during the week when he was gone. She went to the park with Sasha, met friends and their children for lunch, or went to the museum or the art gallery.

"Now I understand what it feels like to be a single parent," she lamented, recounting all the things she and Sasha did together without Bruce. "I didn't intend to be a single parent when I married Bruce. Who would have thought it would be like this?"

Bruce was also feeling embittered. He hadn't expected to be traveling as much as he was on his job, but he knew that he could double his salary if he got all of this extra training. He resented Lori's being angry with him for trying to provide for his family. He had also just assumed that all of the partying they had done on the weekends before Sasha was born would come to a quick halt once they became parents. His parents never got baby-sitters so they could go out, so why should he and Lori? Bruce and his dad had always enjoyed watching sports on weekends, and his mother never complained. At least he was proud of his work ethic, even if his wife didn't seem to be.

If both parents haven't agreed to prioritize the baby when she enters their lives, they'll be out of sync with each other and, most likely, with their child. The major problem with this season of parenthood is that once you miss it because you think other things are more important—because it just doesn't fit your schedule to be there for it or because you are too wrapped up in your own self-importance—you can never retrieve it.

It is a transformative time. At no other time in a child's life will she grow and change so quickly; at no other time does the sand move quite so dramatically through the hourglass. It is a holy thing, this mysterious developmental stage of childhood. It's a spiritual season of parenthood, as both witness this miracle firsthand. But they have to "be there" in mind, body, and spirit to "get it." Sasha's contentment while being bathed, fed, cuddled, and being comforted satisfied Lori's need to know that Sasha was happy: when Sasha was happy, she was happy. Bruce's absences meant he was failing, over and over, to make that same vital connection.

MANY A PARENT is controlled by the pull of a time clock or a traveling job that makes hotel rooms seem more like home. The strain of losing out on the day-to-day ins and outs of life together can dissolve the glue that holds the family together, as Bruce was experiencing. The "absent" parent's lack of focus on the business of the baby also creates a dismal sense of personal failure in the "present" parent, for whom single parenthood is the fallout of mismatched parental agendas.

This was precisely what happened to Bruce and Lori. Bruce's frequent and extended absences and his devotion to his job blasted holes of silence into their relationship. Lori felt all the responsibility of parenthood but none of the rewards of sharing it with her beloved husband. She began to withdraw in anger and refused to tell him all the things that Sasha was now doing, supposedly to "pay him back" for his neglect. She had no choice but to give up all semblance of her prebaby life and the dreams of togetherness that she thought they shared. But for Bruce it was business as usual, and *that* made her furious.

She had counted on their being parents as her parents had been parents—100 percent contribution from each side. Sasha's infancy was passing by, and Bruce wasn't even aware, nor did he seem to care, that he was missing what Lori thought was their most important time with their baby. They both needed to understand each other's dilemmas, however, and the reality of coping with each of their situations.

We helped them discuss various options that might increase their time together, physically as well as emotionally, in raising Sasha: making a family event out of bathing the baby, playing with Sasha in the evening instead of watching TV, making the bedtime routine a family affair, reading books to Sasha, and working together to prepare meals and to feed her. Teamwork would make the tasks seem easier and help them learn to rely on each other rather than seek support elsewhere.

Lori's habit of finding others who would listen and understand her frustration was helpful only momentarily, but it signaled a desperate need for connection with a partner who would share the joy she experienced while soaking up this season of parenthood. Though the honeymoon is over for all couples when they become parents, no laws have been written that say "threesomes" that include the new baby cannot find another kind of honeymoon bliss. Lori and Bruce examined Bruce's perception of his need to provide a lot of money for his family, factored in how financial gains fit into their family's new priorities, and realized that, indeed, money could not buy them love. Still, it wasn't practical for Bruce to abandon all his career-building training; the key was to scale back and strike a better balance.

These decisions are paramount because they set up the responsibilities for each parent's life in Season Three, the Family Manager. Now the "Company" is being formed: by-laws are being written. To maintain equity that will hold its value as parents move from Sponge to Family Manager, both parents must reprioritize personal needs if they are in the way of providing love and nurturing for the baby and for each other. They must learn to take each other's emotional temperature in order to decide how to manage their marriage as parents, not simply as a couple.

Self-Discoveries of Sponges

Your pocket guide to the truths revealed in the Sponge season of parenthood.

➤ **Hang on tight.** As you take the first plunge on the roller-coaster ride of parenthood, the drop into the duties and responsibilities of caring for this new life is fast and furious; regardless of the number of times you've ridden the ride, its power and intensity will take you by surprise.

➤ **Don't worry about your hair.** You may feel that you've lost yourself during this drop into parenthood. But while you're in this season, your goal is to adjust to the feel of the ride. Stay in the moment with your baby. You'll never look better than when you're soaking wet and smothered with love.

➤ **Holding hands is hard.** Despite the fact that you're on the ride to-gether with your partner, hanging on to each other is hard to do as you make this plunge. You may find that letting out screams at the same time brings you closer together.

➤ **Keep a hankie handy!** Expect to get wet in this stage of the ride. No one reaches the next turn dry and unchanged.

Exit Signs

Leaving Duty Swamp. Entering Control Room. The diapers and milk continue to stain your life as your baby defines your daily schedule. But as soon as she becomes upright and mobile, your baby will begin to explore her world, catapulting you into Season Three, the Family Manager. Your parenthood journey will then become defined by the process of civilizing this vibrant, vertical whirlwind of activity, formerly known as the Baby.

SEASON THREE

Family Manager

CHILD'S TODDLER AND PRESCHOOL YEARS

Management by objectives works if you know the objectives. Ninety percent of the time you don't.
—PETER DRUCKER

"WHEN MY DAUGHTER WAS a baby, I couldn't wait for her to start walking and talking. She started walking when she turned one; since she turned two, she does both, nonstop! Now I just wish she'd stay put and be quiet . . . for even a minute. You know the old saying: 'We spend the first two years of our children's lives teaching them to walk and talk and the rest of their lives trying to get them to sit down and shut up!' "

PARENTS OF TODDLERS and preschoolers we interviewed said that they wholeheartedly agreed with this mother's lament as they witnessed their infants changing from dependent, horizontal, immobile bundles of joy to independent, vertical, mobile little chatterboxes. They found that this season of parenthood was not a stage for the "weak willed or fainthearted," as one father wryly put it. Civilizing their recklessly mobile, insatiably curious, unpredictably moody miniature offspring is hard work, physically, intellectually, emotionally, and spiritually.

In the Sponge season, not only are parents shackled to their infants'

91

feeding and sleeping schedules, but their babies' freedom is also restricted by their helplessness. In the Family Manager season, however, independence is everyone's battle cry. All the rules change as children demonstrate their personalities and activate their ability to protest: running away when their names are called; uttering their new word, no; coloring walls, furniture, and curtains with streaks of crayon; venturing into streets; scrambling out of strollers; getting into medicine cabinets. When children reach this stage of development, it's essential to appoint a manager who's in charge of their day-to-day business, because toddlers are inexperienced navigators of their world; they will put themselves and their families in danger in the blink of an eye if left to their own devices. Therefore, parents are inevitably forced to take on a new identity, Family Manager, to safeguard the investment in love, time, and attention they've made in their new family during the Celebrity and Sponge seasons.

They must now ratchet up their physical energy to save their adventurous wanderers from harm, grow eyes in the back of their head to find where they have run off to, and monitor what comes out of their own mouths to provide appropriate language lessons for their little ones. Their lives are transformed by these three central challenges: selling their toddlers and preschoolers on learning social skills; coping with personal performance reviews; and making sure that they stay in charge of the "family business"—maintaining relationships with each other, their parents, and their in-laws; childproofing their home; rectifying their family finances.

Although their toddlers' and preschoolers' needs still prioritize their life choices in the Family Manager season, parents' personal agendas begin to reemerge from obscurity as their children learn to walk, talk, use the toilet, demonstrate manners, dress themselves, share, and get along with others—the end markers of this season of parenthood. Their investment in the family will have then grown large enough to earn parents the new dividend that had been their goal for the past five years: a Big Boy or Girl who is developmentally ready to enter the next stage of growth in the Big World of elementary school.

66 IT'S SO FUNDAMENTAL, what you're doing for another person. And you're able to do it even though it takes a lot. I wouldn't have thought of myself as a person who could guide anybody. And then it turned out that I can. Not that I'm perfect. But it turns out I have answers to some

of [my son's] questions. And if I don't, I can say, 'You know, I have that question, too,' " said actress Meg Ryan.

The self-acceptance that Ryan demonstrates is a healthy tool that will come in handy from this season forward, as you'll struggle to keep your self-confidence high when faced with often unflattering performance reviews from your children. In the past, your relationship with your baby was largely insular. She provided you with intelligible feedback, but you didn't interpret it as a report on how you were doing in managing the family business. Your crying baby may have upset you if she couldn't be comforted, for example, but you probably didn't take her being upset as a sign that you weren't being good parents. You were frustrated, but most often didn't consider her fussiness to be your fault; it was simply a sign that your baby needed something.

Now, however, if your toddler or preschooler throws a tantrum in the grocery store, for example, because he wants to run from aisle to aisle but you say that he must ride in the cart, you become embarrassed, angry that your child would make you look like bad parents by causing such a public scene. Now, you believe it *is* your fault that he's making such a spectacle because you know that you are accountable for training him to become a socially responsible little person. You've come face-to-face with this unwritten law of parenthood: Once a child is upright and mobile, he or she is supposed to behave in socially acceptable ways. So it is in this season of parenthood that mothers and fathers first find their job performance reflected in what their children say and do. You see your own weaknesses and strengths in the behavioral mirrors that your children, ages one to five, hold up in front of you.

Parents, family, and friends only exacerbate this phenomenon. They have said from early on that they could see a mother's blue eyes in her daughter's little face, or a father's curly hair in his son's ringlets. Now you're constantly being reminded by others' comments about your toddler's and preschooler's behavior that you're the primary influences—for better or for worse—on how your child acts in front of the outside world. You've spent the last two seasons of parenthood growing accustomed to the fact that you've genetically provided the "nature" of your child—his or her looks, personality, and temperament—and now you're keenly aware that you also control the nurture—the primary environment in which your child becomes a civilized little human being.

During the Family Manager season, parents have the awesome honor of

watching their little "liquids" turn into "solids." That is why parents' behaviors are so important: their children's character and behavior begin to
solidify; and what their children see and hear becomes part of who they
are and what they do. Soon after this season begins, you realize that it is
incumbent on you to become self-controlled managers of the family in
order to reach the long-term goal of raising socially responsible children
who are increasingly self-sufficient and independent.

Look at Caitlin, an adorable, well-behaved three-year-old little girl, for
proof of preschoolers' power to undermine their parents' confidence in this
stage. Her parents, Pete and Polly, have just had a delightful dinner party
with their good friends Bill and Bonnie. As Caitlin joins her mother at the
door in saying their good-byes to their guests, Caitlin exclaims, "Whew!
I'm glad they're gone!"

"Where would she have learned to say that?" Polly wonders to Caitlin's
dad, shaking her head in dismay. Pete's reaction is just the opposite. He's
not surprised by Caitlin's remark. He knows that his innocent daughter is
simply parroting what she's heard after almost every dinner party they've
ever thrown!

From this season of parenthood forward, little ones will reveal their
parents' character, as Polly learned from Caitlin. Are they Family Managers who are genuinely courteous, kind, empathic, trustworthy, patient,
and honest? If not, their dreams of having children who embody these virtuous behaviors will be in jeopardy. Children are constantly learning how
to act by observing how their Family Managers live their lives.

WITNESSING THE MIRACLE of their child's budding mind and body
during this season of parenthood spawns a new reverence for human
nature within Family Managers. "It was absolutely incredible to watch,"
said one mother of a four-year-old. "My son's questions began at age two
and have never stopped. You can just see his mind developing. He wants
to go everywhere, understand everything. His zest for life, his joie de
vivre, inspires me to appreciate the beauty of a dandelion, the excitement
of seeing a bunny scamper across our porch. I feel like I'm four again, just
discovering the world for the first time."

Indeed, toddlers and preschoolers evoke in their parents a childlike
sense of wonder and the spirit of having the world at their fingertips. However, parents must reconcile identifying with their child's unbridled joy in

discovering the world with knowing that they are responsible for their child's actions and environment. Although you might share your child's curiosity over what would happen if a peanut-butter sandwich is put in the VCR, for example, as a parent it's your duty to prevent such mishaps. Parents discover that being accountable for creating and managing a family business is another leg of the roller-coaster ride of twists and turns, ups and downs, of parenthood that they've been riding since the Celebrity season. They never know from moment to moment exactly when the plunges will come, exactly where their curious George or adventurous Grace will take them as they discover the world together.

BEING SELF-CONTROLLED when their offspring get out of control requires Family Managers to morph into patient and empathic negotiators every day, many times a day. Instead of throwing tantrums themselves, parents must learn how to "make deals" with their little ones when they test their every rule or refuse with fiery defiance their being told what to do. Early in this season of parenthood, therefore, parents must quickly figure out the "family rules" for such management problems to prevent their household from becoming total chaos. The foundation of this plan for managing their little powerhouses was established in the Sponge season: who would be the everyday caregiver of the baby, who would get up in the middle of the night with him, what would be done when he cried, and when and where would he sleep and eat, for example.

In previous seasons of parenthood, you might have fought believing that your children's changes would definitively change your own lives. Now there's no denying this truth. You find yourself moving to another part of town in order to be in the school district of choice for your child or in a neighborhood with children instead of lots of empty nesters; joining a church or synagogue in order to provide a formal religious foundation for your children; leaving a job you love that demands too much travel out of town away from the family "business."

The rewards of being a successful Family Manager can be far-reaching: "Becoming a mother gave me the confidence to move into other areas," actress Meg Ryan explained. "I felt so capable as a mother, which is something I never thought I would do. I felt like, 'I can do this.' I like it that Jack has a routine, which I never had. Now I have one—because of him. I thrive on it."

WHO'S IN CHARGE?

When a man has children, the first thing he has to learn is that he is not the boss of his house.—BILL COSBY

Children in the preschool years continue to live in a self-centered world in which they demand that their parents indulge their every need, just as they did when they first came into the world. However, they add another category of demands to their parents' lives: they want to do whatever they want to do whenever they want to do it. Preschool children act as if they are completely in charge of running the family business.

During this season, however, the child's parents are the general contractors of this construction project called a family, whose foundation was laid in the second season of parenthood. As general contractors, you have the ultimate responsibility of deciding how to build healthy children: the basics, such as eating with utensils, becoming toilet trained, learning the fundamentals of manners; and other issues, such as where the new family will vacation, how to save money, whether child care is necessary if both parents choose or must work outside the home, and how or even if a child's demands should be met. Your own parents may subcontract with you for various jobs, but ultimately parents, as general contractors, need to be in charge.

Parents are best qualified for the role of head of this family business by virtue of their commitment to their children and, theoretically, their maturity. But many parents feel inadequate, full of fears, doubts, and questions about how to solve problems and make decisions because of leftover psychological baggage from their own childhood. They may try to compensate for feeling that their lives are spinning out of their control by trying to take control of those closest to them: spouses, children, in-laws, parents. Learning how to gain self-control, rather than trying to control others, is the most important first step they can take in becoming effective, self-confident Family Managers. This is the ultimate lesson children teach their parents during the Family Manager season, a lesson that will keep their sanity intact as they wend their way through every season of parenthood.

Case in point: "My mother always told me that I had a bad temper when I was a kid, and now my redheaded three-year-old son, Chad, has shown me that he inherited my temper," one of our Circles group members, Robert, told us. "When we get into a battle of wills, I find myself losing control; and when I get mad, I can't think anymore. Finally, I've realized that *I* need to get myself under control before I can do anything with Chad. My wife, Amy, thinks that my losing my temper with Chad is really scary. She's afraid of what I might do to him when I get angry at him, and it scares me, too."

During the Sponge season, when Robert and Amy wanted Chad to wear his special outfits, all they had to do was dress him in them. When they wanted to go someplace, they'd just pick him up and go. Now Chad has a temper tantrum, complete with banging his head on the floor, when he doesn't want to go somewhere, and he runs and hides when they try to get him dressed. Robert thinks that he isn't being a good parent if he doesn't have control over what his son does or doesn't do. His belief that he had control over Chad in the Sponge season, however, was simply an illusion, because in spite of his helplessness, a baby is still controlling his parent's day-to-day life.

Meredith, a mother in Robert's group, told us that she also struggled with trying to control her child. She thought that she should be controlling what her twenty-month-old daughter, Emma, ate because she was refusing to eat certain foods her mother gave her. Meredith had loved breast-feeding her daughter when she was an infant because it made her feel as if she were in total control of Emma's diet. Now that she no longer breast-fed Emma, Meredith complained to her mother, Heidi, that Emma hated drinking milk and juice from a cup and would eat only macaroni and cheese and peanut butter on crackers, not the vegetables that Meredith thought she needed. To solve the problem, her mother urged her to make Emma eat what was good for her, just as she had done when Meredith became a picky eater. It was then that Meredith remembered sitting for hours staring at a plate of food because her mother had told her that she couldn't leave the table until she had cleaned her plate. But she couldn't imagine making Emma do that.

Instead Meredith found herself screaming at Emma and threatening her—spinning completely out of control—as she tried to force Emma to do something that her daughter obviously didn't want to do. The emotional impact of Emma's asserting her independence shocked Meredith. It was frightening to her that she couldn't exercise control over her daughter's life the way she thought she could when Emma was a baby.

This season confirms the fact that the *only* control parents really have in this parenthood business is self-control; they can never control their children, unless their children choose to give their parents control. Therefore self-control forms the basis of parents' ability to be positive role models of self-discipline, responsibility, and independence. The Family Managers are nominally in charge, but many of their choices are driven by their children's need to learn standards of behavior.

Another father we interviewed, Alphonse, also learned this lesson: "When my son was about five years old, my boss wanted me to do something for a client that I didn't think was right—lie to him. I told him why I believed that it was unethical but was scared to death that he would hate me for saying so. I had always been an obedient kid, always doing what anyone in authority ever told me to do, even if I disagreed with it. But now I had a reason for taking a stand, so I had the courage to speak up. I didn't think that my five-year-old son would be proud of me if he ever found out that I did something that wasn't honest. I always tell him to tell the truth; following my boss's wishes meant that I would have to go against that principle. I felt a sense of pride about who I was and who my child thought I was, pride that came solely from being a father. I finally had to quit because I decided that I could no longer work for an unethical boss. Isn't it funny how your life changes when you see it through the eyes of your child?"

When talk show host Rosie O'Donnell recorded two shows daily, she said that she always came home in time to bathe her two children. Actress Meryl Streep has said that she is adamant about working only certain times of the year so she can be near her children during the school year, because being a mother is never far from her mind: "You don't jettison that. Even my decisions about what films I make are predicated on the fact that I think about how my children will view them, how this particular piece will reside in the world that they live in, and how it will either enhance it or strafe the soul of their future."

LET'S MAKE A DEAL

When you are a mother, you are never really alone in your thoughts. You are connected to your child and to all those who touch your lives. A mother always has to think twice, once for herself and once for her child.—SOPHIA LOREN

"Wash your hands and then you can have a cookie"; "When you're buckled in your car seat, then we can play the music"; "When we've gotten your pajamas on, then we can read a story."

Successful Family Managers spend nearly every waking moment with their toddlers and preschoolers in these kinds of negotiations because they are faced with this decision: Who's going to control whom in this family business? In order to avoid inevitable "turf wars" in which their child becomes "the enemy," parents make deals with their toddlers and preschoolers, offering them a chance to do what they want to after they have done what they need to do.

In the workplace, successful managers are visionaries who are interested in maximizing productivity with the least amount of conflict. As Family Managers, parents have the same mandate: They need to guide their "human resource" toward adulthood as a productive, happy, responsible, caring citizen. So Family Managers begin a four- to five-year training program designed to prepare their toddler and preschooler to be successful in his new workplace: school. These years are the first, and most opportune, time for parents to lead their child through this training program. Our society expects that by the time a child reaches five or six years of age, she will be developmentally ready to practice the skills she's learned as she enters the more formal, structured world of kindergarten. Parents yearning to close a deal when selling their child on what they want her to do have to keep their eyes on this longer-term goal.

R HONDA, A SINGLE MOTHER of a two-year-old, shared this story in one of our Circles groups about training her toddler to dress herself: "I realized that I didn't want to yell at my kids like my parents used to yell at me after I heard myself screaming at my daughter when she wouldn't let me help her get dressed. But it's hard not to get caught up in the moment, not to try to control your child, which I've found is actually impossible to do anyway. Although I was mad because we were in a hurry and she was taking so long, I had to think of the big picture in order to be patient so I could help her learn how to dress herself. I told her that I would put her shoes on this time; then I'd let *her* do it herself next time. Using self-control in making this deal with her got the job done for both of us."

Teaching little people to be socialized human beings demands that parents become more flexible, Rhonda learned, which is no small task in itself. Just what kind of Family Manager you are—honest or lying, flexible or rigid, or fair or cheating—will be tested over and over, another challenge during this stage of your own growth.

"My eleven-month-old, Brittany, was so sweet," reported Cynthia, a member of one of our Circles groups. "She would babble and smile, making all of the terror and work of the first few weeks of parenthood fade away. I was finally starting to adjust and to think I was a pretty good mom. We had our routines down pat, and the days were going really smoothly. But then she took her first steps. We were so proud and excited that I called my husband, Stephan, to tell him. Boy, were we in for a shock. Those first steps of hers have made every day a hair-raising adventure ever since."

"She's clearly running the show," Pat, an insurance salesperson, agreed as he discussed his relationship with his three-year-old daughter. "But I am learning so much," he added, demonstrating that he was trying to understand the thinking of his most important "customer," his preschooler, as he grew along with her.

Being a salesperson was no challenge for Pat; selling to demanding customers was what he did every day as he provided for his family. But if parents have no prior experience or aren't comfortable making deals with people, they'll have a difficult ride through this season of parenthood, fighting the anger and frustration they feel when their deals are not accepted immediately or even resentment that they need to make deals at all.

Zach, a strict disciplinarian whose favorite expression was "My way or the highway," fell into this latter group. His wife, Clarissa, on the other hand, didn't want to be too firm with their two-year-old son, Dustin. She wanted to love and nurture him as she had when he was a baby; only now he was a constant whirlwind of activity, and she was exhausted just trying to prevent him from destroying the house. Zach kept telling her to just spank him when he got into things, but she couldn't bring herself to inflict pain on her precious bundle of energy. Clarissa was afraid that she would stifle Dustin's natural curiosity if she put any restrictions on him. "He's all boy," she would say in his defense.

Clarissa and Zach were blindsided by the effect on their marriage of Dustin's new need for boundaries around his behavior. Clarissa didn't care that Zach's parents had spanked him whenever he needed to "learn a lesson," a fact he used to convince her that it was the right thing to do with Dustin. She still thought it was wrong; her parents had always told her that it wasn't right to hurt a child, regardless of what he did.

How can Zach, a strict disciplinarian, make peace with Clarissa, an "anything goes" parent? First we asked both Zach and Clarissa to describe their goals for Dustin's behavior. They both wanted the same thing: less conflict over the best way to raise Dustin. They also wanted to feel as close to Dustin as they had when he was an infant, instead of always being at war with him over his behavior. We explained that every kind of management strategy parents use involves deal making in this season of parenthood. Zach's "my way or the highway" is, in effect, a deal in which he offers Dustin a choice, albeit a limited one. Clarissa was also making a deal if she promised Dustin that they would go to the park—what he wanted to do—after he had put away his toys—what she wanted him to do.

Successful deal making is based on a win-win strategy: both parents and children are happiest when their own agendas are met. We reminded Zach and Clarissa that they own everything that Dustin wants, and they can offer him the opportunity to have or do what he wants when he has done what they want. Although the "quick and dirty" way of shouting and spanking that Zach's parents used to train him might seem to be the easier path, learning to be successful Family Managers who negotiate and make deals moves them from living the angry, fearful, overly stressed life of parenthood that Zach and Clarissa were experiencing to meeting their ultimate, more positive goals: more kindly, empathic, caring relationships as a family.

Both Clarissa and Zach were amazed at how much more comfortable they were becoming with each other as partners on this Family Manager team once they understood that deal making is an inevitable responsibility of this season of parenthood. As they practiced collaborating with each other on ways to reach their long-term goals with Dustin—independence, self-reliance, and self-control—their own marriage was enhanced.

PERFORMANCE REVIEWS

Nobody can make you feel inferior without your consent.
—ELEANOR ROOSEVELT

Kristen, a former social worker, tells us that being a Family Manager is more wearing, tiring, and discouraging than being a Celebrity or Sponge because she rarely feels as though she's accomplishing anything: "At the office, I could always get things done. Things got finished. Now that I've quit my job to stay home with my two- and four-year-olds, I feel helpless and powerless. No matter how many times I clean up the house, the kids, or me during the day, my little ones mess everything up and I have to do it all over again. And it's like pulling teeth to get the kids to mind me. At work, people did what I asked and I moved on. Now, I never feel like I'm doing a good job at anything at home. It makes me want to go back to work just to feel better about myself."

DURING THE CHAOTIC STATE of children's rapid growth at this developmental stage, parents who are most comfortable in a predictable, efficient, organized, and orderly world find that the constant interruptions, accidents, and mistakes of their offspring make them feel totally unproductive and worthless, as Kristen did. These parents' self-talk—the messages they give themselves about their lives—tells them: When my world flows in a more predictable fashion, I am calm. I feel okay. When it is chaotic, I can't stand it! If they tell themselves that they "can't stand" the mess in their house or the noise that their children make playing with their toys, or they believe it's "their fault" that their children are so noisy and messy, they're bound to feel angry and depressed.

Case in point: Kristen remembered consistently being corrected by her mother whenever she made a mess when she was a child—had an accident at the dinner table or spilled her crayons, for example. She told us that she always hated the criticism and punishment that followed; as a result, we explained, her own children's mess making conjured up those feelings of failure and of thoughts of being a disappointment to the person on whom she so depended for love—her mother. We recall those strong connections to our childhood when our children begin to repeat what we ourselves did as children. The performance reviews we received as children come back like ghosts to haunt our parenthood and can influence or even determine our thoughts, feelings, and actions, as they did for Kristen.

But when parents understand that the only thing they really control is what they think—and what they do about what they think—they can choose to think of the mess and noise at home as annoying but not a big deal, just a normal part of life in this season of parenthood. Life becomes easier when they stop fighting the inevitable and "go with the flow." When they admit to themselves that they "can stand" what's going on, even if they don't like it, and that the chaos of their lives doesn't mean that they're poor parents, they can reframe and enjoy those precious moments with their children.

By repeatedly saying aloud to herself, "This is no big deal. I can stand this. My children's messes don't make me a bad mother. And this, too, shall pass," each time she got upset over the shambles that her children made of her house, Kristen reported feeling less frustrated with motherhood. By thinking of her children's behavior as teachable moments, she started to appreciate the important impact she could make on their lives as a Family Manager.

SUE AND HER HUSBAND, Chang, decided that Sue would stay home to care for their two young children. But doing so was driving her crazy. She couldn't handle being a full-time mom, she said, and wanted to put the children in a Mother's Day Out and preschool program all week, although Chang opposed the idea. He wanted family and only family to care for their precious little tykes.

So the two made a deal with each other: Chang would ask his parents to baby-sit three days a week, and they would go to their preschool the other two days. After she made these changes in her children's daily schedule, Sue felt just as miserable. She told herself that she was a failure as a mother for not being able to tolerate the chaos her children created at home and felt guilty because she believed that her mother-in-law was better at mothering than she was, as were the professionals at her children's school.

But slowly, she told us, she adjusted to this season of parenthood, after telling herself that she could acquire the skills of parenting by watching her family and children's teachers and that her lack of parenting skills was not a character flaw in her. By observing their examples and following their instructions on discipline issues, on how to be more flexible, and on ways to make compromises in her own life, Sue felt more comfortable in her ability to handle full-time management of her family.

It wasn't that she needed to get a job outside her home, Sue told us, it was that she needed to learn management skills so that she could cope and feel competent at home. Learning how to manage the business of her preschoolers' lives, as well as her own, was difficult mental and emotional work for her—a twenty-four-hour-a-day MBA in family management.

"JUST THE OTHER DAY," Fran reflected, "I was out having lunch with my twenty-six-month-old when I ran into an old friend from a former job. I immediately panicked about how my toddler would react, because he didn't always do well with strangers. Instead of smiling and sweetly showing off for my friend, my son screamed, 'No!' and lunged out of his booster seat to the safety of my arms and tried to swat her with his fist like she was an annoying fly. Oh, I nearly died."

Fran told us she wished at that moment that she could go back to those simpler days when he was an angelic infant, who needed just to be held, fed, and tickled to be happy. She was sure that her friend was thinking that she was a bad mother because her child didn't act like the darling, smiling baby he used to be. Fran found herself apologizing for her son's acting so unfriendly, although she knew how silly it was for her to make excuses for his normal toddler behavior.

But she couldn't help herself. No one had warned her that this season of parenthood would make her feel so inadequate. Was it parenthood that made her feel that way . . . or had she never gotten over needing her friends' or her parents' approval as a child?

It was then that Fran remembered hearing her own mother's criticism of parents they would see at the grocery or in the neighborhood when she was a child over thirty years ago. When other children would act up, her mom would look on them with disdain and say that she was glad that *her* children never acted that way. As a child, Fran had learned a clear lesson: To be a good mom meant that your children needed to be friendly, act nicely, and control themselves. No crying, screaming, hitting, or disruptive behavior or you've flunked as a parent.

This desire to give a good appearance begins when children first become aware of how they appear to others, at around six years of age. Showing off their beautiful, competent, well-behaved children is a normal and natural continuation of the need to look good and be acceptable in the eyes of others, rather than to focus on one's own self-acceptance. Of course, if you learn to accept yourself, your self-worth won't be based on the judgment or opinion of others.

However, in the abstract business of parenthood, children are Family Managers' only tangible "products." Therefore they puff with pride when their children reach developmental milestones early; they are crushed when they don't seem to be measuring up to their peers. Taking their children's progress and behavior personally can wreak havoc on parents who believe that their children's every foible is a result of their inadequacy as parents.

Part of the amazing process of learning how to trust one's decisions in life comes from risking being wrong, coping with making mistakes, after trying to make informed choices. The most freeing lesson in life—to accept one's mistakes, one's human failures, as learning opportunities—is the essence of happiness as a human being. It is a hard-won happiness for those perfectionists who struggle to accept that they are fallible and can be loved even when they aren't perfect. If they base their self-acceptance on the performance review offered by their toddlers, in all their chaotic fallibility, they're on shaky ground indeed.

"MY MOTHER SAYS that I was a little brat," reported Latisha, a Circles group mother of a preschooler. "Now I have a little terror just like I was, according to my mom. She says that what goes around comes around."

Her mother's warning signal only served to put Latisha on the defensive with her daughter, Latoya. She was determined not to act like her mother, she told us, and was always afraid to take any advice her mother gave her for that reason. The painful memory of her own mother's criticism of her when she was a child was still razor sharp.

For other parents, like forty-year-old Rhonda, it's the performance review from their own mom or dad that matters the most and brings the most comfort or pain. "I'm still trying to please my parents, even at my age," Rhonda confessed. "I still want them to be proud of me, but I'm learning to stand up for myself, thanks to my child. For example, my mom and I had a major conflict because she didn't think I should breast-feed. But I was determined to breast-feed because I thought it was best for my baby; she thought that I was just being rebellious.

"I decided that my own sense of right and wrong was my report card," she added. "I knew what I wanted and was really proud of myself for sticking with my principles, even at the risk of losing my mother's approval." Rhonda had grown during this season of parenthood in ways that will serve her well for the rest of her life.

The conflicts that arise when parents disapprove of their children's parenting style with their grandchildren can create relationship rifts that are hard to repair. Parents who try to control what their own parents think and believe about how they are handling child-rearing issues will find the task as impossible as controlling young children. When parents are self-confident, well informed, and committed to being the primary Family Managers in their child's life, they can acknowledge and appreciate suggestions from their own parents but recognize that they are ultimately responsible for their child's training program. If there is a reciprocal love relationship between themselves and their parents, they can try to reframe differences in parenting styles, and the disagreements that might result, as interesting and enlightening instead of threatening and rejecting. It all depends on how advice received from parents is viewed by Family Managers.

Children humble us by their ability to trust that we will still be there for them and love them, even while they make mistakes and struggle against us to declare their own independence. While children are teaching their parents to love them unconditionally, they are teaching their parents to love *themselves* unconditionally as well.

Grace's Guilt: Failing the MBA

Grace was an intense thirty-year-old art director who dragged her husband, Phil, into our office to seek help in managing the tantrums and name-calling of their wiry two-year-old son, Gavin. It was clear that he had turned their lives upside down and that they desperately wanted to return to the relative peace and predictability of his infancy.

Gavin's behavior was making Grace feel like a failure as a mother. For example, after baby-sitting Gavin one day, during which he whined for his mommy for hours upon hours until she came home, Grace's mother, Doris, sneered at her daughter: "Your son is wild and crazy because you still work, Grace. I told you when Gavin was born that you should quit and not go part-time!"

Grace was looking for a thorough, objective evaluation of her parenting—the same kind of report card she received from her job—so she would know if she was on the right track with Gavin or if her mother was right. Phil thought that she was so consumed with being a good mom that working at the art studio was a godsend: "You would be crazier than Gavin if you stayed home all the time!" he told her.

Grace knew what he meant. She was obsessive about her work, but she knew that was, in part, because she was transferring some of her anxiety about Gavin to her job. Had she not had an outlet for her frustration, she might have been even more worried than she was. She just could not figure out why she and Phil were affected so differently by Gavin's behavior. Soon to make partner in his architectural firm, Phil had started going out with the guys after work on Fridays, supposedly to prove his commitment to the firm and gain favor with his employees.

Grace thought, however, that he was working so much simply to avoid coming home and hearing about how Gavin bit the child next door or destroyed the television. No matter what Grace did to help sell Gavin on fol-

lowing directions, he wouldn't buy it. Their battles over Gavin began to eat away at their marriage and were clear signs that Grace didn't like taking on all the leadership of the family. She wanted a co-manager.

Was this what parenting was going to be like forever? they wondered. Looking ahead, Grace and Phil started worrying about how Gavin would behave in preschool. Wherever they went with him, they had to be constantly on the alert because they could never predict his next move. They couldn't imagine the day when he would be ready to conform to the structure of kindergarten, and the anticipated teacher reports about Gavin were more than Grace and Phil thought they could survive.

Grace and Phil knew that they weren't happy, but they were pointing the finger at Gavin, not at their own personal conflicts, which most parents experience in this season of parenthood. In this case, it wasn't their son who needed "fixing" so much as their reaction to the crises of being Family Managers. Neither one had thought about the fact that they never did like making decisions, couldn't sell food to a starving person, and were totally dependent on their parents' approval in order to feel good about their jobs and even their marriage. They denied their adult shortcomings in the same way they denied their role in their son's behavior.

Phil wasn't interested in trading in his hat with his architecture firm's logo on it for the father hat on the weekends. That was *his* time, he reasoned, for letting off steam and relaxing. There was this problem, though, called Gavin, who seemed to be demanding that he make changes, mostly in the decision-making department. Phil knew he would have to assert some authority, but he knew nothing about how to respond to tantrums, prevent Gavin from making a mess while eating, or dress him. He knew nothing about taking care of kids.

In fact, he didn't want to even tell Grace how scared he was of this whole parenting gig. His own father had never lifted a finger to take care of Phil and his older sister, according to his mother. Just as his dad had been supportive of his mother, who stayed home to take care of Phil and his sister, Phil had gotten along until now just being supportive of Grace, but never having to actually do anything differently since Gavin's birth.

During the first year of his little life, Gavin was always screaming because of his colic, according to Phil, and Grace had been frustrated by her inability to quiet him. She had enjoyed the shine of being a Celebrity while she was pregnant, but the luster had begun to tarnish during the

Sponge season of parenthood. Now, with Gavin no longer suffering from colic, she thought things would get better; but he had learned to walk early and was keeping her on the run. Managing the family business didn't fit the image of what she'd expected parenthood would be like; being a mother was turning out to be a most difficult venture.

She and Phil saw different images, we explained, when they looked at Gavin. Grace had imagined her son would be a dutiful little preschooler who obeyed his parents, just as she had been a responsible little girl who never gave her mom and dad a lick of trouble, according to her mother. She hadn't felt like a failure as a mother when Gavin had colic, but now that he was so rambunctious, she was convinced she wasn't cut out to be a parent. Her brothers had never been like Gavin, as far as she could remember from being the oldest child in her family or from her parents' stories.

Worst of all, Phil never told her that she was doing a good job; he just wanted to play with the baby—and applaud Gavin's accomplishments—whenever he was home, letting Grace set down the rules. After all, she was at home more than he was, he rationalized. Besides, Phil never remembered his father making any rules or taking any responsibility around the house.

It was clear to us that neither Grace nor Phil was an assertive person; in fact, Grace was still being controlled by her mother's approval, which she wanted even more than Phil's; and Phil was happy only as long as he fit the model he had of fatherhood established by his own father.

Grace needed to share with Phil the expectation that she had about sharing leadership roles, which would help him assume the same responsibility that she did for deciding on important family issues. The longer she waited to do so, the more her resentment would build, and the more she would erect a wall of anger between them.

In this season of parenthood, Grace thought of herself as someone who was first a parent, then an art director. But Phil hadn't been able to relate to the shift in self-concept that Grace had already accepted; he was an architect first, with father a distant second. Therefore, when he said that staying home would make her crazy, he was suggesting that being the Family Manager—making deals with Gavin—was not fulfilling work. It was just "something to make you nuts," he said, his description of caring for toddlers and preschoolers. It wasn't as if Grace disagreed. She had yet to feel any sort of reward for all of her work. She knew, however, that she didn't want to go through the rest of her life feeling this trapped, alone, and overwhelmingly responsible.

The conflict between Grace's husband's advice (keep working) and her mother's (stay home) in order to give Gavin the direction and limits he needed is a familiar one for millions of families in today's world. It is a conflict of agenda, change, and identity, a conflict that cries out for parents to decide together what they want for their family. It is also a conflict that can create a wedge between couples and their own parents that only gets wider as they age. It is not a grandparents' issue, a mother's issue, or a father's issue; this decision of who is going to be managing the family business in this season is one that needs to take everyone's needs into consideration.

In order to feel at peace in this season of parenthood, Grace and Phil needed to see the same image when they looked in the mirror: two parents who were equal partners in their new family business. Both Grace and Phil needed to explain this fact of life to Grace's mother in order for her to understand how to be supportive of this business venture in which she felt so invested herself. Phil also had to address his fears of taking an active part in his family. We recommended that Phil begin attending a series of parenting classes so that he could learn about normal child development and feel more comfortable as Gavin's Family Manager. Grace was best advised to stop waiting for her performance review before feeling good about caring for Gavin. Their investment of time, love, and attention in their son would pay great dividends in the future, we told them. They would also be investing in their marriage, as he and Grace strengthened their partnership through solidifying the family business that now had only a part-time manager.

Jo Ann Gets Heard: Mother/Daughter Conflict

Keen insight into the way that her four-year-old daughter's little mind worked. That's what helped twenty-eight-year-old Jo Ann, a divorced media buyer for a television station in a large metropolitan market, figure out what her preschooler, Debra, who suffered from a hearing loss and speech impediment, was asking her since she had first learned to talk when she was about two years old.

Jo Ann's mother, Nancy, on the other hand, was not blessed with this insight. She couldn't understand anything her granddaughter asked her, which put Jo Ann in a real bind. As a single parent, Jo Ann needed Nancy to care for Debra while she went to work. But she knew that Debra's speech wouldn't get any better unless Nancy could help her with certain words all day long.

In addition, Nancy's own hearing was no longer the keenest at age sixty-eight. But instead of discussing her hearing problem with her daughter, she just demanded that Jo Ann and Debra both "speak up and stop mumbling." The conflict between Jo Ann and her mother was getting hotter and hotter, Jo Ann told us, as Debra's speech problems and hearing loss were making her grandmother more frustrated with her.

Jo Ann knew that she had two problems on her hands: taking care of her aging mother's hearing problems and those of her four-year-old. Her daughter, however, wasn't fighting getting help, as her grandmother was. It was as if Jo Ann's concern for her own daughter were somehow a direct affront to Nancy, who didn't want to acknowledge that anything could be wrong with her or her own granddaughter.

When Jo Ann suggested that Nancy take Debra to the special clinic for speech and hearing disorders at the local teaching hospital, since Jo Ann couldn't afford to take the time off, Nancy grew more adamant about just waiting and seeing what happened.

"Debra will get better as she gets older," Nancy insisted nervously.

Jo Ann felt that she had nowhere to turn. As days passed, she became concerned that the longer she waited to get help, the worse Debra's problems, as well as her mother's, would become. The last thing that she wanted to do was upset her mother . . . but she felt a responsibility as Debra's mother to take charge of this serious situation.

Jo Ann was absolutely right to be concerned about Debra, as well as Nancy, we told her, knowing that this news was both comforting and difficult for her to swallow. We explained to her that this season of parenthood was all about managing the family business, and that was exactly what Jo Ann was trying to do as she saw that her daughter and aging mother must have support from outside the family. Jo Ann needed to care for both generations of her family but address their issues separately.

Working was not a matter of choice for Jo Ann now; she needed to support her family. Her job was her responsibility, as was getting her daughter the help she needed. She agreed that quitting work would not solve the problem. But perhaps there was another solution, we argued. Instead of having to sacrifice Debra's health to save Nancy's sense of pride, Jo Ann could explain to her mother that she loved her and appreciated her opinion about Debra. As Debra's mother, however, she was going to take the lead in making decisions about Debra.

Because confronting Nancy in this way was so frightening for Jo Ann, she realized for the first time how controlled she had been by her mother all of her life. Now their relationship was lopsided, Jo Ann admitted, by the power her mother held because she was caring for her precious granddaughter. So we suggested that Jo Ann be more honest with her mother, in spite of the risk of upsetting her, in order to equalize the balance of power in the family. Jo Ann needed to explain to Nancy that her help was important in caring for Debra and that she wanted Nancy to get help herself. In fact, this crisis could bring them closer together as they took a loving approach to solve a family crisis. We also suggested that Jo Ann talk to her boss at the television station about the health crises with her mother and Debra, since this was going to take time and energy to solve. She needed to get her work covered while she cared for her daughter and her mother.

Jo Ann took our advice. For the sake of her daughter's care, she learned to become more assertive in making deals with her boss, as well as with Nancy. Deciding to share her family's problems with her friends at work and her boss was hard for her because she'd always acted as if she could do everything perfectly and was always in control. She'd been taught well to never let on that her life wasn't a well-oiled machine.

Taking this risk personally paid off in the long run. Her good friend at work, Ronnie, offered to take Debra to the hearing clinic every other week on her day off, so Jo Ann's mother wouldn't have the extra responsibility. She also sold her boss on the idea of having a flextime schedule for several months. Juggling her new schedule was difficult, but Jo Ann found extra strength when she reminded herself that meeting Debra's needs was her primary responsibility.

For a while, she and her mother had trouble with the loss of their previous relationship, and they worked to develop a new way of communicating. As Debra's speech improved, her mother began to trust Jo Ann with the big step of getting her hearing tested and hearing aids fitted. After all, she reasoned, if her granddaughter could get help with her hearing, she was brave enough to get help, too. Jo Ann could tell from her improved self-confidence that her self-image and family relationships were growing more positive as her family manager skills improved.

Manuel's Crisis: Conflict in Management Style

"I am in heaven," Manuel said, beaming. He was a participant in one of our Circles groups who was more than happy to talk about his life with his four children, Lupe, Laura, Lee, and Elena, eighteen months, three, five, and eight years old, respectively.

We had rarely seen a dad as dedicated as thirty-year-old Manuel. "I cannot wait to get up in the morning," he said. "The kids climb all over me and smother me with kisses. I get them all ready for school because their mom, Angelina, is a doctor who has to be out of the house by six-thirty every day so she can make rounds. The kids are all mine until I take them to the sitter's at eight. The older ones walk together to school, which is just around the corner from the sitter's house. After my morning dad duties, I go to work."

We were impressed as Manuel went on and on about the organization of his little family business. "I love making the lunches with them every night," he explained "I know what they like because I was there for every step they took when they were babies. I was a stay-at-home dad until just a few weeks ago when I took a new job."

We asked him how his wife helped with the children's care, which turned out to be a loaded question. "She and I don't see things eye to eye," he said quietly. "Since she's not home much, I've had to take over making sure everything gets done. When she does come home, she tries to change everything, especially in the discipline department. I have to completely retrain the kids after she goes back to work on Mondays. The weekends are absolutely nothing but war."

We could tell that the war between Manuel and his wife was not only upsetting to him, but also disturbing the way he thought that his family was going to be. "The only good part about my wife's job is that it keeps her away from home so much," he joked, with a serious undertone to his voice.

We could see that Manuel was a devoted dad who was drowning in a dilemma. Raising four young children puts most people on overload as managers of the family business; Manuel was also in conflict with his wife over how to get a positive performance review for his job as dad, sell the kids on appropriate behavior, and lead the family in a unified direction.

All three of these conflicts surfaced because of a lack of commitment on the part of his wife to see family management as a collaborative effort. Manuel told us that he'd never realized how mean and bullying his wife could be, a facet of her personality he hadn't seen until they entered this season of parenthood.

"Angelina doesn't understand the meaning of limits and boundaries," Manuel offered. "She wants the kids to be in jail." He told us that Angelina was often angry at what the children did, which put her on the offensive with all of them, including Manuel. This somewhat explosive side of her character was new and frightening to her, too, she grudgingly confessed to Manuel, which was why she was almost afraid to be around all of them anymore. It was easier to be away so she didn't have to work on learning new techniques of self-control. She never lost her cool at work, she told us, confused as to why she couldn't exercise the same levelheadedness at home.

"I guess I use up all of my patience on my patients," she joked. I can't seem to tolerate the confusion at home, everyone going in different directions and screaming for what they want. I can't seem to calm anyone down, least of all myself. My family makes me crazy."

Through our discussions, Angelina learned that it was perfectly natural to feel overwhelmed by the "family business." Her job itself was high stress, but it was something that she'd been trained to do. The demands of this season of parenthood are also high stress, but she felt that she lacked the training needed to do it as perfectly as she wanted. It was easier to go to work, where she could meet her demand for perfection, than to stay home and face potential failure.

As long as parents are at odds over management issues, their company is doomed to have problems. Both Angelina and Manuel agreed that they needed to work together to decide just how to sell their children on positive behavior and what to do if the children didn't buy their sales pitch. We helped the couple practice self-calming techniques, which gave Manuel a way to hold his tongue when he saw Angelina lash out at their youngest for making mistakes, such as spilling his milk; then we taught Angelina some ways to discipline without shouting or spanking. They kept a chart of issues that caused them to behave disrespectfully toward each other. After a few weeks they realized that Angelina's impatience and lack of empathy were the two things that most set Manuel off.

Angelina said that she was always yelled at as a child and couldn't see another way to get children to behave, because she had no other example to follow. She had no memory of an idyllic family situation: being tucked into bed at night with a mommy's good-night kiss or welcomed each morning with a daddy's smiling hug. She remembered both of them always being irritable and short-tempered when they were home, which was not very often because they worked all the time.

Manuel had grown up in a household of shouters, too. But he had vowed never to talk to his children like that because it had made him feel so demeaned. He hated his father's screaming orders at him, an emotion that also evoked tremendous guilt. When Angelina yelled at the kids, he was transported back in time to those unhappy days.

Neither Manuel nor Angelina had a good example from their respective childhoods of adults who could calmly and rationally work things out and negotiate a settlement in a dispute. Manuel, however, had learned from his childhood what *not* to do as a parent. He used his early experiences as a model of what to avoid in his own family.

The couple talked about their own experiences as children and their interpretations of their similar upbringings, realizing the impact that their parents had on their lives now. Until their children reached preschool age, they'd had no idea that they'd be destined to echo the mistakes of their parents, mistakes that upset them each time they made them.

Their children were teaching Manuel and Angelina to make positive changes in their own family: trying to be more supportive, less critical, and in unison when it came to managing everyone's behavior. We helped Angelina and Manuel learn ways to negotiate the differences between them, trying to remember that their joint long-term goal was to raise happy, well-adjusted, successful adults.

Angelina still struggled sometimes with her reactions to her children's behavior and became dismayed at her inability to perfectly order her surroundings as she did at her office. When this happened, instead of being critical, Manuel would try to "talk her down" and work *with* her instead of *against* her. Things weren't perfect, but they had a prescription for improvement.

Overscheduled Eric and Abby: Too Much of a Good Thing

Disheveled and flushed, thirty-two-year-old Eric raced in late to a couples Circles group in his good friend's living room. "Sorry I'm late," he apologized. "But I had to pick up my five-year-old, Jared, and Kate, his three-year-old sister, at day care. She had a real mess in her diaper, so it took us a little longer."

Sitting quietly on the couch, Eric's wife, Abby, flushed deep red. Later she told us that she was embarrassed by Eric's openness, his speaking so easily about matters that she considered private. Just the fact that Jared and Kate went to day care at all made her feel guilty that she wasn't home with her kids all day, every day, as her mother had been. She also felt guilty that Kate was still in diapers and hadn't been toilet trained yet. So many things about being a parent made Abby feel like a failure, she admitted after our discussion group ended and the other parents had gone home.

"I'm sorry that Eric went on and on about the day care," Abby apologized. "Jared goes there full-time, and Kate just goes two days a week. It's not really day care, it's a Mother's Day Out and, well, a preschool."

Eric chimed in. "Yes, we feel it's really quite educational for Jared. We did a lot of research on choices for them and decided that this school would give them the best kindergarten readiness. Jared couldn't begin kindergarten until the following year because he turned five just after the deadline. We see Kate following in his footsteps."

We were mentally exhausted by the time the two finished telling us all of the things that Jared would learn at this Mother's Day Out. They then launched into all the other activities Jared and Kate participated in. Abby and Eric had their children's schedules so micromanaged that it seemed their kids hardly had an hour to breathe. If they weren't going to Mother's Day Out, they were in a play group. Then twice a week they went to massage therapy, and on two other days they attended music class or went to swimming lessons. The pace of Jared's and Kate's activities must be hard to keep up with, we noted wryly.

"No, we don't mind," Abby continued. "Whatever's best for Jared and Kate is best for us. Being parents is the most important thing we've done, and nothing is too good for our children. Everyone is trying hard to give their children more than they had; that's a parent's job these days."

Eric and Abby reminded us that today's parents are bombarded with an enormous array of opportunities to stimulate their young children. In fact, one of the management crises for parents in this season of parenthood is learning how to take charge of the family schedule. They may want their little ones to do everything: go to preschool; attend art, music, drama, dance, and gymnastics classes; take swimming lessons; join a pee-wee soccer, T-ball, or golf team. It's hard to say no to more, better, newer activities. If I want the best for Jill and Johnny, then I mustn't deny them anything, parents say. But what led to this thinking? Parents who are determined to get a good performance review on their parenthood from their family, neighbors, friends, and co-workers in this stage frequently take advantage of all of these options, even if they can't afford it, putting themselves and their children on "overwhelm."

Abby admitted that she had been given everything as a child and wanted the same for her son. Running from music classes to dance classes had paid off for her. She had performed in plays since she was three years old and currently wanted to audition for some community theater. Abby loved the fast pace and excitement of performing and couldn't imagine that Jared and Kate wouldn't like it, too.

Even though she wanted to expose them to everything, a part of Abby missed her children and wanted them just to hang out at home sometimes. "There isn't enough time when we're all together as a family," she lamented. "If we can get our schedule refined enough to keep it running smoothly, I feel like I'm successful. My mom always seemed to get everything done and made it seem so effortless. But when Jared and Kate screw up—like Kate did when she dirtied her diaper at the eleventh hour—I get so angry because it messes up our schedule."

If parents are constantly frustrated, as Abby was, that's a red flag warning her that they aren't honestly facing management decisions that have to be made for the benefit of the whole family and are experiencing the stress and burnout of overscheduling. Eric and Abby admitted that deep down they resented the constant running around that they felt was their duty to Jared and Kate. "We never have a moment to breathe," they said. "We always feel like we're short-changing them if we aren't stimulating them."

We helped this parent team understand that it wasn't wanting the best for Jared and Kate that was driving their family business. Instead it was being controlled by what their family and friends would think of them as parents. They agreed that they had a "keeping up" attitude about their family—they had to match or top what they had been given as children and what all of their friends at the country club and church were doing with their children in order to feel good about themselves. We suggested that trying to impress others or "best themselves" was not necessarily going to lead them to making the best choices for themselves or for Jared and Kate. They needed to make deals with their children that were good for the whole family and stop worrying about what others would think about their decisions.

It was also important for Eric and Abby to take their own emotional pulses and decide what a healthy rate of activity for them as parents might be. Differences in parents' temperament and personality determine how they tolerate the pace of family activities and can create stress in their relationship unless they reach a consensus of how often they want their children to be in scheduled activities. Slowing down the pace of an overly active life by creating a schedule that is comfortable for the whole family can reduce the threat of overscheduling burnout for parents.

Likewise, their children's pulses need to be monitored: what is overscheduling for one child might be just right for another. For example, Tricia and Tyler, four-year-old fraternal twins, were signed up for music, art, and soccer camps, according to their mother, Trudy. She couldn't understand why Tricia kept whining about going to these fun activities and pleading with her to stay home and play with her best friend next door. Tyler, on the other hand, wanted to try every activity his mother suggested. He never seemed to get enough and was happy with his schedule. In fact, when a day of soccer camp was rained out, he moped around the house as if he were a lost puppy

Children's behavior is a good barometer of burnout. Trudy realized that Tricia liked a quieter pace of life, much like herself. When they were both too busy, they were cranky and irritable. Tyler loved to be doing something all the time and didn't like to stay home and relax; Trudy noted that he was much like his dad, Clark. When a child is tense and crabby, as was Tricia, parents need to consider reducing the pace of activities and let him or her simply play for a while, a sure stress reducer. Trudy tried to work out a compromise to her hectic schedule by carpooling when possible, letting Tricia play at her best friend's house when it was her turn to drive and getting Clark more involved in transporting Tyler to and from his soccer practices.

When both parents experience burnout from overscheduling, as in Eric and Abby's case, they can more easily agree on how to slow down the pace of their children's lives, even if the children don't seem to be stressed by their activities. Eric and Abby decided to prioritize spending time at home together, as a family, to help themselves feel calmer and more in control of their lives. "Let's go home right now and skip music today," they suggested to each other with a gleam in their eye. They decided to try to take the management of their family business away from the outside "board of directors" and place it squarely on their shoulders, where it belonged.

A New Day for Dawn: Can a Daughter Be a Best Friend?

"I'm in trouble," thirty-five-year-old Dawn began as she spoke out in one of our Circles group interviews. *"I want Anna Kate to be my best friend. I can't tell her 'no,' even though I know I should sometimes. Since she turned five a few months ago, she refuses to go to therapy that's supposed to help straighten her legs. Her doctor says that they won't grow correctly if she doesn't continue this therapy that she's been getting for three years. She never complained about going before. But now she couldn't care less about what will happen if she doesn't go. She hates it so much, she says, and there's no reasoning with her. I can't even bribe her to go!"*

Dawn was clearly conflicted by this season of parenthood. She herself always got to do everything she wanted to do as a child, so she couldn't imagine forcing Anna Kate to do something she didn't want to do for fear of turning Anna Kate against her.

"I know, though, that I'm the mother and she's the child, and sometimes I should go ahead and tell her that some things in life you just have to do even though you don't want to. But I can't help but spoil her; she's the light of my life and seems to be growing up so fast. I just want to hold on to my little girl," she explained.

We wanted to know what her partner, Mark, thought of the way they were raising their child.

"I had nothing growing up," he said. *"So I want Anna Kate to have everything! I don't think we can spoil her. She's such a little girl, small for her age, and is always a little slow in being able to do things that are considered to be normal for her age. So we think that letting her do anything she wants will make her feel better about herself."*

When parents see their child asserting her independence, as in Anna Kate's case, fear is often the response. Dawn and Mark were afraid that they might lose their daughter's affection by forcing her to do something against her will. So they "bought" her love by allowing her to do anything she wanted, any time she wanted.

As a result of their focusing only on their needs, however, their lives were miserable. They relied on a good performance review from their daughter to feel good about themselves as parents. Dawn and Mark's friends never wanted their children to play with Anna Kate now because of her bratty behavior, which was going unchecked. She was definitely in charge of this family business. But Dawn and Mark would rather have her run their lives than risk losing her love.

To restore the appropriate balance of power to their lives, Dawn and Mark needed to put their daughter's physical problems and needs in perspective. They admitted that they were afraid to make any kind of "deals" with her, sure that if they didn't do what *she* wanted, she wouldn't be able to handle the frustration.

We helped them understand that Anna Kate, just like all children, needed to learn to cope with life's disappointments and adversity during this stage of her development. Her parents likewise needed to learn to cope with their fears of Anna Kate's disapproval, as well as their own disappointment that their child might not meet their expectations.

By separating Anna Kate's problems from her as a person and focusing on them as separate issues, both Dawn and Mark were able to take control of the direction the family was taking. They realized that the family business required them to accept Anna Kate for who she was, despite their worry about her physical problems, and to help her learn about her world in the best way she could. Letting her be the boss wasn't going to accomplish what they wanted for her or what they wanted for themselves. To be good Family Managers, they had to learn to trust their "employee," to delegate, and to trust themselves.

As children near five years of age, the whole family needs to prepare to enter a new passage in their lives. Family Managers who are on the tail end of the third season of parenthood need to reflect on the solidity of the foundation and structure of the family business they've created and commit themselves to continuing to focus on their management goals. As children enter the magnetic field of school, the pull away from home will get stronger . . . and the strength of the home-based business that parents have managed in this season will increase in value as it contributes to everyone's well-being.

Charles in Charge: Money Matters

"No, we should not move just because the kids have to share a room," *Charles, a frugal, forty-year-old self-employed accountant and his thirty-*

eight-year-old wife, Heather, a supermarket clerk, told us emphatically in one of our Circles groups. We asked them if they were comfortable having their three-year-old twins, Chad and Brad, sleep in the same room as their eight-year-old son, Mark.

"Yes! They are all brothers and should sleep together," they replied.

The couple continued to explain that, in their opinion, moving into a bigger home was somehow "giving in" to Chad and Brad, who now seemed to be controlling all of the family finances and decision making. They couldn't make a move without getting them a sitter, paying for day care, buying new shoes, or replacing the toys they ruined by being so rambunctious. The boys were turning out to be more expensive than all of the furnishings in their home, according to Charles. Eight-year-old Mark rarely entered their conversations.

"We know we are doing a terrible job," Heather told us quietly, "because we can't even save money anymore. The diaper expenses alone are making us crazy. We argue all the time about money. Charles thinks I'm spending too much on the children, and I keep telling him that I'm saving him money because of my discount at the store. He keeps nagging me about toilet training the twins so we don't have the diaper expense anymore; but I'm so exhausted all of the time, I'm just not up to it."

"I know how much we have budgeted for everything, and if we could just stay within our budget, we'd have enough to get along," Charles said defensively. "But Heather just can't seem to manage money very well. We could afford a bigger house if we could meet our budget. The twins' expenses have been so astronomical that we've had to go into debt and haven't recovered yet."

"Unfortunately, raising Chad and Brad just keeps getting more costly every day," Heather lamented "It's funny that they are the ones that make us need a new house; but just feeding, clothing, and keeping them healthy cost so much that we can't afford one."

Charles and Heather were shell-shocked by the impact that the twins had made on their lives—from the exhaustion they felt at the end of each day to their stretched finances and cramped living arrangements—management issues that they had under control until their family of three became a family of five.

When their babies were infants, Charles and Heather were the center of everyone's attention; the women's auxiliary from church had come over twice a week to help them with housecleaning, cooking, and baby care. The babies had slept in a bassinet in their parents' room, so feeding and diapering them hadn't interrupted Mark's life. But as the twins got older, everything had changed.

Charles and Heather's marriage was getting run down by their battles over finances. They hadn't been able to discuss much of anything other than money since the twins' births, and they found themselves fighting over the most petty of purchases. Heather resented Charles's "bottom line" mentality, and Charles continued to believe that Heather was a spend-thrift. At this point in their marriage, wrangling over money was creating an irreversible rift.

Charles's parents were both teenagers during the Great Depression, and they thought that they needed to save everything. Charles's mother even had a collection of used aluminum foil that was the joke of the family. Although his family did not consider themselves poor, "Waste not, want not" was the mantra that Charles grew up hearing and was more than will-ing to repeat to Heather at every opportunity.

Heather remembered her family always being financially comfortable; although her mother loved to find a good bargain, she never gave Heather the impression that she needed to. Heather had always been sheltered from financial matters as she was growing up, so she resented Charles al-ways bossing her around about money matters. She was more interested in hanging out with her friends than studying during high school and hadn't been a particularly good math student. This made financial discussions with Charles even more frustrating. She didn't understand half of what he was saying and didn't really care. If the children needed new shoes, she just wanted to buy them.

We asked them if moving would make them happier. Probably not, they admitted. They remembered being perfectly happy sharing rooms with their brothers and sisters when they were young. What was good enough for them as children should be good enough for their children, Charles told us. Heather was not so sure that this arrangement was the best for Mark but didn't want to question Charles's authority.

They put the blame on their children for creating their marital prob-lems, when in reality their treatment of each other was the villain. Each needed to take personal responsibility for the treatment of the other and strive to be more empathic toward each other's points of view about the cost of taking care of the children.

Even though Heather resented Charles and his "bottom-line" approach to everything, she agreed that she could try harder to work on staying within the budget they would create together. She also agreed that looking for a new job that paid more would help her feel as if she were making a greater contribution to the family. We urged Charles to become better informed about the cost of raising preschoolers by shopping for their clothes and other necessities. He knew that he wasn't getting anywhere nagging about finances all the time, so they set up a time each week to pay bills together and discuss how they could budget for the next week. They realized that they had a long way to go to get themselves out of financial difficulties but would increase their chances of reaching their goal by working as a team.

Self-Discoveries of Family Managers

Your pocket guide to the truths revealed in the Family Manager season of parenthood.

- ➤ **Help! I want to get off.** In this season, you realize that even if you want to, you can't get off the roller-coaster ride of parenthood. Someone else is in charge of the speed at which you're traveling, and the track you are on is fixed on a predictable and inevitable course. The only way to enjoy it is to relax and appreciate that this part of the ride won't last forever; the ride will soon be smoother.

- ➤ **They never told me about this part.** You are caught off guard by what you have to do to keep from falling out of the car. The twists and turns of the ride force you to constantly adjust your position as you rush along. Your partner beside you needs to stay calm when you shift positions; if he or she gets out of control, the whole car can get off track.

- ➤ **Now everyone's watching.** Looking good to family and friends as you rush along seems to preoccupy some riders, but the more important task is to hang on tight as you strive to keep your balance. Trying to impress others has to take a backseat to the business of keeping everyone in the car safe. Use discrimination in following the advice that onlookers offer; remember that this is your ride, and things look different from the ground.

➤ **For this I spent four years in college?** The parenthood roller-coaster ride is the great equalizer; no matter how much education or money or social status you have, the ride is pretty much the same for everyone. The only difference for each rider is his or her attitude about the twists and turns: Whether you see them as scary or exciting, overwhelming or manageable, dangerous or doable, depends on the thoughts you have as you rush relentlessly along the track.

Exit Signs

Leaving Control Room. Entering Elementary School. Although children's behavior continues to call out for a Family Manager to reinforce the lessons of their first five or six years, the focus of the management tasks changes from managing children to managing the children's schedule in the new world of elementary school. Parents' shift in identity, from mother and father of a young child to "kindergartner Meg's mom or dad," abruptly changes the direction the family is traveling. As the roller-coaster track turns, parents become Travel Agents and have a new view of the landscape of their family's life: new people, places, events, activities, demands.

Travel Agent

CHILD'S ELEMENTARY SCHOOL YEARS

The events in our lives happen in a sequence in time but in their significance to ourselves they find their own order . . . the continuous thread of revelation.
—EUDORA WELTY

CUB SCOUTS. BALLET LESSONS. Brownies. Field trips. Piano recitals. Day camps. Art projects. Valentine's Day parties. Soccer teams. Teacher conferences. School talent show. Homework. And more homework. This cafeteria lineup of activities, some of which children first sample in the latter preschool years, is now the regular diet of hungry, middle-years children as they explore their world outside of the home for the majority of their waking hours. That's why middle-years children, generally six to twelve years old, turn their parents into Travel Agents in this season of parenthood. You are now the responsible party for planning and executing your children's itineraries, their safe and productive travels that create the stories your children will remember as their childhood.

Your children will continue to route your journey in life, forcing you to relive more of the adventures you remember playing out in your *own* childhood. You may barely recall anything of the first few years of your life, but heading off to school is a major milestone. Who doesn't recall the gut-wrenching spats with other children, sweaty sports contests, greasy school

125

lunches, and nervous talent show tryouts—what it felt like, smelled like, and sounded like to be six, seven, eight, nine, ten, and eleven years old? As you revisit these years with new insight, your kids become young people whose world you can relate to even more readily.

"I loved my elementary school years and couldn't wait to go to the father/daughter square dances when my daughter was in first grade," Roger, a Circles group member, offered. "I remember that my dad loved going with my little sister. It was like I was going back home again, about to relive some of the best years of my family's life. What was so cool was that I felt like I could make them even better for my child because I knew where the land mines were hidden."

Just entering the school itself can evoke a flood of emotions for parents. Lynn had a stomachache throughout her child's first few years of elementary school, which intensified when her daughter, Liz, hit third grade. As she relived her own early elementary school years through Liz, she realized that she still harbored the pain of losing her mother when she was in third grade. After her mother died, Lynn never felt as though anyone were ever "there" for her—helping with homework, taking her to Brownies, being a room mother for her class parties. Her father was so overwhelmed by keeping up with his job and coping with the loss of his wife that he never paid much attention to Lynn and her two older brothers as they were growing up.

Lynn had no blueprint to follow now that her daughter was in school, no role model from her own childhood. "Inadequate. That was how I saw myself during my daughter's grade school years because I thought that it was my responsibility to make sure all was well, even though I didn't have a clue about how to do that. I had to make my life up as we went along. I just felt my way, based on what I would have wanted my mom to do if she had been able to be there for me when I was Liz's age. It was amazing to have this second chance to create the kind of childhood that I always wished I'd had."

TRAVEL AGENTS TOLD US that they felt accountable for helping their children's expeditions through these elementary school years be as comfortable as possible, complete with nice bedrooms, safe carpools, positive coaches, caring teachers. They must face three central conflicts in order to be successful: adjusting to the changes that teachers, friends, and coaches, among others, make in their children's itineraries; coping with their children's normal need to navigate more and more independently; and facing the reality that their children may want to go places that they have no interest in taking them or experience in navigating themselves. Parents accompany their little travelers on their adventures into the big world, feeling more qualified to help them enjoy their trip if they have "been there, done that" themselves in prior years.

If soccer is your child's love, for example, you might find yourselves making friends with the coach, hauling big coolers of drinks and snacks, and commiserating with other soccer parents while knee-deep in mud on faraway fields in rain, sleet, or sun, even if you've never played the game before in your lives. How you feel about doing so will be measured in large part by your expectations for your child, expectations that you might not even be aware of, based on who you were when you were your children's ages. If you enjoyed being soccer stars, for example, nothing would make you happier than seeing your child follow in your proverbial footsteps.

C HILDREN'S DEMANDS dictate to some extent how comfortable or crazed parents are as Travel Agents. Randy, a Circles group father, related his story: "We lived in an okay apartment, but our nine-year-old son and eleven-year-old daughter were embarrassed by it. They wanted a house with big rooms, a closet filled with $150 sneakers and Rollerblades, trips to expensive camps across the country—all the stuff their friends had."

"I don't know how people can afford to have kids anymore. I never felt poor until my kids made me feel poor. Whatever happened to playing in the park like I did? Now they need to be taken to ball fields across town, wear uniforms that cost over $100, and travel to different cities to tournaments. What kind of a racket is this? Everything was great until my child started telling me how to live my life. I would never have asked my parents to take me on a trip just to play in a ball game."

Randy expected his childhood and his children's to be similar, even though his children referred to his youth as the "olden days." Although he was accused by his kids of being "old-fashioned," he resented being asked to book such expensive accommodations for them. He told us that he wished his kids were preschoolers again, a time when they weren't ever exposed to "big kid" ideas that included such extravagant travel plans that he had to arrange.

F OR NATALIE, a particularly articulate mother in one of our Circles groups, the "olden days" held memories she wanted to forget. She remembered how disappointed her father was when she wasn't a great speller as he was. He had won the first- and second-grade spelling championships and expected her to do the same, although art, not spelling, was her love. It still haunted her today, she told us, that he refused to take her artistic endeavors seriously, directing her instead to a career in writing. That was the main reason she was now an editor and not an artist.

Natalie had quit her editing job, however, when she became pregnant with Aubrey. Since then her world had revolved around her daughter. She had grown accustomed to separating from her for brief periods, but the thought of Aubrey being away from her all day, every day, made her feel isolated, almost abandoned.

"I have never felt as lonely as I did on Aubrey's first day of first grade," said Natalie. "I understood that I had no choice—I had to take her to school for the whole day. More startling to me was realizing that I was starting on a whole new journey with her in the world of school. We would meet all kinds of characters on the way—teachers, principals, and students—just as I had when I was her age. But they would be part of *her* world, not mine."

Natalie discovered a universal truth about this season of parenthood: When a child enters first grade, regardless of how many baby-sitters, day care centers, preschools, or kindergartens she has gone to, parents feel the family foundation shift, which causes a ripple to travel through every aspect of their lives. Natalie vowed to accept her own daughter's passions during her years in school, even if they didn't match her own, in order to avoid the unintentional hurt that her father had inflicted on her. What's more, the next time she visited her dad, she was able to discuss this still vivid memory with new maturity. She even decided to go back to school and pursue her dream of a career in painting because she was so thrilled with doing art projects for her daughter's school and received rave reviews for her work.

ALL OF THESE TRAVEL AGENT CONFLICTS—facing reality, changing itineraries, and braving the separation blues—are colored by parents' own experiences as six- to twelve-year-olds. However, knowing that we are walking the same path with our children that we traveled before them brings a sense of familiarity to our lives.

FACING REALITY

*Family faces are magic mirrors. Looking at people who be-
long to us, we see the past, present, and future.*
—GAIL LUMET BUCKLEY

When spats over "who stands by whom" in line at recess send their elementary schoolers into puddles of tears, parents told us that they had the
same sick feeling of having been punched in the stomach by schoolyard
bullies when they were on the playground. Anger that they never knew
they were capable of welled up inside them. Their children's crises evoked
memories of their own childhood laments that reemerged with such clarity
that it seemed as if they had happened only the day before.

Now, through parenthood, moms and dads of all ages are transported
back in time, compelled to solve problems—longing to be more popular,
wanting to be smarter, or needing a best friend—that have been dormant
all of these years. Parents told us that their children's suffering made them
feel helpless, even more helpless than they felt when confronted with the
same issues as children. They were heartsick as they began to realize that
even though they were their children's Travel Agents, they could not perfectly arrange their children's journeys through life. There were bound to
be glitches along the way.

CHRISTINE LEARNED THIS LESSON with her daughter, Lili: "I
couldn't believe that someone could be mean to my sweet child. She
hated to go out on the playground in fourth grade because she was so bad
at jumping rope. All of the other girls made fun of her, which absolutely
made me crazy! I wanted to call their mothers and tell them to teach their
kids some manners."

Christine's own experience with playground teasing had put her in
tears some thirty years ago when she was in fourth grade. Her lack of patience with rude, insolent children and adults today was a remnant from
then, she said, having never really gotten over the taunts and teasing. But
part of her feelings stemmed from wishing that she could put a protective
coating around Lili or rewind her back to her preschool days, when Christine felt more control over who her playmates were and her exposure to upsetting situations like the playground fiasco.

Christine had always assumed that the problems she faced as a child—fickle friendships, poor grades in math, reading problems, and detentions for messy lunchroom tables—had something to do with the times, the particular school she attended, her mean classroom teacher, the wild kids in the neighborhood she lived in, or maybe even her own problems in standing up for herself when she made a mistake. To see her child struggling with these same challenges brought home the fact that growing up is, by its very nature, full of adversities that are rites of passage for all children. Christine now realized that history would repeat itself, and no matter how much she wanted to, she couldn't make Lili's trip through life wholly painless for her or for herself.

Two factors contribute to parents' frustration over how little control they have in how their children experience their travels. First, as much as they would like to be, they can't be "the mouse in the corner" in their child's classroom. The stories they hear at the end of the day—about the awful Mrs. Jenkins, the disgusting boy who sits behind her, or the rejection by the popular girls of her after-school invitation to come home to play—are all hearsay. How their child views the world is totally unique to who she is and determines her reaction to her experiences, just as it does for everyone. Proof that her tales of woe really happened in the way that they were described is not the issue. Parents are forced to mop up the often tearful mess that their child's interpretation of these events has splattered on her delicate heart and relive similar travel hazards from their own childhood. The reality is, as your child's Travel Agents, you only direct her travel plans; you don't control her view of those plans. You're best advised to help her cope with disappointment and frustration, which will teach her how to play the cards she's dealt.

Second, although parents have spent the first three seasons of parenthood trying to keep their child free from harm, now her experiences include a much wider cast of characters who are often unknown to parents. Courtney may be "dying" to go to an overnight at Justine's house, but her parents tell her she can't go because they haven't met Justine or her parents and don't feel comfortable letting her spend the night in the home of "strangers." Courtney wails that her life is ruined if she can't go. So what do parents do? They could get to know Justine and her parents: arranging a play date at their house before allowing their daughter to go to Justine's; calling Justine's mother to learn the rules she has for her daughter; inviting Justine's mother and mothers of Courtney's other classmates to an informal coffee at her house, thereby getting better acquainted with Courtney's new social world.

Parents need to start by giving *themselves* messages to adjust their attitude about their children's discontentment: "It's better to help my child deal with problems than to try to avoid all adversity." "I can handle this—it's no big deal." "If I handle it well, so will my child." "It's not the end of the world—now let's see if we can find something good that can come of this." "I can stand this—I just don't have to like it." "If I demand what I think is fair, it may not be fair for others." "It's better to look at what's good for all." Each is an example of healthy self-talk that you can practice to help yourselves think logically when your offspring aren't developmentally equipped to do so yet.

It's how you as Travel Agents think about these bumps in the road that makes the difference in your ability to cope, to take the long view in problem solving regardless of the magnitude of the obstacles in your way.

NOT ONLY ARE TRAVEL AGENTS not in complete control of the world in which their little travelers navigate, but they also discover that their children may not be the kinds of travelers they had dreamed they would be or have the same destinations in mind. If you always fantasized about acting on Broadway, performing at Carnegie Hall, winning the U.S. Open, or writing a Pulitzer Prize–winning volume, for example, here's when you'll get your first taste of experiencing your dreams potentially fulfilled—or not—through your children as they begin to blossom.

Many parents would admit that their children afford them another chance to "do it all again," to be anything they want to possibly be as they relive their childhood through them. But looking at children as a "second chance" can also be dangerous for both parents and children, especially when children's tastes and interests are different from their parents'.

"I was on the swim team at the country club thirty years ago," Lydia told her eight-year-old son, Curtis. "Now I can't wait for you to join." Having said that, Lydia had to acknowledge that one problem remained: Curtis was deathly afraid of the water and was so uncoordinated that he couldn't get his arms and legs to each do their job in swimming. "The disappointment," said Lydia, "was far greater for me than for him when he told me that he didn't want to join the team."

Unbeknownst to their children, parents may have been building a make-believe image of who their children were through the past few years, an image based on who parents wish they could have been and who they wish their children will become, not on who they really *are*.

Jayne and Arnold, parents of Ethan, a witty, energetic fourth grader, said that they knew what this experience felt like firsthand. When his teacher told Jayne and Arnold that Ethan was in danger of not being able to pass fourth grade because of his poor reading ability, Jayne and Arnold refused to believe the tests.

"Not our son," they explained. "We come from a long line of writers. We've all been writers; our family has it in our blood." In order for Jayne and Arnold to accept their son—reading problems and all—they had to mourn the loss of their dream, a dream that had taken root deep in their soul, that their only son would carry on the family tradition. In order for them to grow through this season of parenthood, they needed to learn how to face the reality that they didn't have the ability to shape their son's life in their own image.

For your emotional and spiritual health, you must accept that each of your children is gifted in his own inimitable way. As Travel Agents, your task in this stage of their development is to discover just where your children need to go in the world, help them prepare for the trip, and arrange how to get them there and back home as safely as possible, physically, spiritually, intellectually, and emotionally.

CHANGING ITINERARIES

It seems to me I spent my life in carpools, but you know that's how I kept track of what was going on.
—BARBARA BUSH

While this developmental stage is often characterized as a somewhat slow period of physical growth in children, as compared with the preschool and adolescent periods, parental growth takes an important leap during these years. A new paradigm for the identity of mother and father is created in this season, one that allows parents to support their child's diverging path: now it's you who needs to adapt when others change the details of your child's itinerary.

In contrast, during the past five years you decided every aspect of your children's travel—where they went, when they went there, and how they traveled back and forth between there and home. Now, as elementary schoolers, your children and their teachers, principals, counselors, coaches, religious leaders, and fellow students are deciding many of the places they will go and when and how they will travel. You're left to plan around the travel arrangements others are making for your children and, ultimately, for yourselves.

The most dramatic example that reminds parents that their children's itinerary may be changed at a moment's notice is the classic parent-teacher conference. It is a harrowing experience even for the most brave hearted. Spiffed-up parents approach the event with a conflicting mixture of excitement at the prospect of hearing wonderful things about their beloved offspring and fear that the news will be all bad, not at all unlike the feelings they had as children about these reports. But now, as Travel Agents, this may be the first time that you receive an official evaluation of how your child is doing on his trip through life, most of which is now being spent out of your watchful eyes, causing you to feel that you are also being evaluated on your performance as his parents.

Clutching their classroom schedule or clean pad of paper, parents wait anxiously outside the door of their child's classroom, exchanging sideways glances that communicate volumes about their fluttering stomachs. They talk to themselves: What will Mrs. McGuire say about John's reading level? Will Sherille have any problems I don't know about? I will die if Mr. Clark says that Andrew can't be in accelerated math. Their children and their educational teams are now traveling companions for most of their children's waking hours. In addition, schools have the power to change children's itineraries as they judge children's performances on the road.

Teachers are required to give parents feedback about how well their children conduct themselves during their trip through the elementary school years, which can dredge up old feelings of inadequacy if parents haven't worked through the performance review conflicts of the last season. Now Travel Agents are faced with these new, more formal performance reviews of their "products," their children: report cards, acceptance on school sports teams and clubs, and after-school detentions. These reports can make parents' stomachs turn and blood pressure rise. To get better performance reviews as parents, they try to turn back the tide to that more comfortable time when they believed they had more control of their children's lives and how others interpreted their children's behavior.

Case in point: When her daughter, Allyson, didn't get Mrs. Parker for fourth grade, one full-fledged control freak in one of our Circles groups, Monica, was upset. "For two years I had been asking the principal for Allyson to have Mrs. Parker," she told us. "Allyson is a good kid who deserved to have Mrs. Parker. It's not fair that she got another teacher after I tried so hard to get her in that class. I'm afraid she won't do as well in the other class."

Rather than let the school dictate Allyson's teacher for fourth grade, Monica demanded that the school move her to Mrs. Parker's room. But when Allyson found out, she was in tears. Her best friend, Kate, was in the class she originally was in, and she didn't want to move. What was Monica to do? She was learning that not always having control over Allyson's itinerary in this season of parenthood made her feel insecure. She wanted Allyson to have friends; it was upsetting to her, though, that being with her friends was more important to her than being in the class that her mother thought she should be in. Monica had to decide when she could or should take control of choosing Allyson's route in life and how she could feel comfortable when the matter was out of her hands.

This wasn't the only time Monica had to face this kind of decision as her daughter's Travel Agent. In second grade Allyson was best friends with two girls, Melissa and Kate. Melissa's mother, Cathy Lee, loved getting together with Monica and Kate's mother, Trudy, whenever the kids had sleep-overs together. The mothers' friendship blossomed into a friendship of couples. The six parents were inseparable at school events and at parties; they even vacationed together so that the kids could do their own thing and leave the adults alone.

By fifth grade the whole happy "family" of friends exploded when the three girls became ex–best friends. It wasn't pretty. Everyone was angry with everyone else over the hurt feelings, snippy words, and jealousies that played out in the classroom and on the playground. Not only were the girls in agony; but when the children began fighting, their parents started to take sides. Monica believed that Allyson wasn't at fault and didn't hesitate to tell the other mothers who was in the wrong. This, naturally, upset the others, and the war was on.

In both of Monica's stories, by taking the long view—what is the lesson to be learned here?—a more mature approach to guiding Allyson's itinerary would have spared Monica much aggravation. The teachers in Allyson's school were all good; Monica knew that was true. Her daughter would be fine in another teacher's class, not Mrs. Parker's; Monica also knew that was true. And Allyson's friends' parents could still be Monica's friends even though the young girls weren't getting along. She, in fact, could demonstrate ways to mend fences by apologizing to the other mothers for getting caught up in her daughter's childish squabbles.

W HEN FACED WITH CONFLICTS over changing itineraries in this season of parenthood, parents such as Monica are fortunate if they've been able to cope with the challenges of managing a healthy family business. For most parents it's difficult to let others rearrange their child's travel plans as his journey moves farther away from home. But having a solid home base of rules and structure for their children and for themselves to return to at the end of a busy day of exploring the world—sports practices, music lessons, and schoolwork—makes a Travel Agent's life less stressful, which helps all of the family stay on a mutually supportive course.

BRAVING THE SEPARATION BLUES

There is nothing more thrilling in this world, I think, than having a child that is yours, and yet is mysteriously a stranger.—AGATHA CHRISTIE

"I spent all of this time investing in my child and now she's gone!" Charlene lamented at a casual coffee she threw at her house for "empty nesters"—parents of children in her daughter's first-grade class.

Charlene, a dental hygienist, had quit her job to stay home full-time when Cara, her six-year-old daughter, was born. Now she suddenly felt lost without her playmate and confidante to occupy her time, she told the group. She knew this day was coming, but she hadn't thought that she would feel so angry, so empty.

We listened to the conversations of these Travel Agent mothers and fathers and others who were facing another bout of anxiety related to their children's pilgrimage toward self-sufficiency and independence, anxiety brought on by the most difficult, defining experience of parenthood: letting go. They had invested so much time and energy in managing their family in the last season of parenthood; now they were discovering how it felt to surrender so much of their children's itinerary to others.

Some Travel Agents told us that they experienced a sense of loss as they tried to adjust to their empty houses for six to eight hours a day. As they grieved this new loss, parents experienced anger that their child had left them, fear that others would become a greater part of their child's life than they were, worry that they would have to redefine who they were, and sadness that their child was growing up: all ingredients of the separation blues. They reported being overwhelmed by each of the stages of grief associated with loss: denial and isolation, anger, depression, bargaining, and acceptance.

For some parents, their denial that their child was moving out into the big world was expressed by dressing her as if she were four years old again and overprotecting her by refusing to let her go anywhere without them, except to school. They felt isolated, alone, separate from their child's new world. Their anger turned into resentment of those people who might get close to her and gain her love: teachers, other parents, classmates. They became masters at bargaining with their child's friends (and parents) to play only at their house, with her teacher so they could volunteer in her classroom and receive daily feedback about progress. These parents said that they felt depressed as they lamented their loss and discovered that they were powerless to change the forward momentum of their child's growing up and away from home.

Finally, these Travel Agents found themselves forced to accept the inevitable: Their child was entering a new, expanded world of adventure, whether they liked it or not, making them responsible for creating a new itinerary for themselves as a part of their child's world. Ultimately Travel Agents are best advised to shift from thinking that they have been *abandoned* by their children to thinking that they are being *led* by them to new adventures as their offspring naturally and predictably expand their world beyond home, the day care center, preschool, and the neighborhood. Parents who have accepted this predictable path give themselves the opportunity to share their children's new activities: school, sports, music, dance, scouting, religious classes.

For many parents, the work needed to cope with the conflict of the separation blues in this season is dependent on how they met the challenges of parenthood in Seasons One through Three. The more they bonded to their little ones during their infancy and preschool years, the deeper the roots of their connection and the harder it will be to let go and separate from those they have grown to love.

Katherine, a Circles group participant, understood the irony in this truth about parenthood. She saw the last vestiges of her son's innocence slip away as he entered third grade and confessed to his mother that he knew the Easter bunny wasn't real and that third graders didn't kiss their mothers good-bye in front of their friends. Katherine found herself going through all five stages of grief as she mourned the loss of her "little boy." She admitted holding on to one strand of his early childhood: telling him that Santa Claus would definitely come to their house on Christmas Eve if he had been a good boy all year. Their family would still "believe" in Santa Claus, just as her family had done when she was her son's age, thus maintaining a link to her past as well as her child's.

O NE WARNING: Don't make the mistake of believing that the separation conflict in this season of parenthood stems from the fact that children are in school for six or eight or even ten hours a day. The origin of separation blues is not in the clock, but results from the changes in agenda that children experience developmentally. They are moving away: separating from the dependency that characterized their previous stages, learning new things, establishing new connections to people and places, beginning to challenge their parents' ideas.

Colby, a father who talked with us after a PTA meeting, told us that he was surprised by his pangs of grief in this season. His second-grade son, Brandt, and fifth grader, Alexis, had played a good-natured game of checkers and snuggled together with a good book each night when they were preschoolers. For the past several years this Travel Agent had helped his wife, Jill, plan the schedules for their children; but a sense that he no longer was important on their social itinerary plagued him. Brandt and Alexis now needed him for homework answers and money for skating parties, not as an evening playmate. Once he stopped thinking that he was being rejected because they didn't snuggle on his lap as they used to, Colby was able to appreciate his children's sense of adventure and appetite for independence that he had experienced when he was their age.

"It still made me nervous," he said, "to watch them spending more and more of their time away from home in places, such as the skating rink, where I wasn't invited."

Although school-age children may seem increasingly competent, they drive parental fear by their independence, as Colby identified. A 1998 *Newsweek* poll showed that 64 percent of parents worry that their kids will get involved with troublemakers or use drugs or alcohol. Even though three out of four mothers of school-age children work outside the home today, their children remain the most powerful priority in their lives.

Some parents become overprotective of their child in this season of parenthood to compensate for the anxiety they generate by having a diminishing sense of control of who's in the driver's seat of their child's itinerary.

"My parents were scared to death to let me do anything but go to school," Martha recalled in one of our Circles groups. "I couldn't join a soccer team with my friends because the coaches were all too mean, according to my mom and dad. I couldn't even play outside after school if they didn't know the kids' parents, and couldn't spend the night out because the other moms would let me stay up too late. My overprotected childhood will not be repeated by my little ones," she added, vowing to try to embrace the "carpe diem" attitude she had heard friends say had colored their own childhood.

Other parents reported feeling hypocritical when the separation blues felt more like separation relief. Those parents whose children had spent years in day care centers or with baby-sitters told us they were overjoyed about their children being elementary school students. Finally, they echoed, they could go to work guilt free: their children had full-time jobs, and they had theirs until dinnertime each day. They no longer felt guilty about being away from the children all day. Now no one was home!

Sometime during this season, however, many parents who had full-time, daily work itineraries of their own reported that their separation relief was starting to fade: being their children's Travel Agents demanded that their schedule be more flexible than ever before. They were then forced to make compromises in their lives—choosing what was important for them to share with their children and what wasn't: Brownie and Cub Scout meetings; parent-teacher conferences; holiday parties; morning PTA meetings; their children's play performances, talent shows, and field days.

THE KEY TO COPING with the separation blues in this season of parenthood is a keen ability to follow the Scout motto: "Be prepared." Looking at the pattern of family life as a constantly changing adventure helps parents understand their identity as the keeper of the compass. Separation blues can become separation celebrations when everyone is comfortable with where the journey is taking him and how to adjust the sails when the wind shifts direction.

Jasmine, the Helicopter Parent: The Illusion of Control

A big smile spread over the face of a fiftyish-looking woman in the second row who had "Jasmine" written in big red letters on her nametag. We were doing our regular PTA sales pitch to parents, asking them to use empathy in disciplining children. It was clear from Jasmine's approving nods that she was an attentive listener.

We learned from the PTA president that Jasmine was Volunteer of the Year award winner. Need cookies baked? Call Jasmine. Need a volunteer for the field trip? Call Jasmine. Need a parent to read to the class twice a week? Jasmine's your gal, explained the president. She was always up at school and eager to be of service, so eager that her child's teachers would dart in the opposite direction when they saw her coming. "Involved" was an understatement when it came to describing Jasmine.

When we got a chance to meet Jasmine, we told her how lucky the school was to have her commitment. "I just love everything about kids this age," she gushed. "It makes me so happy to be near Maxine, my middle child out of five, that I will do anything I can to have an excuse to see her during the day. My oldest two, my stepchildren, are grown. When they were young, it didn't seem as dangerous to raise kids as it does now. My younger two children are just in preschool, so they're easy. Maxine is only ten; how can she take care of herself when there are so many bad kids out there just waiting to give her drugs or cigarettes? I think it's important for parents these days to know the school nurse, principal, even the lunch room ladies. You never know when your daughter or son will need them."

When we asked Jasmine how her daughter liked having her mother hang around school all day, she said she didn't know. "It really never crossed my mind to ask her," she explained. "My husband, Scott, and I know what a scary world it is out there. So we think it's our job to protect Maxine from its harmful influences. It just doesn't seem like anyone cares anymore what kids see on television or what movies are rated. My friends let kids Maxine's age go to birthday parties that show R-rated films or rent videos that scare her to death. When I found Maxine in the bathroom at home, smoking a cigarette in front of the mirror, I knew I needed to be more on top of her. What would be next . . . drinking a beer?"

She went on to explain that she wanted Maxine to enjoy her childhood and not be worried about being taken by a stranger or being shot by a gang member. Those worries were her job! Being well known at her school and in her neighborhood was the only way Jasmine could trust that someone would call her if anything bad ever happened to her precious daughter. Catching her in the bathroom was the last straw that convinced her that she needed to police her daughter's activities more than she had been.

"Any 'good mom' would!" she exclaimed.

At the risk of sounding cynical, we let Jasmine know that she had accomplished her goal. Everyone at the school and in the neighborhood knew her well. Unfortunately they wanted nothing to do with her. Her friends thought she was a maniacal helicopter parent who was obsessed with her daughter and her safety. They were scared to have Maxine over to their home or even let their children play with her, lest something happen and it would be their fault.

Jasmine told us that she used to work in the craft store near her home; but when Maxine was a baby, she couldn't bear to leave her at the baby-sitter's. So she quit and started a balloon bouquet business out of her home. This worked out great. She could be home with the "babies" now. Every time that Maxine wanted to go to a party, a balloon would go with her. That was okay with Maxine when she was younger, just as it delighted her little ones now. But recently Maxine and Jasmine were getting into arguments over this ritual that Maxine wanted to end with a bang.

That wasn't the only thing that Maxine wanted to end. She tried to tell her mother not to stay at gymnastics practice, either. Maxine's testing a forbidden cigarette in her own bathroom was another sign that she was trying to separate from her mother and plan her own itinerary, we suggested to Jasmine. We knew that if Jasmine's intensive monitoring persisted, Maxine's rebellious behavior would, too. Despite the signals Maxine was giving her, Jasmine thought it was her responsibility as a parent to protect her daughter from getting hurt by being there to ensure that no harm would come to her—an impossible and unrealistic goal.

Being overly protective of her daughter came naturally. Jasmine admitted that her own mother and father were strict about whose home she played at after school and what "influences," as they called them, were filling her head with unhealthy thoughts. "I really never rebelled against all their rules," Jasmine said. "I just figured that if they said it, it must be for a good reason."

Today, that kind of respect for the older generation seems to have gone the way of ten-cent hamburgers. Even children in the early middle years are, developmentally speaking, moving toward wanting their Travel Agents to take a hike, preferably away from them. And to avoid being rejected, millions of parents fade to black and let their children roam free.

Wanting to be more independent is a natural and healthy symptom of a child's transition through prepuberty. When a parent's response to this symptom is to totally smother their fellow travelers or stop being a Travel Agent, it can be tantamount to either sinking the boat or abandoning ship. Children need guidance in this stage of their development to know how to make responsible choices when away from their parents and left to their own devices. By frequently traveling with your children in this stage without hovering over them, you can assess just what kind of navigator and tourist your child is. This knowledge is critical data for you to tuck away so you can give accurate directions based on what each of your children can handle responsibly in this stage, as well as in the next.

But you also need to give your anxiety button a rest, telling yourselves: I've been through this myself before, and I've survived. My child can do the same now. I cannot control every aspect of our lives together. I'm responsible for making the travel arrangements, not for going along on every trip. Others in my child's life have to be trusted to take my child part of the way now. By looking at the big picture and deciding what kind of Travel Agent I want to be for my child, I can appreciate this season of parenthood as an exciting opportunity to experience new adventures with my child while revisiting landmarks from my own journey through childhood.

Gabe's Confession: Not Fitting In with the PTA Moms

"When my children were newborns, we lived in a small town where I used to have lots of friends. We carpooled for preschool and did a lot of volunteer work together," Gabe, mother of a six-year-old son, Jason, and seven- and nine-year-old girls, Mikala and Ivy, began telling the group assembled at her house for a Circles meeting. *"On the weekends, a group of us would go to the lake house my parents owned, talk on the phone all week, and plan special holiday meals together. They all had children who were the ages of my children, and they became my family because my parents and in-laws lived nearly 1,500 miles away."*

Then Gabe's husband, Avery, had been transferred to another city when their oldest child started elementary school. She didn't feel she had any-

thing in common with the new neighbors she had met, no one to go to with her worries about her kids. Most of the volunteers she now worked with on charity events had children who were having children themselves. They wanted to talk about holding newborns or watching their grandchildren take their first steps.

Everyone in the group empathized with this forty-year-old's "family" story. Most of them had moved away from home after getting married. The long-distance parenting of their parents and in-laws had ensured self-sufficiency but little closeness, particularly if they had moved often.

Now Gabe's world revolved around struggling with reliving her own tormented elementary school scene. Her own grade school years had been pure misery because she had been such a shy and clumsy child. As a parent, she still felt the same way—incompetent and self-conscious. She had no clue as to how all of the other moms and even dads in her children's classes in the city knew how to play the school-age parent game. But they were good at it, she felt.

Her children wanted her to be involved in their school activities and sports, but Gabe wasn't interested in getting dressed up for the Valentine's Day party or buying a new outfit for Back to School Night, like the other mothers talked about on the softball bleachers. Those were the same mothers and fathers who were encouraging their children by shouting things like "Kill 'em!" "Mutilate 'em!" and "Slaughter 'em!"

She felt totally out of place at PTA meetings as well, as she watched the power struggles of her fellow parents come alive with a vengeance. Who cared who baked the best cookies or ran the most popular school events? All in all, she just felt lost, not sure what happened to the parenthood journey she had so loved before now.

Gabe admitted that she couldn't come to grips with being a mother of a school-age child. That meant, as silly as it sounded, that she was old, a grown-up. But she said that she still felt so young, like a college kid. It had seemed kind of fun to have little kids. She and Avery would carry Mikala and Ivy in their backpacks, and they would go on long walks the way they did in college. Or she would jog with Jason in the jogging stroller, just as she had done with the girls. Even preschool was fun; she had loved watching *Sesame Street* on television and playing games with colors and numbers that both of her children had adored. She had loved the funny cut-out sandwiches, picnics in front of the fireplace, pony rides on her husband's back . . . she started sobbing just mentioning all of the wonderful memories that her children's early years had brought to their family.

"Now they're gone," she lamented. "Gone! Poof! It was like it was all a dream."

We felt tearful, too, just listening to Gabe's reminiscences of the experiences that had formed the core of her family's closeness. Now her task was to create new memories, and this required involving her husband in the travel plans she made—attending school functions, parent-teacher conferences, and sporting events. Working together as Travel Agents, they could support each other through a transition that was particularly difficult for Gabe because of her reluctance to replace her old identity with her new one.

The degree to which parents feel they fit in—at PTA meetings, Back to School Night, holiday parties, soccer matches—makes them reflect on their general status as adults. If they feel as if they are "flunking" PTA, old feelings of not quite measuring up and of being an outsider as a child are dredged up. Parents' personality and temperament play important parts in their happiness as their child's Travel Agents. The most relaxed Travel Agents are the extroverted, self-confident, never-know-a-stranger adults who find the social world of the elementary school a comfortable fit. They have nothing to prove to themselves or to others; sometimes they play leadership roles in their children's schools; often they're happy just to be involved in the action.

Other parents, however, are highly competitive by nature. Because they make everything a contest, they are compelled to best the other parents by one-upping them at whatever they do in their children's world: They bake the most cookies, go to more meetings, bring better snacks to Cub Scouts. This getting drawn into trying to "keep up with the Joneses" is fueled by their need to win at everything in order to be acceptable to themselves, admired in others' eyes, and receive accolades for their performance as parents.

The direct opposite of the competitive Travel Agents are those parents, such as Gabe, who experience feelings of insecurity and inadequacy in the elementary school world because of their own shyness or grieving over "losing" their little girl or boy. They tend to be those who believe that they can't compete and don't want to. So they either refrain from getting involved in their children's school activities or take a backseat in their world while others run the show.

WHILE ACKNOWLEDGING the loss of their children as they knew them, all three camps of Travel Agents need to feel positive about their children's growing independence and support their new itinerary. Because Gabe still wanted to be a Family Manager, however, she couldn't relate to the people she encountered who had moved forward into the next season of parenthood. We encouraged her to let go of her old identity and take the plunge into the warm waters of her children's new lives, a rite of passage that every parent must eventually experience.

Home Alone: "Our Daughter's Led by Strangers"

Looking as if they were fresh out of high school themselves, an energetic, handsome couple, Greg, thirty-five, and Charlene, thirty-seven, sat in the front row at the PTA meeting of the elementary school in which their only child, Amy, had begun first grade a month ago. We were speaking there on the subject of character education, and they nodded their approval at each point we made as if they were being paid to support our particular view of the world. At the end of the talk we naturally gravitated toward each other.

They told us that Amy's school had a reputation for its students' high academic record and excellent teacher performance. But Charlene had one complaint: How could she let the total strangers there influence her precious daughter? Charlene and Greg had been best friends with Amy's Sunday school and preschool teachers, each of whom Charlene had handpicked for her gentle demeanor and keen intuition about meeting children's needs.

Both parents lamented that now new people were exposing Amy to situations that could be harmful to her. Charlene used what happened on the first day of first grade as an example: Amy told her that she had shivered all throughout recess because her teacher, Mrs. Brown, wouldn't let her go back inside to get a jacket. Mrs. Brown couldn't leave the other children on the playground unsupervised to accompany Amy back to the classroom. That was the school rule. Charlene was shocked! Both parents forcefully declared that they felt powerless now that somebody else was in the driver's seat in Amy's life.

To protect her daughter from these kinds of circumstances and to fill the void she had been experiencing since Amy went off to school, Charlene was considering volunteering in Amy's class and trying to get better acquainted with Mrs. Brown and the moms on her daughter's soccer team. She had never dreamed that Amy's going to school would make her feel so vulnerable and as empty inside as she did now in her uncomfortably quiet house. To escape these feelings, Charlene was also considering going back to her former job as an accountant, part-time, if her boss would take her. Now, however, she was feeling so depressed that she wasn't sure what she wanted to do.

Charlene finally understood what her mother had meant when she said, "You will miss Amy more than you can ever imagine." She also felt guilty about all the times she had prayed for the years to pass so that Amy would finally be in school; then she could go back to work and do what she wanted to do. "If only I could turn back the hands of time," Charlene confessed wistfully.

Greg and Charlene were nearly crazy with panic over this inevitable change in their lives. After all, they had once been in elementary school and knew what it was like to discover a whole new world. They knew it could be both painful and exciting. They were informed, rational grown-ups, they thought. But this situation caused them to lose all of their ability to think rationally; it was an emotional nightmare.

As if she were back in elementary school herself, Charlene found herself rebelling against the school policy about recess because she believed that she should decide what Amy could or could not do. "I always have; why should I change now?" she asked us emphatically. That was her job as a Travel Agent, she mistakenly thought, just as it was when she was a Family Manager.

We couldn't blame Charlene for feeling put out to pasture, as so many parents do when their children enter "the system" of full-day school. When Amy forgot her lunch, for example, she had to eat the school lunch that she hated because school policy dictated that parents couldn't bring a sack lunch to the classroom—"too disruptive."

"How dare they make my child suffer?" was Charlene's reaction. She knew, however, that fighting the rules and trying to rescue Amy was only going to defeat her and her child in the long run. Both needed to learn who was responsible for what in their lives. Charlene needed to trust that the school staff was doing a good job in helping map out Amy's educational itinerary, guiding her into being responsible for her belongings, such as her lunch, and teaching her to adapt to new situations. If she didn't help

Amy take these important steps toward self-reliance now, Amy would continue to rely on her to rescue her as she grew older, something that wasn't going to help either of them become self-sufficient.

Becoming a school mother/helper three half days a week gave Charlene an inside look at the workings of her daughter's new adventures away from home. Many parents say that they solve the separation crisis, the feelings of loss and abandonment that are sparked by children whose primary attention right now is outside the home, by volunteering at their children's schools. That seems to fulfill their need to know what is happening to their children in this new environment and help their child's travel companions become more familiar to them, too. It's also a way of denying the need to surrender control for many parents.

When volunteering at school is not an option because of work schedules, parents can still take advantage of every opportunity the school provides for keeping lines of communication open between home and school to help them stay informed. Faithfully reading the school newsletter, checking backpacks for notes from teachers and principal, networking with other parents by using the school student directory, and utilizing the new e-mail and voicemail technology found in many schools give parents little excuse for feeling out of the loop. As their children's Travel Agents, it's parents' responsibility to know the territory in which their children are traveling and who's accompanying them on their journey.

Ken's Disappointment: Grant's New Friends, New Activities

Ken, a career barber whose salon we frequented regularly with our children, kept his friends for a long time. In fact, he had a poker group that had been meeting for thirty years. At fifty-five he was the same age as most of the members who had grown children, but Ken was on wife number three, Maggie, who was all of thirty-two. Maggie's son, Grant, was ten years old and in fourth grade, which was both Ken's and Grant's favorite year in school. Even though Grant was his stepson, Ken treated him no differently than if he had raised him all these years himself.

Ken said that Grant was the son he had always wanted to have. They even looked like father and son: both had lots of thick brown hair that they kept cut short, and Grant had a wiry body that was just like Ken's when he was his age. Ken adored just spending time with Grant, mostly because Grant was a swimmer and hung out at the pool where Ken had also liked to

spend his time as a child. He helped Grant practice his best stroke, the but-
terfly. Even at his young age, Grant was garnering awards at the country
club where Ken and his wife were members, in state swim meets, and even in
some national competitions. Ken had followed the same path when he was
Grant's age. So it was now Ken's greatest joy to watch Grant compete.

Maggie, however, hated the hot and humid indoor pools and was aller-
gic to the sun, so she had secretly wished that Grant and Ken would some-
how fall out of love with this particular sport and take up something more
her speed, like skiing. But so far she had been out of luck. The passion for
swimming had flowed in Ken's family for generations. Ken loved to take
Grant to swim meets across the country, just as his own father, Rory, had
done nearly forty years ago with him. He remembered just how it had felt to
know that Rory was watching him, giving him that big grin of confidence
that he now gave Grant. Sometimes he and Rory would take Grant out to
breakfast a few hours before a meet, a tradition that turned into a special
memory for all three generations.

But then for Ken, the unthinkable happened. Grant began hanging out
with a group of boys who played football, and he wanted to quit the swim
team. He even told his mom that some kids had made fun of him for being
in such a stupid sport as swimming. Maggie was elated at first because her
dream of Grant choosing another sport was about to come true. But then she
discovered that Grant's new gang of friends had a reputation for making
trouble and had been caught bullying some younger children on the play-
ground. Ken even saw them all walking home from school smoking, includ-
ing Grant; and when Ken confronted his stepson, Grant turned sullen and
wouldn't respond.

Ken and Maggie were beside themselves with anger and fear. Their son
the swimmer was heading in a direction that neither could tolerate; but they
felt powerless to alter his course. Grant told them in so many words that they
couldn't pick his friends and that he was quitting the swim team. Ken and
Maggie decided to get tough and ground him "for the rest of his life," or so
they told us. And the war was on. Grant wouldn't go to swim practices any-
more, and his teacher called to inform Ken and Maggie that his behavior
and attitude in the classroom were going to get him in real trouble if he
wasn't careful.

Ken had cherished every day that he could spend with Grant. After all,
he told us, he and Maggie weren't going to have any other children, and
neither he nor Grant would ever be ten again! But this kind of ten-year-old

neither of them wanted. They felt they had lost something very precious to them: the little boy they had adored so much.

We were delighted that Grant had a stepfather who could support him with his whole heart and knew that solid base of support would be the road out of the dilemma these Travel Agents faced. Ken was infatuated with being a kid again and used his keen memory to enhance this season of parenthood. Reliving his own childhood through Grant had taken on special meaning for him because it brought him closer to two generations—his father and his stepson. But Ken's own memories of ten and his desire to replicate those good times exactly kept him from understanding Grant's dilemma.

Maggie was thrilled that Ken provided her son with a traveling companion and cheerleader all in one, but she also felt excluded. Ken had completely taken over being Grant's Travel Agent and had left Maggie out of their travel plans—that is, until Grant got into trouble. Recognizing that changing itineraries is a normal part of this season of parenthood would help them come together as a team in guiding Grant back to the road they knew he needed to be traveling.

We advised Ken and Maggie that Grant's dictating his own trip's destinations right now was a normal part of his development, as was his trying on new friends and behaviors to try to fit in. This deviation from their chosen travel itinerary didn't mean that they were failures as parents, but it did result in their becoming angry and fearful as they saw Grant moving away from them. Ken's insistence that Grant follow the same road that he had traveled as a child only made Grant even more eager to explore a different trail with his friends.

Parents who understand how important peers' influence is on children remember their own pain of childhood: being teased; not fitting in; wanting to be popular; aching to dress, act, and talk like everyone else. Although negative peer pressure and battles with their parents over hanging out with the wrong crowd are hallmarks of most parents' adolescence, many of these issues have now trickled down into the elementary school years, as Ken and Maggie discovered. Millie, a kindergarten teacher we interviewed, pointed out that her five- to six-year-old charges were now making fun of fellow students over the kinds of shoes and jeans they wore, the toys they had, the sports they played, the movies they hadn't seen.

Children's natural desire to fit in, even at this young age, exerts tremendous pressure on parents who want their children to escape being the targets of ridicule. They themselves may still carry the scars of being scapegoats when growing up and desperately want to rescue their children from such suffering. The issue becomes the price that parents are willing to pay to buy popularity for their children.

We encouraged Ken and Maggie to understand parents' responsibility when their children begin hanging out with the "wrong crowd" for whatever reason: they're teased if they aren't a part of that group; they're caught up in the excitement that group represents; they want to belong to that popular clique. Children understand popularity; they just don't understand the risk that may be inherent in associating with certain children if they are engaged in dangerous or deviant behavior.

Therefore, it's incumbent on their parents, as Travel Agents, to ensure their child's safety as best they can: establishing rules about where he is and isn't allowed to go or what he is or isn't allowed to do (such as smoking); designating the specific times he needs to be home; deciding with whom he is allowed to ride to and from his parent-approved destinations. Allowing him to try out for the pee-wee football team that his new friends were on would give Grant the opportunity to be with the gang, but in the controlled environment of team practices and games. They hoped that the coaches for the football team would inspire Grant to continue to work hard in sports and guide him to be a good team player. Ken and Maggie were still apprehensive, however, fearing that they were losing their influence on Grant because of his allegiance to his new friends. Sometimes the hardest part of parenting is allowing kids to make their own mistakes and learn their own hard lessons.

Parents who keep their child's itinerary in focus as they share the driver's seat with other adults find that everyone has a better time on the trip. Despite their protests to the contrary, children in their middle years feel more secure as they travel to appropriate destinations—friends' houses, sports practices and events, movies—with their parents' cheerleading support in the background and limits on their curfew and travel companions in place.

There will come a day, in the not-so-distant future, when children won't be caught dead with their parents! So travel, travel, travel in this season. Be with your middle-years children while you can, before the hormones step in and force everyone into the lava flow of the volcanic adolescent years.

Hannah's Heartache: Lauren's Special Needs

Lauren and Kyle's mother. That's what the button said that was perched on the stiffly starched collar of Hannah's work shirt. She had been to one of our parent education programs at her church and was sure that we could help her through her second divorce. We knew from her comments during our discussion that she was proud of her children and could sense that something was troubling her so deeply that it must concern one of them.

We learned that Lauren, Hannah's eight-year-old third-grade daughter, had entered kindergarten when she had just turned five. The reason that this twenty-nine-year-old court reporter decided to start her in school as soon as she was eligible, she admitted, was that she needed her to be busy all day long while Hannah went to work.

Now Lauren's third-grade teacher at her elementary school seemed to be plotting against her. She was trying to tell her that Lauren had a problem sitting still in class, that her emotional immaturity was making it difficult for her to complete her work, stay on task, and let others do their work undisturbed. According to her teacher, Lauren was aggravating the other kids by wanting to hug them and hang all over them, always fidgeting with their hair or trying to play clapping games while in line. The bottom line? The school counselor wanted her to be tested by the psychologist she recommended to determine whether she had attention deficit disorder.

No one had ever mentioned that before, Hannah told us. Why, all of a sudden, did she have to listen to this counselor who had known Lauren for only two months? Who knew her child better than her own mother? Someone had told Hannah that Lauren's problem was immaturity; she had started school when she was too young and looked bad in comparison with the other children in the class. She wanted desperately to hang on to the belief that Lauren didn't have a problem and would simply outgrow these behaviors. Besides, she was sure schools were overdiagnosing ADD just to get kids to shut up in class.

Hannah had avoided the testing as long as she could but had finally given in. The psychologist was very nice and quite thorough. He patiently went over all of the test results with her, and they concluded that Lauren did indeed fit the criteria for attention deficit hyperactivity disorder. The recommendation was to start Lauren on stimulant medication for school and to work with Hannah and Lauren's teacher to set up behavioral programs in the classroom and at home so Lauren could learn how to keep herself as fo-

cused as possible. Lauren also needed remedial help in math and reading because she had gotten behind the other students in those areas.

Hannah, however, had told the psychologist that no child of hers was going to have her personality changed into a zombie by taking drugs. She'd heard about what happened to kids on medicine for attention problems and wasn't about to subject her baby to mind-altering drugs. The fact that she worked all day as a court reporter across town made her daughter's diagnosis even harder to accept. There was no way she could make it to all of the places she needed to take Lauren that the psychologist suggested: his office weekly for counseling, the doctor to have Lauren checked and to get the prescription for the medication each month, the tutor twice weekly for reading and math. Life had been a breeze with her son, Kyle; all of a sudden she just couldn't cope with the monkey wrench that Lauren's behavior was throwing into her itinerary, especially as a single mom whose ex-husband was already out the door.

Our hearts went out to Hannah. The dose of reality that life was feeding her during Lauren's trip through her elementary school years was hard to swallow. Now Hannah was unsure of Lauren's new fellow travelers in third grade and suspicious of their "attack," as she called it, on her daughter. She had never felt more alone; she knew no other parents who were faced with this kind of problem. At least when Lauren was a preschooler, she had been able to rely on the school's small staff to help her manage her family's ups and downs. Now she had so many people and services that she needed to coordinate; she didn't know where to begin, and it was all on her shoulders.

Her previous trip through this season of parenthood with her son might have made this second time around less traumatic, but Lauren was hitting bumps in the road that Kyle hadn't. Therefore Hannah had to make new travel plans based on her special situation. We advised her to follow the steps she would take if she were planning her daughter's trip through a foreign country, which was exactly how she felt, she told us. Lauren's "destination": Improve her ability to concentrate in school so she could learn as well as she could.

To get to that destination successfully, Hannah needed a map that had more information—exactly what was attention deficit hyperactivity disorder, and where could she find resources to help her cope with it? How long would Lauren need special help to improve her work habits? What support systems did her community offer that fit the schedule of someone who worked outside the home? The answers to these questions would help her feel more capable of handling these new responsibilities that she would never have had if Lauren had not been diagnosed with this problem.

Besides getting her questions answered, Hannah found herself needing to resolve her anger over wishing Lauren could be different, could be "okay like her brother." The fact that Hannah was angry was normal but not very productive, we told her. She needed to channel that anger into getting informed and arranging Lauren's schedule around her work hours.

What Hannah was experiencing was just a small part of what parents of children with special needs are forced to face as they try to help their children through the maze of special programs offered by school districts. To have to adjust to being a Travel Agent with a "normal" child can be difficult, but when faced with the detours, bridge-out, under-construction, and flight-canceled problems that special-needs children present, the task of coping can be overwhelming at times, especially for single parents. Parents of special-needs children find themselves fighting a constant battle with bureaucracies, misinformation, prejudice, and their own shattered dreams of normalcy for their child. Interspersed throughout this picture of doom and gloom, however, is often good news: outstanding resources, understanding teachers, dedicated specialists, extra attention, and parent support groups are available to many special-needs children and families.

The most difficult task of Travel Agents for special-needs children is to accept their children as they are, rather than to deny that they present special challenges for the whole family. In addition, these parents have the extremely difficult task of avoiding favoritism if they have other children who don't have special needs. But the overwhelming guilt parents often feel as they acknowledge that their children in some way "have a problem" drives them into overcompensation, where they can get stuck in the muck, spinning their wheels and ending up forever being Travel Agents for their children.

Being parents of children who are identified as "gifted" can also catapult Travel Agents into a life of overcompensation. Feeling an extra burden of responsibility to supply their "gifted" child with more academic opportunities to take advantage of his or her potential can create anxiety in both parents and children. In contrast, when a child is not identified as gifted through elementary school testing, and the parents insist that their child be included in the school's "gifted program," trouble can begin brewing for both generations.

Parents need to look inside themselves to understand why they want to push their child to achieve more, earlier, and faster or belong in classes for the "gifted." Is it their own bragging rights? Fear that their child might fall behind their classmates in getting into prestigious colleges? Belief that their child needs to be pushed to be successful? The answers to these questions will help parents temper their thinking of "gifted" children only as those in "gifted programs" in school. By reframing their definition of "gifted," including all of children's gifts, not just those identified by formal testing, they can best realize their child's potential.

Kyle and Lauren were different children who needed different kinds of attention. Hannah needed to accept that she had different responsibilities now, with new hurdles to clear in her own journey through the seasons of parenthood. By taking her time to plan how Lauren's change in travel plans would affect her own life, Hannah was able to learn how to avoid the trap of getting stuck in this season in her development.

Self-Discoveries of Travel Agents

Your pocket guide to the truths revealed in the Travel Agent season of parenthood.

> ➤ **Changing travel companions.** Surprise! You don't know how it happened, but the folks who got on the roller-coaster ride of parenthood with you when you began aren't the same ones who are with you now. How did that happen so fast and you didn't even notice? Oh well, they're nice people; get to know them; they'll help you on the twists and turns to come.

> ➤ **Enjoy the view.** The ride doesn't get any smoother than this, so sit back and relax. The ride has slowed down enough that you can be lulled into a false sense of security, thinking that you can handle whatever comes next. Around each turn is a new vista, an opportunity to appreciate how far and how fast you have come to this point on the ride. The ups and downs of this part of the ride only hint at the big drop that awaits you.

➤ **Car talk.** On this part of the ride, there are many more opportunities to get acquainted with your fellow passengers; the ride has slowed enough so that you don't have to keep bracing yourself and shouting to be heard. There are so many new things to see, experiences to share, and people to meet that the ride stays interesting if you stay friendly and open to broadening your horizons.

➤ **Stay loose.** Although you may see another ride across the park, you're stuck on this ride and have to stay to the end. Facing reality and living in the moment helps you appreciate the thrills of your own journey. Every roller coaster in the park has its own highs and lows; it's your perspective from a distance that makes them seem easier or harder on their riders.

Exit Signs

Leaving Elementary School. Danger: Volcano head. By the time children reach the end of elementary school, most parents would give anything to keep their lives as calm and stable as they've been, because they're seeing some eerie warning signs in their children—irritability, voice changes, demands for training bras, zits—that they are entering a new, more tumultuous season of parenthood. Predictably, this is a most frightening transition for parents as they fear that the past twelve or thirteen years of parenthood were all for naught. Their children look, act, smell, and think in unfamiliar ways, causing parents to react to their budding adolescents just as their own parents did to them: prevent them from causing as much family damage as possible as their teens move inevitably through their turbulent passage to adulthood.

Volcano Dweller

CHILD'S ADOLESCENT YEARS

Youthquake: An eruption followed by a twitch, a tic, and much sullen or ashen silence.—BERNARD ROSENBERG

VETERANS OF THIS VOLATILE season of parenthood, which lasts from when children are about ten to when they're around eighteen, usually admit they should have seen the eruptions coming. Their children gave them cues: intermittently acting like their "old" dormant sons or daughters, then turning into active volcanoes spewing forth fire and smoke. They reported feeling personally challenged on all levels—physically, spiritually, intellectually, emotionally—by their transformation into Volcano Dwellers that forced them to adapt to sharing their home with these rumbling, fuming, changeable mountains called adolescents.

But we hate to sound negative. After all, some parents said that this was their favorite season of parenthood. They loved living on the rim of active volcanoes, loved never knowing if, at the ring of the phone or the emergence of a zit, their formerly sane children would have eruptions of insanity, spew forth lava, and go up in flames. They loved being the rescue crew, there to clean up the molten rocks and ash from their children's lives. It made them, in some ways, continue to feel needed.

Other parents said that they had a hard time handling volcanic eruptions of this season. They yearned to live on solid ground again, to breathe
cleaner air without such dangerous gases. They coveted the safe affection
and admiration that their adoring offspring provided before they were
quaked off their foundation by hormonal explosions that led to the emergence of voice changes, pubic hair, breast enlargement. And that's not all:
other ingredients in adolescent volcanic eruptions include mood swings,
outrageous clothing, unusual hair colors and styles, body piercings, and
rebellion against any and all authority.

Parents' genetic and social influences, cultural heritage, personal histories, and ability to cope with the following psychological strikes against
them in this season put at risk the peace and happiness that they've
worked so hard to build to date. Strike one: fearing that they've been failures as parents. Strike two: closing the books on childhood. And strike
three: the nightmares of adolescence coming back to haunt them. When
will it ever end?

Generations ago, the answer to this question was simple: The Volcano
Dweller season ended when adolescents turned eighteen or so and became
financially self-sufficient after leaving home to make their way in the
world—joining the armed forces, going to college, getting married, entering the workforce full-time. Today, this season of parenthood still ends
when teenagers leave home; however, unlike past generations, the majority
of these teens remain financially dependent on their parents. That is why
we have set the end marker of this period of parental development simply
as adolescents' physical move away from their parents, not their achieving
financial independence. Just the sheer fact of their living in an empty nest
has a profound effect on parents' daily lives, redefining parents' work
habits, marital relationships, choice of friends, and leisure activities, simply because their schedule is no longer tied to their teens' comings and goings. This next season is one that Dakota, one of our Circles group
mothers, couldn't reach fast enough.

As a home day care provider, she told us that she was a natural at being
a dedicated Sponge—soaking up every detail of her children's infancies
while caring for two other children in the neighborhood. Being a Family
Manager and Travel Agent had also come easily to her. But her household
was now becoming the talk of the neighborhood high school parents. The
previous year, Dakota had become a single parent after a bitter divorce.
She had no choice but to go to work full-time in order to keep up with the

expenses of feeding, clothing, and housing her teenagers in the manner they had grown accustomed to before her husband walked out, leaving her with the sole responsibility for her children—eleven-year-old Tucker, Cooper, thirteen, and Rand III, who turned fifteen this year.

Nearly every morning at work, she would now receive upsetting phone calls from her children's schools: Tucker was caught in the bathroom with a cigarette, Cooper had yelled at his English teacher; and Rand's friend Bryce had given him a copy of the final history exam before the test. Her own phone calls home "to check in" when the kids were in elementary school seemed so sweet compared with the bitter ones she was getting from school administrators almost daily.

What happened to my innocent children? she asked us. She couldn't remember getting into trouble when she was a teenager. In fact, she was so scared that her mom and dad would criticize her as they did her older brother whenever he did anything wrong that she didn't dare break one of their rules. She told herself that she would never be that critical of her kids because she hated the way her parents pressured her into "being good." But now she was the one who was feeling pressured. Why were her children doing this to her? she wondered. When she asked herself if she'd failed as a parent, all of the signs of the destruction in her family made her answer yes.

Her teenagers reminded her of angry lyrics in the rock music of "her day"—lyrics about the angst of finding peace, changing the world, and breaking free of adult bondage. She had listened to these kinds of songs herself and couldn't wait to break free someday of her own parents' tight hold on her. But for her, those days were over. She couldn't believe that they were now just starting for her children, she admitted to us. It was now "her children's day" to sow their wild oats and right the wrongs of those in authority. Now they were trying to break free of her!

"When did *I* become the authority? When did my stories about riding around on motorcycles or being a cheerleader turn into a *history* lesson?" asked Dakota. This question was echoed by many parents and reflected their confusion and dismay about the fact that their lives no longer seemed to be current news.

If parents ever considered that they were holding on to the last vestiges of their own childhood, this season explodes that pipe dream. Parents can dress the part by buying their clothes at the hip new teen store; act the part by driving fast cars with the top down; or be their kids' "friend" by hang-

ing out with their teens' fellow classmates. But they're just fooling themselves. Parents who continue to identify too strongly with their teens are avoiding acknowledging the fact that they should be acting like the responsible adults that their children need them to be. However, now they are not the perpetrators spewing forth adolescent fire on their volcanodwelling parents; they are the innocent, loving victims who can't believe that this could ever happen to them.

"Before I became pregnant, if I had thought about the fact that I would have to relive the nightmare of adolescence as a part of being a mother, I might have reconsidered and backed out of the whole deal," laughed Tommie, a fifty-three-year-old member of one of our Circles groups. "I went into shock when my daughter turned fourteen and started saying the same ugly things I remembered saying to my mom when I was a teenager—'I hate you, leave me alone, stop trying to control me.'

"Now I was on the receiving end of her explosions," Tommie continued. "And I was miserable, as miserable as I was when I was her age. I guess I could have predicted that her adolescence and mine would not be that different from each other, but what made me even more miserable was the fact that I had no way out but to live through adolescence again with her. I decided that I had to look at the big picture. I knew that my daughter's explosions were signs that she was on the road toward self-sufficiency and independence, my destination when I was her age. So the only way for me to get through this period of her life was to tell myself that I could handle going through the pain of giving birth to an adult. I had to appreciate this agonizing but rewarding process, just as I did giving birth to my child in the first place."

So it is with being a parent of an adolescent. The only way to get to the other side of parenthood—to pass from parenting children to parenting adults—is to learn how to survive life as a Volcano Dweller, treasuring the mysterious beauty of the mountain, as well as the eruptions, the smoke and flame, the noxious gases.

FEAR OF FAILURE

Oh, to be only half as wonderful as my child thought I was when he was small, and only half as stupid as my teenager now thinks I am.—REBECCA RICHARDS

When children make the passage from childhood to adulthood, the drama of this journey isn't lost on their parents. They continue to be forced into making transitions of their own in response to their children's lives. Case in point: Johnny was a "good kid" in elementary school—never got in trouble, did his homework on time, even did his chores when asked. When he turned thirteen, Johnny began to look and act like another child, a child his parents had never met: surly, obstinate when refusing to do chores, critical of his parents' every move.

His parents insisted that Johnny stay the course—do what he was asked. After all, if he didn't learn to be responsible, his parents would be to blame, they thought. But when they reminded him to clean his room and put away his clean clothes, Johnny would play his volcano trick—slamming doors, yelling profanities, and threatening to run away from home.

His parents became confused . . . and angry. This was ridiculous, they said to themselves, hunkering down for the good fight. Johnny *must* learn to do what he's asked. We can't let him get away with thinking he's in charge of the household! Next thing we know, he'll be one of those teenagers who gives every adult heartburn—acting as though he's entitled to the world on a silver platter. He'll be grown and gone soon, and we have to get him shaped up before he goes into the world. If we don't, it will be *our* fault.

For parents like Johnny's who have not yet accepted the fact that they cannot control the changes that are morphing their children into miniadults, their anxiety is fueled by two factors: self-blame and self-doubt. Parents tend to blame themselves and inflate incidences of teenage rebellion into major disasters, creating for themselves a full-time emotional job in this season of parenthood.

"Where did I go wrong?" Sandy asked us when describing his formerly attentive daughter. "Since she turned fourteen, I turned into an embarrassment. I'm like a contagious disease to her that she's afraid she'll catch if she's around me too long, or even at all."

During this season, the I-should-haves abound, as Jill, another Circles group member, told us: "I should have made my daughter, Brittany, follow my rules when she was younger, like my parents made me do. I hated having curfews and having to call home when I was a teenager, so I didn't want Brittany to have to. Now I see why my parents had those rules. If I had done what they did, Brittany would be more controllable now. As it is, she's never home, always with her friends, doing God knows what. She never even wants to be in the same room with me."

Tom, one of the fathers we interviewed, shared Jill's pain but had a different story: "I should have loosened the reins a bit. Now my son won't even go out with any kids. He's scared of them, saying they're all into trouble and drinking. I'm glad he's not doing those things, but I hope he's not too lonely. I should have taught him how to assert himself when he was younger."

Such were the worries of dozens in our Circles groups. Parents lost sight of the fact that their children were still growing and changing, that their adult selves might well be different from their teen selves. They needed to frame their teenagers: as "works in progress." Their adolescents' behaviors—positive and negative—seemed so permanent only because their teens looked so adult-like, with grown-up bodies and deep voices.

Though Volcano Dwellers can and do offer consulting services to their teenage children, they often doubt their ability to do so effectively, because they are so consistently being pushed away and rejected by them. Parents can survive life on a volcano, however, when they stand ready with support and emergency equipment: a sense of humor; a nonjudgmental listening ear; curfews and, most important, a positive spin on the mantra of their own lives: "This too shall pass." Separating themselves from their adolescents' behavior—not taking it personally—is a standard requirement to ensure parental peace of mind.

As teenagers move through this developmental stage, this adage becomes more than a catchy phrase. It is a truth that can save helpless, hapless, and hopeless parents from despairing that the traumas of this stage, the tumultuous growth spurts and emotional craters, are navigable. At their teenagers' high school graduation, the tears parents shed are as much about the relief of letting go of their fear of failure during this last season of the first circle of parenthood as they are about the relief that they have survived being Volcano Dwellers.

CLOSING THE BOOKS ON CHILDHOOD

When his child requests a car, a father will wish that he were a member of some sect that hasn't gone beyond the horse.—BILL COSBY

"The college counselor droned on so long about my daughters' SAT and ACT scores and their chances for getting into college that after three grueling hours of nonstop questions and answers, I finally said enough is enough!" Ginny, a mother of seventeen-year-old triplets, told us in one of our interviews. "I had to leave the room. I couldn't bear having these people chop up my daughters like they were raw vegetables for college soup."

Tears welled up in Ginny's eyes. Putting her triplet daughters' performance on standardized tests, grades, and high school résumés under a microscope brought home the undeniable truth that she could no longer ignore: Her children were going to leave home in less than a year.

"Why am I crying all of the time?" she asked us. Going to college is a good thing, a lucky thing, she tried to tell herself. Being able to afford to send their triplets to college was something that her husband, Noah, and she had worked toward for seventeen years. But now that the time for them to leave home was nearly upon them, all that seemed to be holding her together was the knowledge that her parents had let her go to college far away from home and had survived.

She told us that she'd cried when her children came into the world . . . and now she was overwhelmed again at the thought of them going out into it. Her family of five was the axis of her life. Now that the kids were about to graduate from high school, she felt as if she were losing her compass. She would be left without a true north, no way to steer herself in the direction she needed or wanted to go. She felt the same disbelief she'd felt lying on the hospital bed in hard labor. She knew that the impending experience was inevitable—the kids "had" to come out—first out of the womb, now out of the home. That was an unavoidable fact. She would trade all of the worry and anxiety of the past seventeen years, however, to avoid having to close the books on their childhood. She feared being left alone—she hadn't been alone in nearly twenty years.

As a VOLCANO DWELLER, Ginny was preparing to leave the first familiar circle of parenthood—parenting children—as surely as her children were preparing to leave their last phase of childhood. Neither parents, particularly on their first trip through this season of parenthood, nor their adolescent children are comfortable making this emotional transition, which necessitates a complete identity change.

As pregnancy was for them so many years earlier, adults' transcendence into the second circle of parenthood is a leap of faith. Neither they nor their children are truly sure of what's ahead, which can lead to anxiety for both generations. Adolescents try, sometimes fairly successfully, to shed their resemblance to their former selves in this process, one reason for their own pain. Parents must do the same, while being expected to perform what many parents we interviewed called by one name: damage control.

Damage control adroitly describes the practical work of parents closing the books on childhood. Volcano Dwellers need to keep vigilant watch on the friendships, marriage, family relationships, home, and career they have worked all of these years to build to avoid their being destroyed by the natural disaster called adolescence. When teenagers test parents' patience by their trials and errors in school, on the road, and in the working world, parents tell us their lives become one long stream of putting out fires—a stressful way to spend their time. They share their teens' conflicting feelings over wanting to get through this transition as quickly as possible so they can enter the new world of adulthood together; yet both want to stay in the relatively safer world of childhood.

Karl and Helga, parents who sought our advice after a high school workshop on discipline for teens, identified with this catch-22 of Volcano Dwellers. When their son, Kurt, turned sixteen and earned his driver's license, his grandmother gave him her old car, much to his delight. This gave Karl and Helga the freedom to go out more often with friends on weekends because they didn't have to be Kurt's chauffeur to his job, ball games, and friend's houses. Kurt had earned their trust, abiding by his curfew or calling if he was going to be a little late. They couldn't understand why their friends were always complaining about the problems they were having with their teens that forced them to cancel last-minute plans because they were grounded or weren't responsible enough to be trusted to stay by themselves without getting into the locked liquor cabinet.

But Kurt's newfound freedom was more than he could handle: his grades began dropping; he wanted always to be with his friends; he started coming home at all hours of the night. When Helga took away his car keys because he had come home so late, Kurt immediately appealed her decision to Karl, who gave him back the keys, not wanting to risk losing the affection of his precious son by upsetting him. Helga was furious and felt that the two of them were now aligned against her. Because he believed that his father would rescue him from Helga's iron rule, Kurt began to push harder for more freedom. When Helga told him that he couldn't spend the night with a friend, he screamed an obscenity at her and flew out the front door anyway. Helga wanted Karl to lay down the law with their son; although he agreed to talk to him, Karl never did.

"I was ready to run away from home myself," Helga confessed. "I got so I couldn't stand Kurt or Karl. If this stuff keeps up, I won't even go to my son's graduation from high school because I'll be so mad at him. Karl and I haven't spoken a civil word to each other for weeks because of Kurt."

Parents quickly burn out from being so focused on their relationships with their teens that their other relationships suffer—marriages in particular. As in Karl and Helga's case, arguments over discipline can drive as sharp a wedge between parents as an extramarital affair: the trust that parents had built can be instantly eroded by the daily battles over how to contain their volcanic child. They're always on guard, parents told us in Circles groups of adolescents' moms and dads, which makes them a nervous wreck during this season of parenthood.

Trying to relax with friends feels like a joke, much like their attempts to go out and have a good time when their offspring were infants. Volcano Dwellers were always worried that something would go wrong and they wouldn't be there to control the damage. It's easier now, many said, just to stay home. At least then they'd be "on watch" if their teens tried to "pull a fast one on them" or got themselves in trouble simply because these adolescents believed that nothing bad could happen to them, the "personal fable of adolescence."

The sum effect of teenagers' normal volcanic eruptions on their parents is a "hunker-down" mentality, a mentality hardly conducive to marital bliss unless parents are a unified security team who cooperate in protecting their relationship from harm as vigilantly as they protect their offspring. All marriages feel the effect of teenagers' rumblings. But in cases in which an adolescent is already the "least favorite" child—abusing alcohol or other drugs; in trouble with the law; failing school; or playing the uneasy role of the stepchild who never did accept one of his stepparents or is told by the parent, with whom he doesn't live, that he doesn't have to follow his stepparent's rules—marriages can get hopelessly buried by the stress of doing damage control.

In addition, teenagers test the standards of courtesy and decorum that their parents established in the Family Manager season of parenthood, just as they did as toddlers and preschoolers a dozen years ago . . . with bigger bodies, louder voices, and a spicier vocabulary, of course. To cope with life as Volcano Dwellers, parents need to start by repeating the same reality-check mantras that they used to maintain self-control when their children were out of control in all seasons of parenthood heretofore: "This too shall pass. Keep the faith. We have traveled the teenage road ourselves and are here to tell the tale." Performance reviews take on a whole new meaning when it's your kid caught with the six-pack at the prom.

Volcano Dwellers are in prime position to end this first circle of parenthood with one lasting souvenir, an honest appraisal of their children's childhood, which they are leaving behind. Parents spend much of this season caught up in a reflective mode, which actually helps them pull their teens through what seems to be an interminable time span. They remember that they too struggled to be independent and self-sufficient, all the while deep down inside wanting their parents to reassure them that they were there for them when they needed them.

REGARDLESS OF THEIR socioeconomic status, race, religion, age, or sex, parents in this season have now relived it all: their own infancy, toddlerhood, and elementary, middle, and high school once again, as they watch their little ones try to be all grown up. Only through this season of parenthood do they have the opportunity to reflect on their childhood lives in this "complete" way, sometimes over and over again, depending on the number of children they raise. They think, of course, that they are just "parenting" their teens. What they are really doing is taking stock of their own childhood, in toto, before they move on down the road of their lives, as well as their children's.

THE NIGHTMARE RETURNS: TEENS ARE BORN-AGAIN TODDLERS

Memory is more indelible than ink.—ANITA LOOS

Volcano Dwellers learn never to underestimate the power of a good memory. They remember feeling a deep sense of confusion and rejection when their infants turned into toddler whirling dervishes. In this season of parenthood they find themselves in this familiar, gut-wrenching nightmare again, this time with their teenagers—born-again toddlers with driver's licenses.

Adolescents' bodies change as rapidly during this stage as they did during the preschool years, when children grew almost double in size in four years. New hair, breasts, voice, muscles, feet, language, weight, and zits transform their former children into new physical beings, just as their infants sprouted into vertical adventurers from horizontal crib potatoes. Parents whom we interviewed told us that they felt surprisingly caught off guard by the behavioral metamorphoses of their teens, particularly by that of their first child who enters adolescence. Their children's normal trip into puberty gave the parents flashbacks of going through the pain of being volcanoes again.

The ultimate cause of the nightmares that impact Volcano Dwellers in this season is the same as it was in toddlerhood: their children's push to be independent. When and how they allow their teens their freedom is the fuel that ignites the conflicts between teens and parents in this season of parenthood. These power struggles over boundaries feel insulting and outrageous to parents, even though it wasn't that long ago that they were on the giving, not the receiving, end of this emotional abuse! They remember when they, too, couldn't bear being home by their curfew time or being near their mom and dad in public, for example, and in the next breath asking to borrow $10 to go to the movies. Parents' memories of this stage can be a helpful backdrop of "normality" for their teens' angst.

NOW PARENTS ARE UNEQUIVOCALLY considered to be the "grown-ups," the parents they swore as teens they would never be. Listen to Jean, a forty-five-year-old nurse and mother of two who attended one of our Circles groups: "It didn't really hit me until March of his freshman year when my fifteen-year-old son, Justin, started planning his sophomore schedule. I said to myself: My kid? Getting ready to drive? I'm still best friends with some of *my* high school classmates who started driving at the same time I did. What happened here? Only a minute ago, it seemed, this kid's not even here, awaiting life itself. Then he blasted his way into the world, making sure that his father and I give up our self-centered ways, thank you so much. One recent morning, I found myself wondering what kind of God would let this happen to me, let my kid get so old that he was about to get into two tons of steel and glass to cruise down an asphalt highway. I was beginning to sound more like my mother every day, especially the nervous parts. God, it made me feel so old. What kind of nightmare was this?

"It started getting worse instead of better. At the beginning of my fourteen-year-old daughter Jessica's freshman year, she told me that my clothes all seemed so dull, brown, and dowdy. And, she said, my skirts were too short for a *mother* to wear and my pants looked like her grandma's. My lipstick was too red, too, according to her, and I was wearing too much makeup. What happened to the flower of my youth? I thought to myself."

Like Jean, most adults recall thinking during their teen years how awful it would be to get as old as their parents. Then suddenly they are the parents of an adolescent who reminds them that they are now the "old folks." This situation is intolerable to many baby boomers today as they try to maintain a sense of self-worth in a youth-worshiping culture that decries aging and warehouses the old. As noted in a Yankelovich Partners 1998 survey, "the generation that in youth didn't trust anyone over age thirty wants to make sure today's kids don't regard them as quaint relics." As parents in this season of parenthood wrestle with their own aging and seek to recapture their youth, they often begin to imitate their teens in looks and actions as they begin the infamous "midlife crisis" over their identity. A *USA Today* story on the survey results quotes Ross Goldstein, a San Francisco market researcher who studies intergenerational relations: "The boundaries between generations have broken down. Adults are no longer a clearly distinct group from their children."

The truth is, adolescents are ready triggers for the predictable identity crisis so expediently described as midlife. As parents see their children growing increasingly independent and fondly recall their own wild and crazy adolescence, they seek to recapture those carefree times by rejecting their adult status and reverting to adolescent behavior themselves: trading for new girl or boyfriends, coloring their hair, getting liposuction, living at the gym, going barhopping. This desire to reject the natural course of aging in favor of perennial youth, as represented by their children, drives the often immature and dangerous behavior engaged in by many adults during this period.

"I've still got it!" is their war cry as these aging parents receive the admiring glances of others and suck in their sagging bellies and lift up their boobs in front of the mirror. Thus marks the matching struggle for identity they share with their adolescent children. They are hell-bent on recapturing their youth so that they won't appear old to their teens. Adults can get away with thinking of themselves as young and "with it" much more easily in their forties and fifties if they don't have the sharp contrast of what youth really looks like that their teens show them on a daily basis.

Diana, a forty-nine-year-old mother of a seventeen-year-old daughter and a fourteen-year-old son, admitted that she never really thought much about her own wrinkles because she was so busy making sure that her children's lives went smoothly. But as her family became more self-sufficient, she began to have more time to herself, time to analyze herself; much to her chagrin, she didn't like what she saw. When did her waist disappear? she asked herself, suddenly horrified at the difference between her own clothing size and her daughter's. They used to share clothes; but not anymore. She was also aghast at the color of her skin or, as she said, her spots of color on her skin and the gray flecks in her formerly all-brunette hair.

Diana found herself grieving the loss of her youth, experiencing those stages of grief that she remembered from the time her children began kindergarten. First she denied that any of these changes bothered her, but she found herself wanting to avoid going out in public with her teens for fear that others might discover the truth she was facing. When her son asked her if she was going to dye her hair the way his aunt did when she began to "get gray," as he called it, she felt herself becoming angry and defensive about the changes that she had never thought about before. She decided to dye her hair blond and began wearing heavy eye makeup and coverup foundation, to recapture her looks. Her plan backfired, however, when her daughter took her aside before going to church one day and told her that she looked ridiculous as a blond and to wipe that stuff off her eyes because she was "scaring" her.

Horrified at her daughter's criticism, Diana felt she had reached an impasse; she didn't want to get older, and her attempts at hanging on to her youth had blown up in her face. She was damned, however, if she was going to give in to aging without a fight, she told us. Instead of focusing on what she looked like, Diana started to pay attention to how she felt: energized, vital, capable of still enjoying the activities their family had loved over the years. She organized family waterskiing, horseback riding, and even hot-air ballooning adventures over the next month, revealing muscles she'd forgotten she had as she discovered a path to feeling good about this transition point in her life.

In contrast, many of the Volcano Dwellers we interviewed also found themselves reflecting on their lives; but when they did, they found that the pleasures that they had once enjoyed were gone. They saw their youth rapidly slipping away as they watched the fun their teens were having—playing a furious game of basketball with their friends, jumping on the trampoline, Rollerblading, skateboarding, eating bowls of ice cream at midnight and not gaining a pound—and were overwhelmed by an urge to return to the carefree days of their own adolescence. They longed to return to the innocent days when their own parents were responsible for making everything okay if anything went wrong, a time their memory had wishfully colored into an endless summer.

Some parents refused to accept that this version of their teen years is a myth. Ernie, one of our Circles group members, told of a friend at work who had found a young woman who made him feel youthful once more. He ended up divorcing his wife, alienating his children, and losing most of his friends just so he could be a "kid" again.

Ernie had also tried to turn back the hands of time, but in a way that did less harm to his family. "I bought a motorcycle," he confessed. "I loved the wind in my face and the feeling of freedom it gave me, and it didn't mess up my family. It did mess up my leg, though, when I fell off on the street. That was the end of trying to feel young again for me."

During this season of parenthood, rather than focusing on what is being lost—their children's innocence and their own youth—Volcano Dwellers are best advised to take the long view as they consider the promises that the future holds for them. The irony of this season is not lost on parents who appreciate the fact that they long to be younger at the same time that their children desperately want to be older. Although it is predictable and inevitable that parents will find being a Volcano Dweller smudges the book of childhood, that is why adolescence is as infamous and important as it is. When parents have survived this season with their marriages, friendships, relationships with their teens, and their own sense of self intact, both generations should feel proud of their accomplishment.

A S THIS SEASON OF PARENTHOOD ends, the first circle of parenthood is about to be complete; a new circle is now about to begin. Parents need a positive outlook to survive this transitional season. For those who resist the formation of a new circle, the following seasons will leave them feeling bereft, as if they missed a change in the script; they are not quite in sync with the lead, their new adult children. If they follow along the scenes of the new script, the deepest meaning of the drama will unfold. They will know the truth in the phrase, "Every woman used to be somebody's little girl, and every man used to be somebody's little boy." They have been the witnesses to this miracle of life firsthand, and it has changed them as much as it has changed their children.

In the next season of parenthood, Volcano Dwellers' offspring will return to the personality and temperament they had as adventurers in the elementary school years, quieting and allowing to grow dormant the volatile, fire-breathing volcanoes of adolescence.

Carrie Seeks a Simple Life: No More Hand-Holding

"My life suddenly became one tragedy after another, and I was the one who was expected to be the family grown-up on all fronts," said Carrie, a forty-five-year-old mother we interviewed. She was right: her family was living off of her salary because her husband had lost his job after twenty-two years as a sales representative for a medical supply company; her mother-in-law depended on her to handle her grocery shopping because she couldn't drive anymore; her seventeen-year-old daughter was failing high school because she was hanging out with a new group of friends who frequented the mall instead of going to class; and her grandfather's life was about to fade away after ninety years.

Carrie was looked up to as the person "in charge," the only one who could "fix" her family's health, bad fortune, and poor choices. And there was more on her plate that kept her from sleeping at night. Her mom's memory loss, the depression of her best friend's husband, the stroke her neighbor's father recently suffered, and the fact that her co-worker at the office got laid off because she took too much time off to care for her daughter's mysterious illness—each crisis was something else she had to rescue, nurture, fix. And it was all driving her crazy!

Carrie wished that she could turn to her own parents for support and guidance, just as she had when she was a little girl. But now her parents had problems of their own, and her mother's favorite answer was "It'll be okay, Carrie. You'll see. Everything will turn out." Carrie had grown to hate her mother's positive but empty platitudes. She had never felt so alone. She and her mother were totally different. Acting as if nothing were wrong and keeping her life under control in her own quiet way were her mother's ways of handling problems, Carrie told us. But Carrie always took everything to heart, felt as if she had a "built-in" need to right everything that was wrong in her world.

Her main focus was now her daughter, Alice. Carrie believed that if she could only "make Alice perfect before she left home," then at least she would have accomplished something. So Carrie became more critical, more demanding, and angrier as she attempted to polish her gem of a daughter to an artificial glow.

It was Alice's all-out rebellion at this additional buffing that ultimately forced Carrie to stop and take stock of her need to solve all problems. Carrie hadn't yet grasped what many parents conclude when they enter this season of parenthood: Many things in life are beyond their control, and no matter how much they want to fix the world, as they might have been able to do when their children were babies, they now find themselves powerless to do so. Carrie's mother knew this truth but had never taught it to Carrie, who could now thank her teenage volcano for teaching her this lesson.

Absence does make the heart grow fonder in this season of parenthood and changes the relationship between parents and their children. Because Carrie's mother was no longer around to patch up everything for her daughter, Carrie was left to her own devices to mimic her mother's pattern of trying to make life perfect for her daughter. She found that she had to "grow up" along with her offspring, get used to the fact that her "little girl" was gone, as was her own time to be a "little girl."

To ease their adjustments to their changing world, many Volcano Dwellers find themselves self-medicating with chocolate, caffeine, nicotine, alcohol, or illegal drugs in order to numb the anxiety or pain. Carrie told us that a couple of gin and tonics each day seemed to ease the sharp edges of this nightmare of aging and loss of control that characterized her life. She didn't want to face the reality of any of her problems—least of all the failure that her daughter had become.

We helped Carrie look at Alice's rebellion as a part of her transcendence to her own new stage of life, young adulthood. Alice was "trying on" new friends as she attempted to solidify her own identity before moving on. Carrie needed to trust her knowledge that the foundation that she and Hank, Alice's father, had laid down long ago was solid and would support Alice as she traveled through this tumultuous developmental stage.

Alice needed to know that the boundaries that Carrie had set were firm, even though it was hard for Carrie to be the bad guy, the authority figure. Alice had always gone along with the deals her mother had been making with her since she was a toddler. Now Carrie tried to make a new deal with her as she attempted to remain Alice's friend, appealing to her to follow the school rules and to take responsibility for going to school so that her mother would have one less thing to worry about. But Alice wasn't buying this deal. She didn't seem to "get it" and told her mother that she had everything under control and not to worry about her.

Control was indeed the issue. Carrie finally admitted that she had never really controlled Alice, even when she was a toddler and was resisting giving up diapers during toilet training. However, Alice was now wreaking such havoc in her life that she knew she couldn't deal with her other problems until she had taken every step she could to manage this one. She met with the vice principal of Alice's school, and they worked out a plan for the school to help Alice be accountable for her school attendance.

Although her mother's efforts to stop her daughter's tailspin toward flunking out of school because of excessive absences angered Alice and made her more rebellious for a while, Carrie was relieved to have the support of the school in handling Alice's problems. Her daughter made her realize that she needed and could accept help from others in times of crisis, something that Carrie's mother never would have done. Accepting herself as different from her mother was Carrie's first step in taking control of her own life.

Mary Pat's Friendship Fiasco: Threatening Teens' Travels

"Why was she so angry with me?" Mary Pat implored, questioning the bad turn that her forty-one-year-old friendship with Marilyn had taken. She had known Marilyn since they were in kindergarten, had nearly grown up at her house. The two had drifted apart when they'd gone to different colleges. But when Mary Pat's mother died about two years ago, Marilyn had provided a ready shoulder.

"Now whenever she calls, I'm in the middle of something," Mary Pat shared matter-of-factly. *"But when you have a fourteen- and an eighteen-year-old, you're going to be busy. Jared plays soccer, so it seems I'm always taking him to games or getting him ready for them when she calls. This summer has been the worst for the two of us. We've also been getting Caroline ready for college; she leaves in five weeks!"*

Mary Pat explained to us that Marilyn was angry because whenever she called (it was always she who called), Mary Pat had no time to talk. Marilyn had told her old friend that she felt she really didn't care about her. "If you did, wouldn't you make time for me?" she'd pleaded.

Mary Pat explained to Marilyn that she was on the last lap of being at home with Caroline. She had to make sure that she spent as much time as possible with her and Jared, who needed her supervision in order to stay on top of his chores and homework.

Marilyn started laughing in response. "If it's not been said by now," she told her, "they won't hear it anyway."

The fact that Marilyn, with no children of her own, had little tolerance for teens suddenly created a chasm between the two old friends that Mary Pat found no bridge would connect.

"How insensitive could a person be?" she asked us. "Didn't she know what a tough time this was for me . . . getting ready to let go of my precious first born? How rude for her to lay a guilt trip on me about our friendship when I was nearly having a nervous breakdown over making sure that my teenagers stayed safe and smart."

The game that Marilyn was playing reminded her of little fires that Marilyn would ignite when they were in high school themselves. They always ended with one of them being mad at the other for breaking a promise to go shopping or to do something for the other in class.

"It might as well be decades ago," Mary Pat told us. She had moved on since then and was trying to teach her kids not to play these games with other people. She couldn't understand why Marilyn hadn't moved on, too. She seemed to be frozen in time, in a time that Mary Pat had no desire to relive.

Change is inevitable. Growth, however, is optional. Mary Pat's and Marilyn's agendas were out of sync because of the changes that parenthood had made in Mary Pat's priorities. This situation presented both friends with the option of learning to develop a new attitude about friendship. Mary Pat's children came first—before friendships, before personal attention. But Marilyn's indifference to her current priorities reminded her of their age-old spats.

Now, just talking with Marilyn made her as miserable as when they were battling over the same boyfriend or were on the outs with each other because Marilyn found fault with her clothes, her hair, or her friends.

Marilyn's criticism of Mary Pat's devotion to her children told her that their lives had simply gone too far in different directions. She respected Marilyn's choice of never having children, but that meant they had even less in common to support a friendship.

For Marilyn, defining her life according to the developmental stages of her children, as Mary Pat was doing, was a foreign concept. "Why would you give up your own agenda for someone else's, wrap your identity around being a parent when your kids will just leave you someday?" she needled her friend.

Although Mary Pat couldn't see it, Marilyn resented losing in the competition over Mary Pat's attention, in much the same way they'd competed over boys and grades while they were teens. Competition between friends often rears its ugly head during the hot lava flows of the teen years as parents and their friends play the one-upmanship game over the amount of free time they have to give to friendships, as well as who's got the "best" kids and, therefore, in their minds, is the best parent. Scorecards are kept and compared of their teen's grades, college selection, ACT or SAT scores, involvement in school activities, sports prowess, gifts of cars, extent of community service involvement, numbers of awards and trophies, visits to grandparents, and absence of police records.

The same competition between friends on the playing fields of PTA, soccer, spelling bees, room motherhood, and report cards that began while parents were Travel Agents becomes amplified as the number and kinds of activities in which teens are involved increase. This competition among parents can get ugly, very ugly, as the tension of life on a volcano threatens all vestiges of rational thinking. Formerly reasonable people have been spotted shunning friends whose children were named cheerleader, elected as prom queen candidates, and accepted on sports teams when theirs weren't. Parents who are still struggling to resolve their need for a good performance review that began in Season Three—needing their child's "products" to be approved by others in order for them to be acceptable in their own eyes—risk damaging their friendships by continuing to view parenthood as a contest.

T EENAGERS NATURALLY DEMAND their parents' attention just when they want it less. Therein lies the crux of friendship conflicts for Volcano Dwellers. At the same time that they need to supervise their teens' activities, listen when they need to be heard, and advise them when they seek counsel, parents also need their friends to help them through the rock slides and hot lava flows they are encountering. Therefore friends and Volcano Dwellers alike need to shower each other with empathy and understanding; it won't be long before parents of teenagers become empty nesters with more time on their hands and a tremendous need for companionship to fill the void in their hearts.

Audrey and Chuck's Midlife Dilemma: Looking for Love in All the Wrong Places

Audrey and Chuck, both forty-six, confessed that their marriage was in trouble because their sullen, fifteen-year-old ninth grader, Shawn, was destroying his family's peaceful coexistence. He barely spoke to Audrey and Chuck, except when he needed money or wanted to complain about the embarrassing car they were driving. Their three older daughters were happy to be tucked away at college, removed from their hostile baby brother who broke, borrowed, ripped, or lost everything in his path, including the birthday presents they sent him from school and things they left behind in their rooms.

Those childhood treasures were hardly cheap, since Audrey and Chuck each sometimes worked sixty to seventy hours a week in order to maintain their large home in the suburbs and smother their children with all the clothes, computers, and expensive toys they had ever wanted. Chuck had slaved without recognition for fifteen years as a foreman at the local auto plant. Audrey still regretted that she hadn't been able to climb the corporate ladder to become an office manager, at least, at the long-distance provider where she worked, because she refused to work on weekends so she could be with Shawn. Both were beginning to question whether all of their efforts to provide the "ideal life" for Shawn, in particular, were worth it, especially after receiving frequent calls from the high school principal and counselor about Shawn's obnoxious behavior in school.

Chuck and Audrey began to feel that they had wasted the past fifteen years of their lives trying to raise Shawn. Daily arguments over whether they should have been less strict or more attentive were becoming the norm. As the two parents described the constant conflict in their lives, they reminisced about the battles with their own parents. When they were about Shawn's age, war had broken out in both families over their being able to date each other. Neither of their parents had believed that Chuck or Audrey was good enough for their daughter or son.

"I can't believe that my youngest child is now that age," Audrey de-clared wistfully, adding that this fact alone made her feel ancient. "Our parents are supposed to be the old, responsible adults," she mused.

Living with Shawn was like reliving the nightmare of their adolescence. The pain inspired in them a desire to do something wild, crazy, and irre-sponsible like they used to, if only to reassure themselves that they still had the best of their lives ahead of them.

Chuck had always liked his little boy and had even coached his baseball and soccer teams to state championships. But now that Shawn was no longer a little boy, he wanted nothing to do with his father. The fact that he found his father an embarrassment was a developmentally appropriate mile-stone for Shawn to reach, although it had a disturbing effect on Chuck. He couldn't understand what he had done to transform his loving, adoring son, who had copied everything his dad did, into someone who suddenly rejected him and made him feel worthless.

Audrey and Chuck are parents caught between two unpleasant worlds dur-ing this season of parenthood: the nightmare of their own past adolescence and the unsettling reality that they are old enough to have a child who is living this nightmare for himself. On any given day, they never knew whether their sweet, loving child would transform into a hairy, snarling monster. Because they felt dissatisfied with their own personal and profes-sional achievements as they reached midlife, Chuck and Audrey let this kind of ridicule and rejection affect their assessment of the value of the time and money they had spent on their son.

In addition, Chuck started to question the value of his relationship with Audrey, particularly in light of what his best friend, James, was up to with his latest fling, Tabitha. While his home life was in such chaos, Chuck found himself fantasizing about sitting on a beach in Mexico with James's girlfriend. And James, also a parent of a stormy teenager, didn't help much as he related every last seamy detail of his affair to Chuck while they worked together at the plant.

After Chuck told us about his friend James and his affair, we pointed out that even though James thought that trading in his wife, Leann, for Tabitha would wrest him of his responsibilities as a father and help him circumvent his wife's badgering, he would soon see his plan backfire. His children would keep drawing him closer to them as they sought to redeem themselves in his eyes, blaming themselves for his abandoning them. As their mother, Leann, would be part of his history, even if they divorced and lived thousands of miles apart.

Escaping into an affair is a "solution" for some Volcano Dwellers who find life on the rim hotter than they can bear. Longing for an escape to a cooler environment, many Volcano Dwellers try a more familiar route from the Travel Agent days—justifying their lives on the hot seat by trying to create "trophy children"—pushing them into programs for gifted children, premier sports teams, beauty contests, and talent shows—in whose glory they think they will find a cooling shower. Much of their self-esteem is mistakenly based on being able to produce these successes: star athletes, honor students, leads in musicals, cheerleaders or yell leaders, homecoming queen or king candidates.

When Audrey and Chuck were faced with Shawn's rebellious behavior, they became caught up in this unhealthy way of thinking. They hoped they could solve this crisis by rebuilding their child into a person who could go out into the world and make them proud. I didn't have a child so that he could end up being a loser!" Chuck professed adamantly. But the fact was, Shawn was totally in charge of whether or not he would be a trophy child for his parents, just like all children.

There is a cost that both children and parents pay at some point when children tire of the trophy track, rebel against their parents' pressure to perform, or internalize all of this pressure and become angry and resentful. They remind parents of who's really in charge of whom simply by declining to participate, exploding from their years in the pressure cooker of their family's expectations, or cutting off communication. Parents cannot actually create trophy children, nor can they stop children from becoming such successes; they will be much happier when they enjoy their children for who they are and love them unconditionally.

OUR INTERVIEWS WITH other families experiencing the volcanic eruptions of adolescence illustrate the hard work, tenacity, and self-control needed to preserve marriages and adult/child relationships through this infamous period in the growth and development of both generations. Parents who take personal blame for the misadventures of their teenagers block their ability to be objective about their children's behavior. Issues surrounding power, control, and identity create an atmosphere of tension that is unsettling for both children and parents.

Once again, logic must prevail. Volcano Dwellers' most effective tool is their self-talk. Parents offered their favorite mantras: "This too shall pass" (still the number-one favorite!). "I've done the best job I could; if I could have done better, I would have." "If I keep my eye on the future, I can see that this kid will become an adult in spite of me." "The warm, caring relationship we had when he was in elementary school is what it will be like when he's an adult." "I love my child even though I may hate some of the things he says and does." "Someday her room will be clean; she won't be living here anymore."

In his push for independence, Shawn would continue to be prone to volcanic eruptions; Audrey and Chuck needed to join forces in helping him safely continue his journey to adulthood. Survival for Volcano Dwellers in this season of parenthood is more readily assured when they work as a tag team, much as during the Family Manager season.

For parents who want their lives to be neat and orderly, it can be agonizing to face the reality that life on a volcano is almost always messy, unstable, and perpetually in need of a cleanup crew. But many parents told us that after twelve or more years of working in the salt mines of parenthood, they expected their "big kids" to finally give them a break. To realize that just the opposite is true is a rude awakening for those who can't take the long view of their lives.

Ramon and Marina on the Rocks: Perils of a Rescue Mission

Ramon and his wife, Marina, stopped us after a presentation that we gave on the fallout from grounding teenagers. Their sixteen-year-old son, Tonio, was a good kid, Ramon told us, who wanted the same privileges that his sister Angelina, now twenty-two, was given when she was his age, but he wanted none of the responsibilities.

Big and lovable, Tonio just wasn't as mature as his sister, reported Ramon. We could tell from Marina's shaking head that she did not agree; she told us that babying Tonio was Ramon's full-time job. Every argument that they had ever had in their marriage had occurred in the past five years, Marina admitted, because she was sure that Ramon was ruining Tonio, just as his parents had ruined Ramon's baby brother, Miguel. Enabled, dependent, and incapable of being self-sufficient, Miguel had never held a job in all of his thirty years. His parents still supported him financially; and when he got his girlfriend pregnant, they even paid the hospital and doctor bills.

Ramon was afraid of repeating his parents' mistakes, Marina said, but added that he couldn't help waffling under the spell of normal teenager guile when their son needed something. Tonio's charm, debating skills, and ability to manipulate could force his dad to do anything for him that he wanted. Ramon admitted that he couldn't bring himself to follow Marina's advice and ground Tonio or let him suffer some other consequence of not being rescued whenever he got into a bind. That seemed to be happening on a regular basis since he started driving: he had wrecked his car twice; had gone to court three times for failing to pay traffic citations; and, most recently, had gotten a little too close to the curb, as he said, and ruined one of the tires and wheel on Ramon's new car. Ramon was constantly shelling out money for body shop work and attorney's fees to bail Tonio out of trouble.

When we suggested that Ramon could break his habit of rescuing Tonio if he wanted to, Marina emphatically agreed. "Since he won't, I'm worried that Tonio will turn into a hot-shot, privileged brat" whom she hated to be around. Marina remembered those kinds of kids from her high school, the ones who intimidated other people just because they felt superior. She had always felt so insecure and fearful around these swaggering, bragging teens who acted as if they were entitled to rule the world.

That was another problem. Her teenager sparked in Marina memories of her high school years that she had long forgotten. She remembered always being worried that she wasn't pretty enough or popular enough, and the boys had reinforced those insecurities by teasing her about her glasses and pimples. Her parents had insisted that she was crazy, imploring her to just ignore those "mean kids." But their advice never worked; those same fears of failure infected Marina's life now as she thought about Tonio's life. She felt as if she were right back in the middle of the most insecure time in her life. She worried that Tonio would be to his classmates what her bullies had been to her if Ramon continued to reinforce his sense of entitlement and prevented him from suffering any consequences for his irresponsibility.

Unfortunately, the insecurity of teenagers in this stage of their development has a contagious effect on their parents. Even if they had been the most self-assured Celebrities, Sponges, Travel Agents, and Family Managers, Volcano Dwellers must beware: Their teenagers' irresponsible behavior can create cracks in the foundation of parenthood that mothers and fathers have been building for over a decade.

Both Ramon and Marina were clueless about how to repair their previously solid parenthood ground that Tonio was eroding. Do you rescue a teen to prevent him from suffering the consequences of his actions, or do you turn a child into an entitled bully when he knows that he has no consequences for his actions? When parents rescue their children, they are only rescuing themselves from feeling guilty that they are letting their children suffer. Parents who take the long view of parenthood understand that the suffering they allow their children to experience by not rescuing them helps their children become responsible adults.

Despite the fact that Miguel's lack of self-confidence and insecurity presented Ramon with a vivid example of the potential downside of parental rescue missions, Ramon thought that good parents didn't let their children suffer from their mistakes. He had been in the habit of rescuing Tonio since he was a preschooler. When Tonio would leave his toy trucks out in the rain, for example, Ramon wouldn't be happy about it but would always buy him replacements if they got rusty or lost. That seemed like the right thing to do when Tonio was four or five. Now that he was sixteen, it was breaking Ramon's heart to think about his son having to pay the price for being so irresponsible with his car. And Marina was making him feel guilty about "fixing" everything for Tonio, just as his parents had always done for Miguel.

Ramon knew that Tonio would be away at college soon and would be lost without his dad around to save him when he got into trouble. By seeing the big picture, we suggested, Ramon could look into the future with Tonio and tell himself that the next two years held the promise of many opportunities to teach Tonio the important lessons he needed to learn before both father and son could move forward in their adulthood development, something his parents had never learned. Until Tonio was able to leave home and navigate on his own, Ramon would not be free of the misplaced responsibility for Tonio's behavior that he had been carrying on his shoulders since Tonio's toddlerhood. It was time to give himself a break, we advised.

Marina had different issues. Fearful that Tonio would morph into the bullies of her own youth, she was focused on grounding Tonio from his car and friends so he would learn to appreciate his freedom and become more responsible. This attempt to gain control of Tonio's behavior wouldn't accomplish those goals—it would only serve to ease her anxieties every time he left the house. Grounding also puts parents in jail, as they have to play wardens to their prisoners, lest they escape.

We advised Ramon and Marina to refocus their lives on what they wanted Tonio to learn—responsibility and self-discipline—instead of what they feared he'd become, the Miguels and bullies of the world. Because Ramon's model for parenthood didn't feel comfortable to both of them and Marina's jailhouse-rock solution and resurfacing insecurities were creating anxiety over her lack of control, the couple found themselves in uncharted territory as Volcano Dwellers and decided to seek help in developing a new road map for themselves and their son. By tossing grounding and rescuing out of their tool kit for survival in this season of parenthood, they felt lost, with no way to repair the foundation they had built for Tonio. We advised them to work with a counselor to restore the trust between them as Volcano Dwellers so that they could collaborate in doing damage control with Tonio, as well as make the transition to the Family Remodeler season as a coordinated team in just a few years.

Hunter Loses a Pal: Confidante or Daughter?

Hunter's daughter, Christina, turned thirteen in November. By Christmas Day Hunter was ready to turn in his resignation from his teaching job of ten years at his daughter's junior high school.

Christina gave him a daily lecture, he told us, about what he could and could not do, wear, and say at school. Seeing that he'd suddenly become a short-order cook for everything in his child's life, Hunter contemplated talking to the school principal, Mrs. Wetmore, about the changes in Christina. He wanted the reality check, but he worried about exposing his inadequacies. If she thought he couldn't handle one teenager—his own daughter— would she question if he could handle a whole class? Would she think that things would be different if his ex, Robbie, were still around to offer the family a "woman's touch"?

Besides trying to understand how he was upsetting Christina just by what he wore to work, Hunter had never felt so insecure since he was in junior high himself. He had relied on his daughter's approval and friendship, he said, because it had been just the two of them her whole life. Hunter was so proud of his relationship with Christina; no other fathers he knew had the kind of bond that he shared with his daughter. When her mother had told him the devastating news that she didn't want to be "tied down" to a baby and had walked out for good, Christina had provided Hunter with a reason to go on in life. She meant the world to him. "I do everything with a little hand in mind," he had told his friends whenever they had wanted him to go somewhere with them on weekends as she was growing up.

Hunter had transferred to a junior high school that was closer to the preschool that Christina had entered when she was three; he could then spend less time traveling back and forth between her school and his. All of his love and devotion to structuring a safe and caring family of two with Christina during the Sponge and Family Manager seasons of parenthood were rewarded when Christina began doting on him in elementary school. She insisted that he come to all of her school plays and get to know all of her friends so he wouldn't feel that he was an outsider at class parties. She made him feel so special: sharing homework problems and girlfriend tips kept her close to his heart as her confidante and trusted friend when he was a Travel Agent. In fact, they had become inseparable buddies for the past three or four years . . . going out to eat, to neighborhood picnics, and to her soccer matches together nearly every weekend.

So where had his sweet little girl gone? Hunter asked us. Was this the end of their friendship? What had he done to deserve this? Why did his daughter seem so angry with him? Hunter braced himself for each day's eruptions, facing each outburst quietly, because he was unprepared to lose a friend and a daughter. His life had become the nightmare of twenty years ago, when he never knew from day to day if he would feel like strangling or hugging his own mother. Now being the ringleader of his daughter's changing circus acts felt just as chaotic and dangerous as his own adolescence often had.

In fact, he doubted if he was qualified to be a teacher anymore. All of his life, children and teaching had meant the most to him. Now he kept comparing all of the other kids' parents to his daughter's father—himself. He wanted to measure up as a father more than as a classroom educator.

His life's goals upended by a thirteen-year-old? It had been a blessing in disguise, he told us, that his wife's leaving him when his daughter was just a baby forced him to become so close to his little girl. But now that she was getting older, he wasn't sure how to play the role of second or third fiddle in her life.

Every parent's life becomes emotionally chaotic during this season of parenthood. As Hunter's daughter was going through her own identity crisis, trying to establish just who she was in relation to the world, her father was traveling down the same path. The nightmares and insecurities of his own adolescence returned to him as he questioned his capabilities in his chosen field. Ultimately he felt inadequate as both a teacher and a father.

Like Hunter, other parents told us that it wasn't bad enough that they had to live through this stage as children. As parents, it felt a billion times worse. Not only did they know how insane it felt to be a teenager, but they also knew that they were helpless to stop it from happening to the person they loved the most—their teen.

We asked Hunter about his particular struggles as a Volcano Dweller. Was their physical proximity—living together in the same school as well as at home—keeping his daughter from being able to separate from him and hampering his growth in his chosen field? Hunter decided to stay in the school but establish some guidelines for the interactions between him and his daughter while he was there so they occupied more separate orbits.

They made two lists. One itemized those things that were an important part of his school day that were nonnegotiable—saying hi to her and to other kids in the hall, wearing jeans on casual Fridays, accompanying his classes on field trips, eating in the lunch room with some of "his kids" if they asked him to, playing music of his choice in class before and after school, sending notes to her at school if he had messages that couldn't wait until the evening. The second list included things that he and Christina could negotiate—discussing Christina's test results with her teachers before she saw them herself, walking home from school with her, sitting at her lunch table with her friends.

Hunter forced himself to address his sadness over the loss of his daughter as his friend and accept that their relationship was undergoing lots of change. During their list-making exercise, he started to see the big picture that we encouraged him to adopt: Christina's wanting to separate from her father meant that she was a normal teenager, not that she didn't love him. By understanding that her developmental path had always defined their relationship, Hunter could prepare himself for this predictable passage in his life, in spite of the fact that he would rather have his little girl back again.

We suggested that he and his daughter talk about the transition that their "buddy" system was going through. He reassured her that he was close by to listen whenever she wanted to talk. Simply ignoring the change in their relationship had caused their conflicts to grow. Though he thought of himself as a private person, we suggested he determine several trust-worthy friends who could listen, advise, and support him. This would help him adjust to the changes in his life and ease the transition from using his daughter as his sounding board to creating new, caring friendships with adults. Finally, doing so would provide a role model for his daughter to create a support system of peers as well.

Jana's Legacy:
Teenage Werewolves Prowl the Country Club

Jana's husband, Richard, an executive with a large computer company, ex-plained to us in a couples Circles group meeting that he and Jana had known each other since high school, where they had fallen in love and be-come inseparable. They had graduated from college together, married, and moved to the suburbs, where Richard had started working for the company that he was still with today, twenty-five years later.

Jana loved the beautiful house that they had finally been able to afford after twenty-five years of marriage but hated the pet name "Mother Di-nosaur" that he gave her because, as he put it, "people like Jana are al-most extinct. No one ever stays home to take care of their house anymore these days."

We learned that Jana came from a long line of home lovers. Her family stuck together like Velcro; she had always dreamed of contributing at least two children to the family legacy. She'd wanted to replicate for her children the warm and cozy environment of the rambling home in which she spent her childhood. She felt as if she were the luckiest mother in the world when Madison, their first daughter, was born eighteen years ago. Their other daughter, Chatham, joined them three years later. Richard's thriving career created all of the opportunities for creature comforts that both she and Richard had been blessed with while growing up.

Jana was a stay-at-home mom to Chatham and Madison as they grew up. "Though all of my friends worked in charity projects from Junior League to the Race for the Cure, I kept my activities to a minimum so I could be available for the kids. Room mother at school, PTA president, and Brownie leader—these were the jobs I cherished," she said.

Being a devoted mother and wife fit her perfectly. This was what she'd seen her own mother, Doris, doing, and this was what she'd always wanted for herself. Now, however, the life Jana had built, complete with a million-

dollar home, was empty. Chatham and Madison were rarely home, their parents explained, because they always wanted to go to friends' houses, where they could just "kick back." All of the "fragile stuff," as they called the antiques and glassware that Jana had displayed in every room of the house, made their friends scared that they would break something.

Break something? Why would they break something? Jana had thought at the time. Didn't they appreciate how much time and effort she had spent in making their home perfect?

From her point of view, her daughters couldn't have cared less. Jana found that her children blew her off—preferring to smoke marijuana and hang out with the "stoners," as the police called their friends. Madison's taste in clothes was straight out of Nashville, and she'd bought a pickup truck to go with her country-western act. She was into dieting, too, losing so much weight that Jana was concerned that she was becoming anorexic. She had read about the high number of teenagers who never felt that they were ever skinny enough, so they just kept dieting.

Chatham was Madison's little clone. She, too, was getting too thin, according to Jana; when Jana wanted to buy Chatham a new car for her sixteenth birthday, she wanted a used pickup truck like Madison's. Jana and Richard said that they found themselves always yelling at their kids to use their manners, to write thank-you notes, and to just be civil. The girls seemed to be oblivious to everything their parents stood for.

Jana and Richard did not understand what had happened to turn their previously charming children into snarling werewolves. When they were Chatham's and Madison's ages, they would have never talked to their parents as their children talked to them: telling them that their clothes "sucked"; refusing to eat anything their mother had made because it had too much fat in it; threatening them with such lines as "If you don't get out of my face, I'm out of here!" when Jana or Richard would suggest that they help with the dishes or pick up their shoes from the living room.

No longer having obedient children who would listen to them or even take good care of themselves as they had done when they were the girls' age left a deep void in Jana's and Richard's lives. Jana tried to gain control over her teenagers by taking away their "wheels" when they talked back to her, dragging them to counseling to "get their heads straightened out," allowing them to see their boyfriends only once a week, forbidding them to wear their country-western clothes to school, yanking their telephones out of their rooms, and moving their curfew down to ten even on Friday and Saturday nights. She justified all of her efforts to "turn her daughters around": young adults should respect their parents by following their example just because they are their parents, she told us. "I never defied my parents when I was a teenager, and look at how I turned out," she said. Her own rose-colored memories of adolescence were so happy and carefree. Now she just felt like an explosion could happen at any moment.

Jana and Richard used to feel that they had their lives under control. They had a marriage that was as big a hit as the couple's stock portfolio. With her dedicated commitment to her family, Jana thought that nothing could spoil her joy of being a mother. But when her children became adolescents, she learned that she simply wasn't happy unless she was in control. This was a lesson that she would rather have learned at an earlier season, she told us when we pointed out that she had already achieved "addict" status as a critical, overprotective boss.

We knew that Jana and Richard were baffled by their daughters' behavior. They had described themselves as "good kids who had never done anything that didn't follow in their parents' footsteps." Even to this day they spent time at the country club, playing golf and tennis with their parents. We reassured them that parents who stand up for their ideals, their beliefs, and their values and are proud of their belongings and achievements are good role models for their children. But they cannot control whether or not their children embrace their same interests and values.

Pushing those values on teenagers and demanding that they conform to them only makes them want to withdraw and reject the stifling pressure, even if they agree with those values, for the sake of their overarching goal: control over their own lives. It's all a matter of kids' familiar struggle to feel that they are in the driver's seat, which began as toddler tantrums, was fueled in the middle years, and blasted off in adolescence.

This season of parenthood felt so different to Jana and Richard, however, because they had neither rejected their own parents' way of life nor been given any hint that their children would not accept theirs. They blamed themselves for their children's problems. We advised them that children, especially during adolescence, choose their own path to follow in spite of parents' best efforts. Engaging in self-blame only prevents parents from moving on to help their children find healthy ways to express themselves.

At our encouragement, Jana and Richard began to see a therapist who specialized in eating disorders. They turned their focus away from trying to make their children into perfect, submissive replicas of themselves and toward accepting each child as she was at this present moment: a country-western music and pickup truck lover.

In cases of controlling parents, such as Jana and Richard, adolescents' separation from their parents' identity often manifests as open rebellion or movement into self-destructive behaviors. Such teens often believe that the only things they can get good at or take control over are what they do with the one thing they think they own outright: their bodies. Excessive dieting, illegal drugs, tattoos, and body piercing are all signs of their struggle to find an identity.

We suggested that Jana and Richard address ways to cope with the loss they were feeling as their "little ones" became young adults. It was natural and normal for them to be grieving the end of their daughters' childhood. Their attempt to control every aspect of their daughters' lives reflected their denial of this inevitable transition to adulthood. Jana's vindictive dictums to her daughters revealed the anger that was bubbling just under the surface of her mask of gentility. She believed that she was "making a deal" with her daughters, much as she had done in the Family Manager season, as she imposed her "rightful authority" as their parent. "Aren't parents supposed to insist that their children do what they are told?" she asked us.

We recommended that Jana and Richard continue to work with their counselor on becoming more accepting of themselves as parents of teenagers, whose duties as Volcano Dwellers include containing the damage from their offspring's eruptions, and not being responsible for controlling them. When they had worked through their stages of grief over the loss of their little girls, they were then free to better put a more positive spin on their children's lives, thinking of them as unique and interesting rather than as unconventional and upsetting.

Benjamin and Fatherly Love: The Sandwich Generation

When he stepped up to our table to chat with us during a workshop, Benjamin, a jovial-looking assembly-line worker at a local manufacturing plant, blurted out that he had a problem. This forty-something single father, who had a big heart tattoo on his arm bearing the names of his kids in the center, was crazy about his sons, ages eight and five, and his thirteen-year-old daughter. Focusing solely on his kids was difficult because screaming for attention in the background were his mother and father, who were both suffering from the effects of mild strokes in their assisted living center halfway across the country.

Benjamin was having trouble coping with the loss of his parents as he had known them. He didn't want to travel to see them because that would mean being away from his daughter and sons. His daughter was changing so much that he felt as though he were losing her, too! She refused to go to Sunday school now, saying that it was for little kids. The adult world already fascinated her. She was always pleading with him to let her wear makeup, to go to the mall with her friends, and to wear clothes that he didn't think were appropriate for her age. She had a new, sixteen-year-old boyfriend, too, of whom Benjamin didn't approve. She was too young to be dating, he told us emphatically.

He realized why his parents were so angry when he had tried sneaking out at night with his friends when he was his daughter's age. Now she was doing the exact same thing to him! And he had no one to help him through it, to share the responsibility, since his wife, Ruthie, had passed away three years ago.

Like so many parents today, Benjamin was seeing the circles of life from both perspectives, as a father and a son. It is a gut wrenching spot to be in and takes energy and patience to sort through everyone's changing identities. Parents' skills learned as Family Managers and Travel Agents come into play as they juggle their busy itineraries with their budding child actors, athletes, musicians, or artists.

In order to survive this season of parenthood, Benjamin needed to be more flexible, revising his expectations for what constituted a "good meal," a "clean" shirt, or an "orderly house." He also needed to revise his standards for what a "good father" was, to see this season as one in which his children's independence is celebrated and his parents' dependence is seen as a natural process of aging.

As parents and children begin to separate physically, the loss of their children's dependency pinches the soul of parents who believe that they need to be needed by their children in order to be a "good parent." If parents operate from the platform that a child's self-sufficiency and independence are valued higher than his dependency during this stage of his life, then this season of parenthood doesn't have to be a time of mourning but, instead, can be one that supports everyone's search for a sense of self.

Benjamin was wise to be concerned about allowing his daughter to do everything she wanted to do: hanging out at the mall and wearing makeup were activities that he could support, within certain limits, however, but dating was "off-limits" for the time being, as he considered it a freedom that he decided no thirteen-year-old needed to have. For her birthday, he paid for her dream makeover at a cosmetics counter, for example, so she could be taught ways to use makeup that were appropriate for a teenager.

Benjamin also found that he needed to change his shift at the plant in order to provide the supervision of his teenager that was necessary, in his opinion. He was glad that he had enough seniority to be able to request the shift he wanted. We suggested that he also take time to work with the social worker in his parents' assisted living facility to keep on top of their health needs, long-distance. As a Volcano Dweller, Benjamin had the opportunity to step back and reprioritize his life, because all three generations of his family were affected by his daughter's passage through adolescence.

One of the pitfalls of parenthood in every season is the push/pull conflict of parents wanting to strengthen the bonds between themselves and their children by pulling the children closer while knowing that they need to be allowed to leave the nest, or gently pushed out, so they can someday fly on their own. Kids' constant, innate drive to be independent, self-sufficient—to "live my own life," as they say—can be seen as positive or negative depending on the needs of the parents and how they define being a good parent.

Helping children reflect on and learn from their mistakes, or rescuing them from suffering from the consequences of their actions, are two different ways of approaching self-sufficiency. The bottom line for parents: Supporting self-sufficiency and independence requires them to become artful jugglers of privilege and restriction as children try out new ways of seeking their own identities. Children show their parents how self-sufficient they are by handling age-appropriate freedom responsibly. As the first circle of parenthood ends, parents' happiness and peace of mind depends on how well both generations have done in balancing staying close and letting go.

Self-Discoveries of Volcano Dwellers

Your pocket guide to the truths revealed in the Volcano Dweller season of parenthood.

➤ **I thought we'd already gone over the *big* drop.** On the roller coaster of parenthood, the first big plunge seems to be the most frightening, but you soon discover that it was only a small hill compared with the free fall of this season. The fear is lessened a bit because you know that you survived being jerked around by the ride so far.

➤ **Oh man! I'm not sure I'm going to make it.** You thought the last part of the ride wasn't too bad, but these last dips and turns really put you to the test. You begin to wonder if you'll make it, and you pray that it will be over soon.

➤ **I'd forgotten how wild this ride was.** You've been on this ride before, but you don't remember it feeling quite this scary. You remember feeling insecure and fearful your first time through, promising yourself that you wouldn't get on it again. But here you are, riding it this time with a new seatmate. Somehow it's not any better, although you know how it'll turn out.

➤ **Is this ride about to end?** You can see the end of the ride, but you keep losing sight of it as you follow the contortions of the track that you can't yet escape. Toward the end of this ride, even though it was really rough at times, you'll begin to get emotional as you think back over where you've been and how many challenging bumps and swerves you have witnessed and survived.

Exit Signs

Leaving Volcano Zone. Construction ahead. The Volcano Dweller season marks the end of the first circle of parenthood: parenting children. The exit signs are clearly marked as adolescents begin packing to leave home, not for just a few hours a day or to go off to sleep-over camp for a while, but often permanently. This is the beginning of the next step on the journey of independence that children and their parents have been traveling . . . and the end of their living as "one big happy family" together.

Parenting Adult Children

Family Remodeler

CHILD'S YOUNG ADULT YEARS

The future is made of the same stuff as the present.
—SIMONE WEIL

WHEN A CHILD LEAVES home—to go to college, marry, or start a full-time job—he forces his parents to respond to something that they haven't experienced for many years with the occasional sleep-over or camp respite: the quiet of an empty house and empty time slots on their calendars. Their task ahead is to take that empty house and empty time and fashion a remodeled family out of it. The Sturm und Drang of their lives—their offspring—now create the opportunity by their absence for parents to look at their family as an inside remodeling job of identity, intimacy, and independence, a psychological fixer-upper. The first phase of the human interior decorating of the family structure is now worn out after over eighteen years of wear and tear.

Donetta, a mother of twenty-four-year-old and twenty-one-year-old college students in one of our Circles groups, explained her own rebuilding project this way: "When my youngest left for college, everyone kept asking me what I was going to do now that I didn't have kids around anymore and my job was done. I didn't really feel done, just different, as if I had run a marathon and was trying to get my heart rate down."

Since her children were born, Donetta's world had consisted of providing the structure that made their lives workable: feeding, clothing, cleaning, and protecting them, as any "good mother" would do. But after the turmoil of adolescence and the departure of her youngest for college, being a mom became more emotionally high maintenance than she'd expected. What was most striking to her during this new Family Remodeler season of parenthood was how much time she spent worrying about her children. In fact, she said that she realized that her worrying about them was taking the place of her hurrying to "do something" or "be there" for them when they needed her.

Her old definition of being a "good mother" or "good father"—always being in close contact whenever the need for a responsible party arose— no longer seemed to apply. Donetta was forced to redefine herself in relation to her children because of the distance that separated them from each other psychologically as well as physically.

She told us that she had understood that worrying was always a part of parenthood, constantly playing in the background of her life like distracting elevator music. When her children were younger, her worrying about them subsided when they were safely at home where she could protect them. But now that they were perpetually out of sight, her worries had become constant companions, as the blueprints for this season of parenthood remained on the drawing board, providing only sketchy details of what her family would look like in the future.

Like all Circles group participants in this season of parenthood, Donetta asked herself: Were the kids eating okay? Were they wearing coats when it got cold? Were they drinking and driving? Did they have enough sense to stay out of dangerous parts of town? Would they come home on holidays? Would they come home for good?

Parents also reported being worried about what their own lives were going to be like during the upheaval of family remodeling: Would they get so lonely without their children that they wouldn't be able to stand living with the empty spaces of their lives? Would they yearn for the old, worn, but comfortable and familiar structure of the family as it was? Would they have anything left to say to each other when it was just the two of them once again?

The interplay between change and continuity stirs up fear of the unknown in the hearts of Family Remodelers. Parents reported that now they had to learn how to cope with their adult children's trials and errors in practicing what they had been preaching: how to be self-sufficient, independent, responsible adults. Their children's successes or failures in school or at work determined how dependent they were on their parents for their livelihood, thereby directly impacting their remodeling job and how they perceived both the past and the future.

Some parents told us that as long as they were footing the bill for their children's college education or living arrangements, they felt as if they were on partly familiar ground. They had a justifiable say-so in what their children did with their lives, when they did it, and how much it cost to do it: spend a semester of college abroad, move out of a dorm room into an apartment, take an internship in a distant city.

Now these parents must relate to their satellite children as adults, regardless of how securely they want to attach their apron strings to them. Their ex-children's lives were being planned around their own agendas, with their parents usually being the last, not the first, to know their whereabouts when they chose to provide that information. The dynamic of this new adult-adult relationship with their children is ideally based on mutual love, trust, and respect, as Helen illustrates in the following story:

"I knew that it was foolish for me to worry about my nineteen-year-old son and my new life," Helen told us in one of our interviews. "So I had to force myself to let go of my fear that I wouldn't be able to make this transition to a new phase of my life. I had to trust my child's instincts to make good decisions for himself and my resourcefulness to build a new, meaningful relationship between us. I think that I was having more of a problem with his letting go of me than he was!"

The issue of control is again a key factor in this season of parenthood, as it is in every season, when parents struggle to "hang on" to their teenagers—keep them safely at home and relate to them as they did when they were young children. T. Berry Brazelton, renowned pediatrician and author, acknowledged his struggle with the approaching empty nest:

"One of my children said the reason that I had such a tough time with them is that I had a difficult time letting them go . . . and I was not able to control them. Control is a very big issue with me. Let's say I won't be writing a book on teenagers."

After the many heated exchanges that occur during the Volcano Dweller season, an important point to consider during this letting-go process is the rationale behind the advice often given to spouses: Don't go to bed mad! According to psychotherapist Tom Scott, "It's very hard to let go of a relationship that is fractured. Parents wait for things to correct themselves, and sometimes that never happens. Young adults may fear that they won't ever want to come back home if their relationship with their parents isn't repaired before they leave. The adults need to take the lead and initiate the healing process."

When teenagers' wars with their parents are ongoing through a stormy adolescence, initiating the healing process before their teens leave for school or a job far from home becomes difficult as Family Remodelers review the years of giving and sacrifice for which they feel they've only been punished by their children's behavior. Tyssa, the mother of twenty-year-old Paul, related that his teen years of defiance over his parents' overly restrictive rules were so wearing that she had been ready for him to be gone since he was fourteen. Paul had been a good student, adamantly opposed to drugs, and a faithful member of the church choir, but he had always set his own agenda and had rebelled against all of his parents' efforts to control the friends he hung out with and the clothes he wore. He was "his own man," he told them. When he was grounded for breaking his curfew, he would erupt, shout obscenities, and claim that his parents didn't trust him.

Tyssa had grown so angry over his outbursts that she often told him how much she hated him and wanted him out of her life forever. Paul had told his father that he couldn't wait to make his mother's wish come true. "I began to worry that when he graduated and went across the state to college, he really wouldn't come back home, and I would never see him again," she lamented. "That wasn't what I wanted. I just wanted a nice kid who'd do what I thought was best for him and not give me a hard time about it. So I tried to back off of what he called my 'stupid rules' and make up with him before he left. But he wouldn't have any part of that. He was so mad all of the time while he was home that I couldn't even talk to him. Now that he's away at college, I e-mail him every day to try to rebuild our relationship. I don't know whether he'll change or not, but I'm willing to keep trying to change the way I relate to him."

In many cases, storm clouds begin gathering during teenagers' senior year in high school as the imminent departure for college or other destinations creates the natural stress associated with change. Parents often become more possessive as teens become more irritable, creating conflict that makes all parties almost eager for the separation, as Gerilynn, the forty-eight-year-old mother of nineteen-year-old Arianna, put it so succinctly: "It's God's way of telling us that it's time to move on. If we hadn't gotten on each other's nerves so much during that year, having her go off to college would have been so hard for both of us. And when she came home for her first break, we were all so glad to see each other, that it was like old-home week."

Parents who look at their relationship with their children as an ongoing process of letting them go and holding them close, even as they become adults, will openly apologize, forgive, and communicate their unconditional love, regardless of the difference of opinion or disappointment that parents may feel over their children's choices or attitudes. That healing process defines their relationship as one in which both parents and their newly minted adult children communicate with mutual respect, which does not always include mutual agreement. To appreciate each other, both generations need to acknowledge their growth from the previous adult-child framework of their relationship and put a new adult-adult welcome mat down by the front door of their respective living quarters.

SOME PARENTS ADMITTED to us in our interviews that they were so reluctant to adjust to the growing pains of changing parenthood that they related to their newly hatched adults as if nothing were different, nothing had changed, even though their children had moved away from home. Ruth is a case in point:

"We had always dreamed of having a house near the seashore," explained this Circles group member. "So when our daughter went to school in Florida, we had our excuse; off we went to join her. But two years later she flunked out and moved across the country to be near her boyfriend. We were as devastated about the loss of our dream to still be near her in this phase of our lives as we were about the scar we believed that her decision would leave in her life."

Ruth admitted that she wasn't interested in remodeling her family yet, so moving to be near her daughter had given her the physical proximity that enabled her to continue mothering her daughter the way she used to on a regular basis: feeding her delicious meals, going shopping with her, and helping her with her English essays. Ruth told us that she just wanted to see her child all the time, have the familiar smell of her perfume waft over her, even hear her whining about how hard her life was as a poor, overworked college student who was forced to live in a dorm with the roommate from hell.

A word of caution: Joseph Walsh, Ph.D., dean of the School of Social Work at Loyola University, Chicago, warns, "If the youngest child heads off to college in August, wait at least a few months to pack up the house and move to the Sunbelt; don't make such a major change in September."

Walsh is alluding to the time, energy, and creativity needed to adapt to the demands of being Family Remodelers: coping with the messy, disorganized upheaval of this season of parenthood and beginning the actual psychological and emotional process of rebuilding. Parents' new identity becomes that of general contractors of a new family structure. Their adult children now need them to be their safety nets, a demand that can become so time-consuming, it can pull the parents away from their remodeling project, thereby interrupting their new work.

THIS PROCESS OF CREATING new family relationships between adults isn't accomplished without experiencing a sense of loss over letting go of the old floor plan of the family—the day-to-day duties of child-rearing. To cope with their mixed emotions as they see new support beams where old walls once stood, parents must size up what kinds of mentors or consultants their children need, especially considering how their adolescent volcanoes have or haven't quieted. They must also learn how to remodel the empty nest without the children incessantly squawking for immediate attention. Finally they are forced to get a crew together to carry out the remodeling project—spouse, friends, clergy, and co-workers—so that their new family life with adult children can grow atop the emotionally secure foundation of the solid, comfortable edifice they began building in the Sponge stage.

Just as they did when they established that foundation, Family Remodelers begin this season by establishing the structure of the second circle of parenthood, parenting adult children. They are beginning parenthood anew, on the ground floor, as an infant in the parenthood of adults, just as their children are beginning an infancy, or first stage, of adulthood. This season of parenthood ends when young adults become financially independent, often at great emotional cost to parents, as experienced by Adrienne: when she asked if she could be of help to her offspring, this mother of twenty-seven-year-old Brendan was told, "Don't send me money, Mom. I can make it on my own."

"It was making me sick not to help him out," Adrienne told us, "because I knew that he wasn't able to buy new clothes or any decent furniture. I was mortified when my friends visited his ramshackle apartment."

Adrienne's story illustrates the difficult transition parents must make to "letting go" financially at the end of this season of parenthood: if they can afford to buy their adult children a better lifestyle, they feel guilty if they're not actively doing so. Therefore this season of parenthood can last for decades, as long as adult children are tied to their parents' money-lined apron strings and parents continue to need to assuage their guilt through controlling their children's economic wherewithal. It will end only when young adults decide that financial independence is important to their sense of having a separate identity from their parents and control over their own lives, or parents adopt the long view and see their children's financial independence as a necessary and healthy goal for their family to reach.

THE EMPTY NEST

Sometimes, only one person is missing, and the whole world seems depopulated.—ALPHONSE DE LAMARTINE

At the end of his teen years, a child's relationship with his parents reaches a significant turning point as this young fledgling spreads his wings and flies away. Whatever his destination, he leaves his parents with the same result: the infamous "empty nest."

This legacy of the first circle of parenthood is characterized by parents' personal interpretation and reflection on their multiple losses: the loss of their live-in children, the loss of the sense of family that they had worked so hard to build, and the loss of their own youth—a loss that they had flirted with during the Volcano Dweller season.

"In retrospect, I thought her childhood would never end," said psychotherapist Tom Scott about leaving his daughter at college for the first time, "thus implying I wouldn't be getting any older. Well, guess what? I'm older, and she is gone. Whether I was ready or not, it was time to say good-bye."

Why does letting go of their children, even though parents know it's good for them, hit parents so hard, leaving them in a state of mourning? We believe that the reason lies in parents' struggles to maintain continuity in their lives in the face of unavoidable but predictable changes their children's lives precipitate. Now the issue of control that had dominated their lives ever since their children's toddlerhood becomes a moot point: not only are they unable to exercise psychological control over their children, but because their children aren't physically near them day in and day out, they don't even know what they are up to in their first public experiment in independent living.

Kyle told us that when he woke up each morning in his own bed but without his son sleeping upstairs in his bed, he felt as if he were lost; it was as if he had been transported in the dead of night to a new home. Everything felt strange, unsettled, in a state of disarray. He wasn't sure where he was in the world or where his son was in his world. Now that his son was on his own, he irrationally thought that he had caused this exodus of the most important person in his life by bankrolling his college education.

Kyle said that he had often dreamed of his son's departure when his little guy had been in the agony of colic during his infancy, biting neighborhood children as a toddler, or insisting on playing his music at eardrum-shattering decibel levels as a teen. Now he would give anything to have the olden days back again, to appreciate the moments of parenthood squandered by wishing them away.

Soon after his son left home, Kyle reported that he and his wife experienced nightmares on a regular basis as they worried about everything concerning their son's life. Most of their worries were centered around thinking that their son's moving out—and therefore their loneliness and misery—could have been avoided.

"If only my wife and I had been more supportive and nicer to him instead of yelling at him about everything. We even paid for him to leave!" he lamented, chuckling. "What were we thinking? He could have enrolled in the local community college and lived at home. I feel like we brought all of this misery on ourselves, *and we can't do anything about it.*"

Whether their son had attended the local community college or had moved across the country to go to school, eventually his developmental path would most likely take him away from home, just as it does most young adults, we assured Kyle. Being a Family Remodeler becomes a positive venture for parents who focus on the future life they are building: striving to learn about and appreciate the new adult who's being created as he trips, falls, and gets back up again on his adventures. They need to tell themselves that they can handle this new construction project and that the remodeled family is a predictable and inevitable consequence of their children's growing up.

Parents of adult children in our Circles group also found themselves using other sensible techniques to maintain family continuity: planning special weekends, family trips, or holiday feasts; going to visit their college students on parents weekend; eating out with their children at their offspring's special places; and serving old favorite foods at home. They used these strategies to reassure themselves that they had done everything to entice their children to continue to feel connected to the family; they wanted their adult children to want to come home to recharge their family batteries. The irony of it all is reflected in the parents' past yearnings for their children to grow up, act their age, get serious. How many parents remember saying, "Don't come to me with your problems. You're mature enough to solve them yourself."

All of the members of our Circles groups who had become Family Remodelers told us that it felt as though a part of them had died when their children left them with an empty nest. What they didn't understand was that a Family Remodeler's job is to re-create her life and make room for the return of her child as an adult. Mary, a hardworking superintendent of schools, experienced soul-deep grief when her nineteen-year-old son left on a backpacking year traveling across Europe. She felt abandoned and found herself studying old photos and making sure that she could still remember her children's voices, to reassure herself that she still was "the mother" she once knew.

Katy, a mother of an eighteen-year-old first-year university student living away from home for the first time, reacted differently. She remodeled her nest by filling the void in her life with new lines of mother/daughter communication that maintained this profoundly important sense of continuity. She showered her with symbols of her love: a toll-free phone line so she could call home; on-line e-mail service for both of them; and weekly care packages of clothes and brownies all helped Katy feel that the nest wasn't permanently empty.

Many parents welcome their children's leaving the nest because they had fought such bitter battles with them over hairstyles, curfew times, phone privileges, grades, and all the other pesky details in the previous season of parenthood. But even these parents experience the grief that comes with great loss. It's only when the grieving process ends that parents can begin the necessary tasks of remodeling their lives.

How parents were themselves parented when they were young adults, as well as their individual personalities, color their ability to cope with this transition in their lives. They begin thinking: What were my own experiences during this time in my life? Why did I go to college far from home? Did my parents openly grieve when I left home for college, for a new job outside of town, for the army, for marriage, or for my own inimitable quest for self-discovery? Did I easily adjust to having this new freedom? Did my parents find new ways to feel needed by laying guilt trips on me, whining that I "never call," "never come home," and "don't care anymore"?

If parents have fond memories of trying new adventures, boldly facing independent living, and being encouraged to spread their wings way back in the olden days during this first phase of their own adulthood, the bouts of grief, depression, and anxiety that often strike them in this season of parenthood have a greater chance of being resolved. Instead of getting upset about a child's departure, these parents are better able to support their child's potential for growth as well as their own. But the process is still frightening and exciting for both parties. Parents are wise to remember that "to become separate in a psychological sense is a lifelong process of becoming—continually building on, reaffirming, and refining a sense of self," according to Karen Levin Coburn and Madge Lawrence Treeger, authors of Letting Go.

Now, however, parents and children are faced with the awesome prospect of actually getting what they had wished for during the past sixteen years or so—their independence from one another. If parents' own first trials were traumatic because their parents were miserable in their own "empty nest," their perspective on this season will predictably be one of dread as they relive their experiences through their child's new independent journey.

By understanding and acknowledging just where the origins of their view of this potentially liberating season of parenthood actually lie, parents can create a new blueprint for themselves and their responses to the expected and universal crisis of the empty nest.

HELP! WHO NEEDS ME NOW?

Independence? That's middle-class blasphemy. We are all
dependent on one another, every soul of us on earth.
—GEORGE BERNARD SHAW

So many empty nest parents wonder: After twenty years of my children's
needing me to provide them with protection and love, who am I if I no
longer have baby birds to care for? This familiar conflict of adapting to a
change in identity resonates with all Family Remodelers. Even though
parents in this season must shift from parenting children to parenting
adult children, they continue to be affected by their offspring's changing
plans, grades, career choices, friends, lovers, and the absence of contact
with them. After so many years of "saving the day," applauding the job
well done, or comforting a disappointment, parents tell us they initially
feel lost without someone to take care of, someone who needs them. They
often cope with their feelings of being disoriented, without a road map for
their lives, by choosing a dangerous path lined with outrageous choices
"now that the kids are gone."

Options that would never have even dawned on them when they had to
"behave like a mom" or "act like a dad" because the children would be
hanging around to observe their actions may now suddenly seem plausi-
ble, even attractive, as parents try to remodel the family. They take risks,
such as acknowledging an infatuation with a young co-worker at the office,
which can lead to a full-blown extramarital affair. The risky behavior often
provides parents with the attention they miss getting from their children.
The empty spaces in parents' hearts that have been created by their children's exit from home can get filled in a flash with flammable materials.
Methods to comfort themselves—spending too much money, excessive
gambling, overeating, compulsive exercising, selling the house and buying
an RV, going skydiving—can occupy the free time they now have on their
hands and serve to provide a sense of excitement, albeit fleeting, in what
many believe is an otherwise boring life.

If a spouse has lost interest in rekindling the old flame that brought a
couple together to have children in the first place, this season of parenthood can become a disastrous time for the marriage. Decades-old marriages in which both spouses' "need" for each other has long since worn
off are often replaced by new relationships that provide heady feelings of

romance—a powerful substitute for the emotional fuel parents may not be getting from their now empty nest.

"Suddenly there was nothing for us to talk about," Norm admitted, commenting on what happened to his relationship with his wife during this season of parenthood. "We would look across the dinner table at each other, a table set for just the two of us, and be speechless. The thread that held our marriage together was our children. Suddenly that thread became frayed and the marriage came apart. We were not prepared for our children to make as big an impact in our lives by their absence as by their presence."

"Since our twins went away to college for their freshman year a month ago, my husband and I have yet to sit down at the kitchen table to eat dinner," confessed Katherine. "The first night we were all alone in the house, we made our favorite culinary treats and were looking forward to a romantic tête-à-tête by candlelight. But setting just two places at the table gave me a sense of loss, not romance. I decided to move our tryst to our kitchen counter where we could dine on our two bar stools—a place usually reserved for more expeditious snacking—to circumvent the ardent pangs of loneliness gnawing at my insides. Changing our dining venue to the bar counter seems so silly, so insignificant. But we both feel that creating this 'dinner table built for two' is a sign that we are opening a new chapter of our lives, a symbol of the fresh start we are making in our twenty-five-year-old marriage."

Depending on the compatibility of the couple, they may now be able to turn toward each other in a sort of rebirth of their marriage, as illustrated by Katherine's story. They may remodel their practice of religion, make a commitment to volunteering, rekindle old friendships, catch a travel bug, or delve into a hobby, such as painting or writing. Or one parent may become the "child" of the other, the focus of that parent's nurturing and devotion, which can be damaging to the equilibrium of the couple. In this latter case, nurturing parents may have gotten into the habit of thinking that being needed is what makes their lives meaningful, what makes them feel fulfilled, what makes them who they are . . . moms or dads. However, this belief in the "need to be needed" is not really a need at all; it is only a *desire* to be needed. When thought of as a desire, not a necessity, being needed becomes less a demand in a parent's life. "I like for my children to want my help, but I can stand it when they don't" is a much healthier way of viewing the changing parent-child relationship than thinking, "I need for my children to need me. I'm nobody if they don't."

As young adults gain independence and self-sufficiency, parents who are able to adopt this more rational view about "needing to be needed" are able to devote their attention to reconstructing their own lives without the foundation of their identity crumbling and threatening the collapse of their world. The irony is that parents have often wished to be free from being needed by their children; now that they are being forced to redefine their identity in this way, they are at a loss as to how to define themselves. After all, it makes sense; they've spent the last eighteen or so years with being needed as the cornerstone of who they were.

For many of the Family Remodelers we met who have nurturing personalities, their desire to be caretakers for others was fulfilled by getting a puppy, planting a garden, volunteering in a geriatric center, baby-sitting, or even taking on a new career. Linda, whose twenty-five-year-old daughter, Jodi, was now living in a distant city, decided to go back to graduate school to become a social worker. "I just love helping people, and I can't think of a better way to spend my time. My husband is all for it because I've been hovering over him since Jodi left for college," she informed us.

REWRITING THE RULES

Every beginning is a consequence—every beginning ends something.—PAUL VALÉRY

From Sponge through Volcano Dweller, everyone knew his or her rightful place in the family: who made the rules, who planned the adventures, who was in charge of damage control. But now that their children are in orbit around the home planet and parents have become Family Remodelers, all bets are off. For the first time, the relationship between parents and children doesn't flow along the conveyer belt of childhood, doesn't follow a set of grades that a school district dictates, a set of developmental milestones, or a set of laws that are enforceable. Whether relationships between parents and children exist at all is entirely a matter of choice (unless there are financial ties) predicated on the emotional, psychological, intellectual, and spiritual connection that exists between both parents and children, a connection that is rooted in the Sponge season of parenthood. The now independent, but frequently intersecting, circular orbits of parents and their adult children need to give each other the space to "do their own thing."

"My girls are so happy," remarked Wanetta, a mother of nineteen- and twenty-one-year-old daughters. "It's amazing to hear about their adventures backpacking in the Grand Canyon and planning a semester in Spain. It makes you feel so good that they have good friends and are able to do such interesting things with them on their own. Sure, they come home for vacations from school. But then they're off again, doing their own thing."

E VERY DAY PARENTS feel the impact of the relative success or failure of their children's experiments in using the tools of self-sufficiency, responsibility, and independence that they demanded their parents give them over the past two decades. How adept they are at using these tools to navigate treacherous relationships and cope with school and job demands, for example, dictates the time parents can spend on their central task of being a Family Remodeler.

Parents may find this season of parenthood more chaotic than they had hoped as their adult children bounce back and forth between their parents' nest and their own. Some just need respite care between college semesters or jobs. Others can't take the cramped lifestyle in their Spartan dorm rooms compared with life in their mom and dad's suburban palace, complete with automatic washer and dryer and built-in laundress. Still others are unable to function without their parents' face-to-face, emotional, intellectual, and spiritual support.

These so-called boomerang children, who decide to drop out of college, quit or lose their jobs, or end their marriages, occupy that "spare" bedroom and fill the nest once again with adult birds, sending their parents into a frazzled frenzy of remodeling and creating more questions than there are ready answers: What do we do with our daughter now that we've just made her bedroom the home office? How does our son's return affect our vacation plans? How do we relate to our daughter—as a child or an adult—when she's showing us that she's not the responsible, self-sufficient, independent young chick we thought had flown the coop?

As their safety nets, parents are usually best qualified to ascertain the condition of their fledglings' wings: Are they returning to their former state as dependent children or simply wanting a place to land for a while to shelter them from stormy weather? Their children's needs dictate whether parents can return to being a Family Remodeler while their children rest and refuel.

It's important for parents to keep in mind that their adult children are still adults in the making, just as their infants were children in the making in the first stage of childhood. No one can predict just how bumpy adult children's first flight will be: what the winds of change will do to their lives. It is a leap of faith for both children and adults; this season of parenthood demands the very same flexibility and common sense from parents that they have been using to cope with the effects of their offspring's growth and development in their lives since the Sponge season. The ultimate goal of Family Remodelers—refurbishing the launch pad after sending their big rockets on their test flight of self-sufficiency, responsibility, and independence—can be reached when both adult children and their parents can demonstrate mutual understanding of their respective tasks.

BLENDED FAMILY REMODELING: HER VICTORIAN, HIS RANCH

By the time they reach the Family Remodeler season, parents' marriages have often disintegrated under the assault of debris from their erupted volcanoes. They may have remarried, only to find that they now have stepchildren who are navigating through their first phase of adulthood as well. One important distinction between biological and stepparent wars in the first circle of parenthood, parenting children, and the second circle of parenthood, parenting adults, is that a cease-fire is declared in custody battles when children reach eighteen years of age. The impact of children's growth and development peppers blended families' lives in the same way it flavors the lives of biological families because the same conflicts arise. In the Family Remodeling season, stepparents and biological parents must adjust to the empty nest; being needed as their young adults' safety nets, not caregivers; and finally burying the hatchet of control they've been trying to use for decades to shape their children.

However, when a child's biological parent and stepparent compete—"Why are you paying for your daughter's college when you wouldn't help pay for mine?"—over what's being given to one parent's biological child and not the other, remarriages can be put on shaky ground. To create a climate of understanding and empathy and strengthen remarriages in the Family Remodeler season, couples need to communicate openly about how their respective children have impacted their lives throughout parent-

hood: How did they cope with their shifting identity in the Sponge season?
What kind of performance reviews did they give themselves as Family
Managers? What effect did the separation blues have on them in the Travel
Agent season? With this knowledge, spouses have a context against which
they can compare their parenthood histories. What's essential is not necessarily to reconcile differing impacts and parenting styles, but to appreciate
two unique perspectives. The goal is to undertake team remodeling, so that
rather than grafting one structure onto another, the couple actually works
together to build a third house that blends both perspectives.

SPECIAL-NEEDS REMODELING

When children have special needs and their parents can't reach the end of
the Family Remodeler season—financial independence from each other—
their lives revolve more tightly around the capabilities of their children.
The conflict precipitated by an empty nest may never arise for these parents if their child isn't capable of living on his own and no funds are available for hiring a caregiver or placing him in an assisted living situation. If
either is in place, however, empty nest conflicts are sure to complicate
their lives.

Marianne was a mother who had been a Volcano Dweller for fifteen
years, she told us, until she finally convinced herself that her child, Mae,
needed her own space, as did she and her husband, Aiden. In sizing up
the situation, they came to grips with their reality that Mae would never be
able to make the decision to move out, to comb the streets and find a job,
or to qualify for entrance into college owing to her mental and physical
disabilities. Therefore, for both generations to navigate through the Family Remodeler stage, Marianne needed to make the arrangements for Mae
to live in a group home, with the continuous financial support of her
parents. Marianne and Aiden would be stuck in the Family Remodeler
season for the rest of their lives, because Mae would never be able to
move far forward in her development, a bittersweet fact of life for them to
swallow.

Just as bittersweet, however, was their adjustment to their empty nest
after Mae moved to the group home, the moment Marianne and Aiden had
been waiting twenty-seven years to reach. They had to keep telling themselves that their decision to help Mae to forge her own circle of friends, albeit one they would have to subsidize for the rest of her life, was the
healthiest for everyone. Marianne and Aiden found that not being needed,

as they had been since Mae's birth, was a relief, mentally and physically; but they still worried about how Mae was doing in her new environment, just as parents of all adult children do when their offspring are no longer under their wing. Although they may be gone physically, all adult children—special needs or not—are *never* absent from their parents' lives emotionally and spiritually.

Carol's Swan Song: Long-Distance Love

Consider the case of Carol, a sensitive, forty-eight-year-old single mother who had recently become a divorced "empty nester." Her voice cracked as she described the intense emotional experience of imagining that her twenty-three-year-old daughter, Sarah, and her twenty-one-year-old stepson, Drew, were still upstairs in their bedrooms, either on the phone or comparing notes on friends or high school teachers.

"I should still be downstairs doing their laundry and making them their favorite spaghetti casserole," she insisted. "It seemed as if they grew from kindergartners to college students in the blink of an eye."

Where did the time go? she asked herself pensively whenever anyone mentioned her children. Carol and her ex, Jim, had married when both of their children were just preschoolers. She was virtually the only mother Drew had ever known. His biological mother had died following complications of childbirth just six months after he was born.

After being so close to her children all of their lives, she was now trying to figure out how to be a long-distance mother. Although she and her children e-mailed each other almost every day, the only time she ever felt close to them was when she organized the old family photo albums. That task had become a nightly respite because poring over the children's smiling faces brought back so many happy memories.

She had hoped that she and Jim, who had walked out on her just eight months earlier when she uncovered his adulterous affair, would be sharing this journey back in time together. It was funny that she could recall few meaningful traditions or even passionate moments that she and Jim had created in their marriage; the lack of photos of the two of them reflected that emptiness.

To make matters more difficult at this lonely time in Carol's life, Sarah had refused to move back home to be with her during the divorce, the most devastating time in her mother's life, as Carol put it.

"How can I convince her to go to our local community college instead of the big university five hundred miles away from home?" she pleaded.

Deep down inside, Carol confessed to us, Sarah was right to stay where she was. She now had a whole world of her own at school and needed to follow her own dream. But she was never very good at handling change, particularly when it came to the children, Carol admitted. She had always told her best friend, Sonja, that she wanted to freeze the kids at the age they were, whatever that age was. She felt so helpless and thought there was no hope that she could ever learn a whole new set of skills to handle the children's problems as they grew.

Her own feelings of inadequacy as a parent stemmed from her childhood sense of never measuring up. Her parents had been overachievers, but Carol had been fairly average: getting B's and C's in school; not participating in any sports or school activities. She hadn't wanted to go to college because she wasn't a good student and hated school so much.

She saw her stepson, Drew, following in her footsteps; he also hadn't been a very good student and had recently informed her that he was thinking about dropping out of college but didn't ask her what she thought about this idea. She had held her tongue when tempted to tell him what a big mistake she thought that would be, reminded of her own rejection of her mother's warning about the dangers of choosing not to go to college in order to marry Jim. She wanted Drew to learn to make his own decisions; but the fact that he didn't ask for her input made her cringe every time the phone rang. She feared that it would be Drew and she would feel compelled to try to talk him out of his dumb decision. She wasn't sure she could sound convincing.

While worrying about Sarah's and Drew's impulsive decisions was a full-time job for Carol, a new crisis complicated her life even further. Her mother, Esther, was diagnosed with severe depression after overdosing on one of her medications. Carol knew that her mother was upset about the loss of her husband, Ward, Carol's father, but she had no idea how much her mother had needed to lean on her. After the overdose, Esther told her daughter that she was the only one who could understand how devastated she was over losing Ward because Carol had also just been through the loss of her husband.

Carol was overwhelmed by these changes in her relationships with her mother and children. It was ironic that her mother now needed her just as she was losing her own connection with Drew and Sarah. The realization

*that her mother related to her so well and that her life was becoming so par-
allel with her mother's made Carol feel ancient. Just being a mother and
stepmother of two "twenty-somethings" made her feel older than she had
ever felt before. But she refused to buy into the fact that she was so old that
she and her mother were now on the same wavelength. Somehow that
seemed to defy the laws of nature. She was supposed to be the child and her
mother was supposed to be the mother, not the other way around.*

Carol now needed to reinvent herself as a parent of new adults during this
new season of parenthood using two tools from the past—the ability to adjust to change and the ability to be a self-controlled adult. Although she
didn't initially realize it, Carol wanted Sarah to come back home so she
could take care of her and give her the love that she had never gotten from
her husband. Carol felt rejected by her daughter's refusal to do so, but we
suggested she needed to congratulate herself; Sarah had gained wings just
when she was developmentally charted to do so. In fact, it is through the
model of her daughter that Carol was able to remodel her own life.

We helped Carol understand Sarah's need to establish a boundary between her mother and herself in order to form her own independent identity, her sense of separateness. As Sarah develops her self-knowledge, her
consistent sense of self, she opens the door to establishing intimate relationships with others while maintaining her own sense of personal integrity. Children must physically and psychologically leave their parents
to accomplish this task and to be able to return home as adults in their
own right.

We advised Carol to focus on volunteering, creating new friendships or
strengthening tried-and-true ones, and reflecting on what she wanted her
life to look like after remodeling, particularly as she coped with the grief of
"losing" both her children and her husband simultaneously. We helped
her see that she would go through the stages of grief that are well docu-
mented: denial ("I will be okay if I just go back to school"); anger (which
she was experiencing toward her daughter for leaving her and toward her
son for not asking her opinion); bargaining ("maybe if I don't say anything,
Drew will stay in school and not make the stupid mistake I did of rebelling
against my mother"); depression ("I'm helpless and hopeless in dealing
with change"); and, finally, acceptance.

Carol was the one who could determine the amount of time she spent
getting upset about Drew, Sarah, Jim, and her mother. Over time, she felt a

new sense of self-confidence and hope through practicing a self-controlled reaction to the changes in all those relationships.

By giving up feeling sorry for herself and wishing that her situation were different, Carol realized that she could still change, even at what she had thought of as her "tender age." It gave her a feeling of being born again, of shedding the skin of self-doubt that had haunted her since she was a child. In fact, she could help teach her mother ways to become more self-sufficient, just as her daughter was helping her do so by her example.

We find it exciting and profound, as did most parents we interviewed, that both generations are going through the same process—remodeling the family—at the same time. As adults try to mentor and consult based on their own journey through young adulthood, they discover that their off-spring now open up new vistas of exploration: education, travel, religion, politics, business, entertainment, and community service, as they fashion their own identities, separate and distinct from their parents.

Jack in the Box: The Boomerang Child

What's Jack doing back from school? That's what everyone in one of our Circles groups was asking Luke about his eighteen-year-old son, Jack. We found out why in short order. His son had happily gone off to his first year in college in another state, the Ivy League school he had dreamed of attending since he was in middle school. He was ecstatic to have even been accepted at such a prestigious university after applying to ten other schools in order to "have backup options," as Luke called them, in case his dream didn't come true.

But Jack's tearful calls throughout the semester climaxed in his pleading with Luke and his wife, Diane, to drive to school at winter break to get all of his stuff. He was so homesick that he couldn't eat, sleep, or go to class. He just wanted to be home, he told his parents . . . and couldn't bear to go back in January!

Thirty-six hours later their boy was back home, out on the couch. They decided not to fight his flight from school. Paying for college was an expensive proposition, Luke told us. If they didn't have to write tuition checks, it was fine with them, he said. But something else was more upsetting to Luke. He confessed to the group a surprising consequence of his son's decision: He felt like a failure, felt responsible for his son not making it through his fresh-man year. Jack's dropping out made Luke feel as though he hadn't prepared him for what college would be like, how to adjust to changes and cope with homesickness.

Father and son had spent hours each day since Jack was a sophomore in high school poring over catalogs of colleges near and far, so he would have an ample list of choices. But finding the perfect match was only half of what became a full-time job for Luke. The application process had made him crazy. Writing essays, creating a résumé—he knew that his son couldn't do these steps alone. So Luke had devoted countless hours to it himself.

In fact, Luke was so caught up in his son's college adventures, before and after he left, that he bypassed any symptoms of dreading or experiencing the empty nest syndrome. Instead he felt the vicarious thrills of college life as he was transported back to his own college days through helping to plan his son's course schedule and receiving fact-filled e-mails and phone reports about the dorm food, fraternity pledging, and pickup football games.

Although he was worried about Jack's complaints about being so miserable at school, Luke remembered that he had also needed time to adjust to being independent. The most miraculous part of his empty nest was that Luke was independent again: he could spend a whole day with Diane at work in the family business and actually get a lot done because he wasn't distracted by needing to pick up Jack, be home at night to supervise a group of teenage kids, or get up at the crack of dawn to drive to swim practice.

When Jack left, Luke literally became obsessed with work, sometimes spending sixteen-hour days at his business. Without the college search process to occupy his evenings, he would meet Diane for dinner at some of their favorite little places, nothing fancy, and they would both go back to work until about ten. Work became the surrogate child who "needed" both of them.

The idea of having to change their agenda back to supervising or at least being sensitive to the comings and goings of their son was not on this couple's radar screen. They had successfully adapted to this new season of parenthood, feeling a sense of accomplishment that they had done a good job raising a good son who was on the road that they had always hoped he would travel.

Luke admitted that he certainly had taken a few detours when he was his son's age, but for different reasons. His own father had lost his job the year before Luke had graduated from high school. That had put such a financial strain on the family that they couldn't afford to send him to more than one

*year of school at the local state university. After working and saving for col-
lege, Luke had put himself through school; these memories were bittersweet
for his parents, who apologized many years later for not being there when
Luke needed them.*

*Now, when Jack was handed a college education on a silver platter and
didn't take it, Luke feared that his son would never make anything of himself. Jack not only didn't want to go back to school; he was now interested
only in getting a job at the local burger joint in their small town. Luke worried about what kind of future he would have.*

*"I didn't want to lecture him about all of this because I wanted to be a
friend, not his old, critical parent now. But isn't it still my responsibility to
be his parent, even though my son is nearly twenty years old?" he asked us.
"After all, I'm nearly fifty and should know what's best for him."*

*It was clear that the family had worked so hard at making choices for
Jack that he hadn't learned to make choices on his own. Now it was all in
vain, Luke told us.*

The empty nest syndrome affects parents of new adults in two distinct
ways, according to our interviewees. Some adults go into a deep depression, mourning the loss of what used to be. Others, like Luke, seem to have
been dreaming of this moment when their children would make their way
into the big world and easily adjust to creating a new schedule of work and
leisure time. It is these parents who reach this season with a remarkable
sense of relief over the fact that their responsibility for helping their child
"grow up" seems to be over. Because they perceive that their job of raising
their child is now finished, they find a new kind of energy for rebuilding
their lives—family, work, marriages, friendships—but not for parenthood.

As Luke and Diane learned, parenthood simply changes but never
ends. Luke was having trouble understanding Jack's attitude; he could relate only to how hard he had worked thirty years ago to get to go to college.
As we talked with him about accepting his son's decision, Luke revealed
that his parents had basically left him alone when he was Jack's age. His
mom and dad were so consumed with the financial strain of the family that
they generally ignored him because they were working so many long hours.

We explained that Jack clearly needed his parents to help him with his
transition to adulthood; he needed them to be his mentors and consultants.
We advised Luke and Diane to reframe Jack's decision as one of hope, not
a signal of failure. Jack's relationship with his parents was solid enough

that he felt as if he could come home and rediscover the foundation he needed to gain emotional strength before striking out on his own again. Although his parents had both passed away, Luke admitted that he knew how proud his mom and dad would be if they knew that their only grandson wasn't wasting his college education but was waiting until he could appreciate it.

Boomerang children are those who have tried to fly but have found that they aren't yet strong enough for sustained flight into their own adult world. Coming back to the nest to rest and gain strength may be necessary before launching off on the long flight of independence. For those parents whose children quit college or decide not to go to college at all, the transition to parenting independent adults may take longer to complete than they had originally thought, as in Jack's case. As adult children work at the relatively low wages generally afforded to those who don't graduate from college, they find that independent living often remains an elusive goal. The expense of having their own apartment while paying for transportation, food, and utilities often forces them to remain at home with parents and with parental rules, thus keeping parents from their goal of remodeling their lives.

The inability of adult children who live at home to become independent creates conflict with their parents who are unable to make the transition to their own rebirth into independence and into the second circle of parenthood. Living at home through the financial support of parents only prolongs the adolescent period for young adults and perpetuates all of the problems inherent in that volcanic time of life. But if everyone is happy living together, and independence is neither sought after nor encouraged, parents may remain Volcano Dwellers indefinitely.

So when do boomerang children become toxic to themselves and to their parents? When do parents need to force their children out of the nest? There aren't pat answers to these questions, for they depend on the length of time adult children want to live with their parents and the length of time and tolerance both parents and their adult children have for living together. In addition, each generation's attitude about independence determines when a boomerang child is toxic to himself or his parents and when parents need to force their child out of the nest. Ultimately, unless they live separately, neither generation will become independent from the other, and the psychological growth of both will be stunted.

In our culture, parents have generally come to believe that they have failed if their children don't leave the nest and that their children have failed as adults for not being able to do so. But this season of parenthood proves how winding the road to independence, self-sufficiency, and responsibility still is for young adults. Family Remodelers are, more often than not, inevitably forced by their adult children to take their own sweet time, some more years than others, to reorganize their lives without their adult children near them on a day-to-day basis.

Fran's Folly: Wedding Jitters

"My husband, Jeff, and I eloped," Fran told us at our workshop on transitions for parents of high school graduates. "It's ridiculous to spend that kind of money on a silly wedding when a justice of the peace can give you the same outcome," this fifty-three-year-old dental hygienist explained.

We learned that regardless of what she thought about the frivolity of an expensive wedding, if that was what her oldest daughter, twenty-three-year-old Marli, wanted, that's what she would get. Fran never wanted Marli to say that her parents didn't care or they were denying her fiancé, Clayton, and herself what all her friends had—a fairy-tale whirlwind of showers and lace and pearls. Deep down inside, Fran admitted being thrilled and excited that the romantic Clayton and her old-fashioned daughter were finally giving her the opportunity to have the wedding she never had.

When Clayton asked Jeff and Fran if he could marry their daughter, Fran told us that she almost melted. Jeff had never asked her parents that time-honored question. The tears that she and Jeff shed that night were still confusing to Fran. She and Jeff had wondered: Were they crying because they were really "losing" their daughter now? Or were they so upset because Marli and Clayton were going to have the romantic wedding that they had ended up denying themselves by being so practical thirty years earlier when they were first in love?

We reassured her, as did the rest of the group, that all of these reasons for their tears were valid and normal, although upsetting. Fran knew that she would have to come to terms with these issues. She found herself arguing with Marli over every little thing about the wedding . . . which she admitted wasn't surprising, given what a perfectionist she was. She said that if she and Jeff were going to spend this ridiculous amount of money on it, they should be allowed to make some decisions!

In our meeting with Fran after the workshop, we explained the benefits of helping plan her oldest daughter's wedding with no strings attached, no guilt-inducing techniques used to stifle a sense of partnership and encourage subservience on her daughter's part. By dismissing a big wedding as "frivolous," then taking over the planning so that it will be "perfect," Fran was satisfying her need to remain in control of her daughter's life and extend her dependency on her "perfect" mother.

By complaining about the cost, Fran bound her daughter to her through guilt with a "you'll owe me forever" attitude. We helped her understand this consequence of continuing to manipulate the family dynamics by making sure that Marli knew how much her mother was sacrificing for her—not a desirable start into healthy independent living for both generations.

Fran prided herself on the fact that she never really experienced an "empty" nest—her kids were always calling from college to cry about not feeling well, having too much homework, getting into fights with roommates, or not having anything to wear. The Family Remodeler season of parenthood in which parents transition from parenting children to parenting adults was a nonissue for her because she hadn't even tried to empower her children to become self-sufficient, responsible, or independent. To do so would mean that Fran would have had to change and give up her false sense of control of her family.

The unhealthy dependency of her adult children developed because Fran never moved through the Travel Agent and Volcano Dweller seasons; she was firmly rooted as the Family Manager, with no motivation to change. When she described her own mother, we could see that Fran had gotten little attention as a child. As one of seven brothers and sisters, she had navigated on her own most of her early childhood years, with no one really paying much attention to her unless she behaved outrageously, which, she said, she tried to do whenever possible.

As a mother herself now, she wanted her children to have all of the attention, approval, and problem-solving support that she never got but always craved. Her elopement fit her personality—take charge of her world and do what she thought was best! We helped her understand that creating a close adult-adult relationship of mutual respect, love, and trust would take hard work on her part as she tried to move from Family Manager directly to Family Remodeler.

F OR PARENTS WITH controlling personalities, such as Fran, relating
to their children as independent, self-sufficient adults is as painful as
getting a tooth pulled without anesthetic. They will avoid doing so at all
costs because it makes them too anxious to face the unknown. They don't
know how it will affect them emotionally, whether things will work out perfectly if they don't exercise the numbing power of control, and they are un-
certain whether they will be able to handle the pain brought on by adult
children who are making decisions that might end up to be "wrong" or
bring them suffering. Treating their offspring as helpless children enables
them to avoid facing the unpredictable crises of their children's adulthood;
therefore they try to push their control buttons whenever possible.

Planning a wedding is an event made in heaven or hell for controlling
parents, depending on memories of their own wedding, which are inevitably dredged up when adult children spring the news of impending
nuptials on their parents. Wedding disasters come back to haunt prospec-
tive mothers and fathers of the bride or groom, or they can be made all
weepy and nostalgic over their dreams of repeating their "perfect wedding." The extent to which parents exercise control over their children's
wedding plans is determined by their pennies and personalities, as well as
by their personal histories. If parents want and can afford to produce an
extravaganza, for example, and if their adult children agree, then the experience can be beautiful and memorable for all, matching the kind of wedding they had or wished they'd had, as in Fran's case.

Conflict arises when parents and their adult children have different attitudes about what constitutes a "perfect" wedding. Controlling parents
are usually perfectionists who believe that the only way their world can be
perfect is to maintain control over every aspect of it. In Fran's case, the absence of her "perfect" wedding was a made-to-order setup for her to go
overboard in creating a wedding extravaganza as she sought to undo her
past through her daughter.

B EING "RIGHT" and doing the "right thing" by their children puts
pressure on perfectionist parents to control their offspring, lest the
kids make mistakes that make them appear to be bad parents. Now their
absence of physical proximity to their adult children takes away any semblance of being able to control their world and thereby make their world
perfect for their children. That break may be what many perfectionist par-

ents need to finally let go of thinking that their children need to be perfect in order for them to be acceptable in their own eyes and in the eyes of others, a harmful belief that may have haunted them since their Sponge days.

Fran's definition of being a "good mother" was mired in her perfectionism and need for control; she still saw her daughter as her "little girl" who couldn't possibly plan her wedding without her mother's direction. If she gave up controlling the details of her daughter's wedding, she would have to admit that her daughter was no longer a "little girl" and could function independently without Fran. She admitted that she feared the wedding would be just the tip of the iceberg. Once Marli proved to herself that she could manage just fine without being under her mother's thumb, Fran knew she would have to change and accept that her daughter was now an adult.

Helping Fran make this transition from being a parent of a child to a parent of an adult would not only help her and Marli cooperate on the wedding plans, but would also serve to put their relationship on a healthier course. But changing her attitude and behavior wouldn't happen overnight and wouldn't be easy. Reconstruction is messy. But when the project is finished, Family Remodelers are glad they were able to persevere.

Glenna's Midlife Crisis: Agendas in Conflict

"My marriage is in big trouble," Glenna told one of our Circles groups. "My husband, Allan, wants to have an affair. I know it. He's always complaining about how we don't have anything to talk about except the kids, our twenty-two-year-old daughter, Jill, and our twenty-four-year-old son, Clint. He acts almost jealous that Jill has a steady boyfriend and talks so much about how in love they are. I see him flirting with every young waitress. He and I met when I was a waitress in college. Now, after twenty-five years of marriage, our flirting is a thing of the past. I just feel grateful that we're still together. Now that we're both forty-seven years old, we have so much history with each other."

She continued: "I was looking forward to these years with the kids out of the house for us to do some major redecorating and taking up bicycling again as we had in college. It's as if Allan and I have a totally different agenda. I'm looking to him to build our new life together; he's looking for ways to outdo his kids and show them that he's not old.

"What does he have to prove? And to whom?" Glenna asked all of us. "He told me that everything, the whole world, is at our kids' fingertips. He

sees them getting better educations than he did, which he seems to resent."
Allan was always slow in school because of a bout with polio that con-
tributed to a sickly childhood.

Glenna told us that she had the exact opposite viewpoint. She had grown
up in a single-parent household, raised by her father after her mother left
the family to "find herself" when Glenna was about eleven. Her dad, a psy-
chologist, was always there for her and her sisters. He pushed them to do
well in school and to have a kind word to say about everyone.

Though Allan had always provided well for his family, Glenna's dad
had been worried about his daughter's future with Allan. He had encour-
aged her to keep her job as a nurse throughout her kids' younger years. Her
nursing skills had come in handy with Jill, who had severe asthma and res-
piratory problems. Like her father, she had been there for Jill and Clint.
Now, she said, wasn't it her turn to get some attention?

Glenna was so proud of her children's accomplishments; going to Prince-
ton and Yale on full scholarships was nothing that she could ever have
imagined in her wildest dreams. But neither were her husband's roving eyes.
Just when their lives could get so good, he was turning hers into her worst
nightmare.

The infamous midlife crisis that is often first experienced by a Volcano
Dweller takes on a different dimension as the children leave the nest and
the "hard work" at home *seems* to come to a close. We asked parents in our
Circles groups to describe the triggers of their midlife crises during this
season of parenthood. Some parents told us that theirs began when they
kept saying to themselves, "I can't possibly be old enough to have a child
in college," as they helped their son or daughter set up a dorm room or
apartment. The milestone that their child had reached reminded them that
their lives were more than half gone. Panic set in, parents told us, and they
admitted demonstrating their joie de vivre by wearing T-shirts that said
motivating phrases, such as "Life is short . . . eat the dessert first!"; buying
Cosmopolitan to read up on how to play flirtatious games with the opposite
sex; and dreaming of sailing expeditions with the well-muscled beach bum
across the street.

In addition, they tried to fill the void in their lives created by their children's flight from the nest, realizing that they no longer had to appear responsible in front of the kids. They fantasized that they could join a nudist
colony, dye their hair, and buy a little sports car without having to hear

their children moan and groan about how embarrassing their parents were. This realization also freed them from having to be on their "best behavior," to be the responsible adult role model that they had to sweat and strain for eighteen or so years to maintain for their children's sakes.

Frayed marriages had permission to disintegrate now that the children were adults and were no longer on the premises to voice their objection to their parents' decision. Couples may have told themselves that they would stay together "until the kids left"; now they had their chance to bail out of what they considered to be a bad partnership. They had such a long period of close-out—since they first decided that their partner wasn't the kind of person they thought they were marrying—that mending the fabric of their marital lives seemed more costly than throwing it away. Affairs often popped up during this time, parents revealed, as they looked to find ways to regain happiness in their otherwise drab lives. Now some of those occasional liaisons became committed relationships without the excuse of "waiting for the kids to grow up" to keep them low-key and secret.

Reestablishing a marital relationship was awkward for couples when fathers had been orbiting the nest while mothers and the children were building a relationship without their spouses. When the young birds left the nest, these mothers and fathers found it difficult to find mutual interests as they once again found themselves alone together. Such was the case with Allan and Glenna.

Allan felt threatened by those who had achieved more than he had, in his estimation. His early years had been so rife with put-downs and insults from his own authoritarian father that he was still yearning to heal those old wounds. If he indeed was looking around for a new love interest, we told Glenna, Allan was doing so to re-create a youth in which he could be deemed acceptable, to get a second chance. However, feeling good because he could capture someone else's love would give him only a temporary boost and would create more problems, as Glenna could already see.

Glenna felt as if she were experiencing déjà vu. Here was her husband trying to find himself, just as her mother had. She knew how much it had devastated her family when her mother had deserted them. Even though they were adults, she knew that her children would be horrified if they discovered that their father was even thinking about deserting his family.

We encouraged the couple to devote thirty minutes a day for "dream time," time in which they couldn't do anything but plan for their future together. Glenna finally could tell Allan her ideas for bicycling trips, which came as a surprise to him. Allan's dreams for the future were to travel and see as much of the country as he could, something they hadn't been able to do because of their children's sports schedules. As they continued to talk, it became more obvious to them that their dreams could be fulfilled together through biking excursions with the local biking club. They ended up buying a bicycle built for two, which in a silly way helped Glenna feel that Allan was committed to the marriage. Allan also hadn't understood how much Glenna needed him; their new athletic play toy was a perfect metaphor for the new ride that Glenna and, eventually, Allan decided to take.

The more time Allan and Glenna spent together, the more he recalled why he had fallen madly in love with her in the first place. "Oh, I remember you!" Allan found himself exclaiming as they started to laugh about their aching knees after a bike trip they had just taken and to reminisce about their long bike rides off campus when they were in college together. "We could ride for hours and not even notice it, we were so much in love then," Glenna recalled.

Allan's knees also showed him that trying to outdo his children might not be such a good idea after all. As he felt better about his life with Glenna, he found it easier to focus on the positive aspects of his marriage. Instead of feeling the need to compete with his daughter's love life, he became aware of the satisfaction he found in the mature love that he and Glenna were recapturing. We advised him to reframe his identity as a parent: rather than thinking that his love life was over just because his daughter had one, he could be happy for the joy and security her relationship was bringing to her life, just as it had for him and Glenna when they were her age and was beginning to do again.

Nick and Lucy's Traveling Circus: Pulling up Roots

"When Nick suggested moving to California, I thought he was nuts," Lucy told our Circles group. "And the reason he wanted to move? Our three children, twenty-four, twenty-six, and twenty-eight, were in graduate school there. At the age of sixty, he said that he just wanted to start a new life with me in another new place while we were both healthy and be near the children at the same time."

When their children were preschoolers, Lucy and Nick had lived in Saudi

Arabia while Nick was working for an American oil company. They never planned to live there for more than five years, but the opportunities for see-ing the world appealed to their adventurous natures, so they bounced around from country to country until all three girls were in high school. Then they moved back to America and settled near family in the Midwest. Now Nick and Lucy were lost without the kids nearby and without the ad-venture that had fueled their lives together.

"Our family was like a traveling act for nearly a dozen years," Nick said.

Lucy agreed. They were fortunate to be able to afford the luxuries of the finest hotel suites and summer homes in Geneva, Paris, and London while Nick did his work. Although Nick and Lucy had an opportunity to move back to Europe after the kids had all graduated from high school, they had both decided not to do it. They had never been so far away from their chil-dren; Lucy never slept well anymore because she worried so much about them as it was. They knew that they would go nuts if they were any farther apart.

Lucy liked being near her own parents, however, and Nick's parents lived only a few miles away. How much longer would they have together before some "old-age trouble," as her mother-in-law called it, struck one of them? Lucy was used to making friends in new places but thought it was weird to be "following the kids" to California. What if one of the kids met someone at college and moved to the East Coast?

Lucy was willing to admit that the days of their family being a tight, controllable unit of four were long gone; she told Nick that he could sleep at night only because he was in total denial! He was pretending that they were still the same traveling show, when actually, Lucy knew the act had now broken up.

The time when children move out and away has a profound effect on their parents. In this case, Nick came up with the solution to soothe the psycho-logical and emotional pain of his empty nest syndrome, as well as the pain of not feeling needed: Follow the children!

Many parents we interviewed had the same dream as Nick; they just never followed through to make it a reality. Instead they suffered their loneliness in silence, waiting for the phone to ring, planning their week so they could be home at the "best" time for their children to call, and send-ing their children e-mail messages and care packages each week.

Lucy began to be physically ill—developing insomnia, stomachaches, and headaches—worrying about all aspects of their children's lives. She felt the loss of her daughters' presence as if there had been a death in the family, even after seven years. She was in fact grieving a kind of death—the death of the family as it had been.

In an odd way, Lucy was farther along the road to successful family remodeling than Nick. Lucy's task is to stop mourning the past and accept that both parents and their adult children must test the separation waters in new ways. It takes time for parents to adjust to living in an empty nest while their adult children practice using the tools of independence, self-reliance, and responsibility. Nick, however, is still in denial, trying to prolong life as a Volcano Dweller by moving closer to his kids. He needs to accept the reality of an empty nest that would stay empty from this time forward.

Who Rules the Roost: New Bylaws for the Empty Nest

"Am I still the parent, or did I get fired?" Ellen, a fifty-three-year-old mother, joked at our parenting workshop in her office building. "My nineteen-year-old daughter, Jan, just came home from her freshman year at college. She thinks that she can still stay out all night if she wants to. My first reaction is to tell her that she can't, nor can she have boys in her bedroom or alcohol in the house or take over the bathroom. When she asked me what I thought she'd been doing in her dorm suite for the past nine months, I just died!

"I've lost touch with who she is. I thought that I taught her to follow my rules and to have decent values. It's like the roles are all confused. I feel like I'm a little kid and Jan's the adult, running around town, enjoying life to the fullest. Am I living in another time? I remember when I was nineteen, colleges didn't allow boys on the girls' floors, nice girls didn't drink until it was legal, you were required to clean up your room, and universities had strict curfews."

We shared with Ellen this thought: Just as Jan had demanded her new legs as a toddler, so had she found freedom while living away from home that she was raring to keep.

"Absolutely!" Ellen agreed with us. "But how do I get her to follow my rules in my home when it's hers, too? Anyway, she is an adult, as my husband says. She can legally do anything she wants—except drink alcohol. I

need her to want to come home, to still feel like this is her home. She's my only baby . . . and I cannot bear to lose her."

Ellen also couldn't bear to lose her own new sense of freedom in her re-modeled empty nest. For example, even though Jan couldn't afford to buy a car, she was continuously borrowing hers now that she was home for sum-mer vacation from school. That left Ellen stranded—and resentful.

It was funny, Ellen told us. Her daughter's habit of borrowing her car, using her makeup, taking her hairbrush, or leaving a mess in the kitchen hadn't bothered her when Jan was living at home. But since Jan had gone away, she felt a new sense of independence: the kitchen and bathroom had been almost spotless, she knew where to find her things, and she could go wherever she wanted to go whenever she felt like it. Ellen discovered that was just the way she liked to live.

Life in an empty nest was surprisingly calm and refreshingly quiet. She remembered that her mother had said the same thing about her own journey through the empty nest stage. She had never told her mother about her ad-ventures in college; her mother had said that she didn't want to know.

It was so weird, Ellen admitted. She had counted the days until Jan was coming home, missing her so badly all year long. She was realizing, how-ever, that she had remodeled her life since Jan was "launched" and the old family habits didn't fit anymore in the new decor.

As far as Ellen was concerned, when Jan came home from college, life would just revert to normal—defined as "the way it had been before Jan left for school." It would be the same as when Jan took a six-week trip with Ellen's in-laws one summer during high school or when she went to camp the summer after eighth grade. Time may have passed, but Ellen thought that she and Jan would still be the same mother and daughter they were when Jan left.

As we talked with Ellen, though, she began to understand that she and Jan *had* changed: Jan had started a new chapter in her life, and so had she. Seeking order was a part of the remodeling of her new life, just as making independent decisions was a new part of her daughter's. Both were laying the groundwork for the beginning of a new circle, a new generation of adults. Ellen had adjusted to not having her daughter around while she rebuilt her life and appreciated the quiet and the time in which to do so. But she hadn't appreciated what her remodeling project would do to their relationship.

Ellen had to remember that although her daughter was an adult, she still needed practice in being responsible, as evidenced by her behavior at home. Ellen also needed to help Jan understand how she had changed after Jan had left and to show her the newly "remodeled" family rules and expectations. On the other hand, Ellen needed to respect Jan's budding sense of independence as she helped her give up her egocentric teen ways to become a more respectful adult.

This task is so arduous and universal that it's even formally addressed in college orientations around the country. As part of the orientation activities for first-year students and their parents at the University of Southern California (USC), for example, hundreds of parents pack an auditorium to listen to USC counseling staff members introduce the twin topics of letting go and reunion, and their accompanying anxiety, confusion, and excitement for parents and their teenagers. At this workshop, Parenting Through the College Years, dozens of mothers and fathers sob their way through apologies for being so emotional about this transition in their families' lives. Veteran parents report that the experience is still gut-wrenching for them, although their new freshmen are, in many cases, their third or fourth child to be "let go."

In one session, many admitted that just the sight of their teenagers' shoes made them melancholy during the summer before their offspring's first year away from home. They would look at their tired sneakers in the middle of the kitchen or living room and burst into tears as they thought about the fact that soon those shoes and their contents would be gone, not unlike the feeling one mother said she had many years earlier while looking at the worn-out wallpaper in her daughter's nursery before getting ready to strip and redo.

One father adamantly warned the men in the audience not to think that just because they were dads, as opposed to moms, their teenagers' intermittently leaving and coming back home would have little impact on them. "We have feelings, too, you know. I thought I'd be just fine. But then it hits you at weird moments. When I went to the supermarket after my daughter left home for USC, I broke down in tears in the dairy section, realizing that I didn't really need to buy the cream cheese I put in my cart because she was the only one who ate it. Then when she came home for her first break, I couldn't wait for her to go back so I wasn't spending a fortune in groceries."

Just as in any remodeling project, parents are best advised to focus on the excitement of their work at hand and how comfortable the newly renovated family will someday be. They need to breathe deeply and try to relax as they and their children move into new quarters, in spite of the confusion and disarray that accompany this season of parenthood.

Self-Discoveries of Family Remodelers

Your pocket guide to the truth revealed in the Family Remodeler season of parenthood.

> ➤ **Gotta keep going; no time to waste.** After the ups and downs of the first circle of parenthood, you finally make your exit from the roller coaster you've been riding for eighteen or so years and move to the quieter ride on the Ferris wheel of the second circle. There's no time to walk around the park, feet on the ground, enjoying the sights for a while, however, because your children force you to get on another ride before you've even recovered from the first one.

> ➤ **Now there are just the two of us.** This ride is different because your children aren't with you to share every minute of the fun, but you can see them and hear their screams of delight as they race to ride their own rip-roaring roller coaster. You and your seat partner finally have a chance to get close again as your ride starts and stops on its way to the top. But don't let this ride fool you; it's not smooth sailing. Reacting to the long-distance noise of your adult children, trying to keep your balance, and getting reacquainted with your seatmate make this ride challenging.

> ➤ **It's still crazy after all these years.** The ride rocks and rolls as it starts and stops to let new people on. You're so disappointed that it's not the mellow, quiet, and cozy ride you'd expected. You'd hoped this ride would provide a respite from parenthood, but you are still white-knuckling it as the ride picks up speed and you see your children moving farther away from you.

> ➤ **On the way up, the view improves.** As you approach the midpoint of this ride, you start to get used to the rhythm of the car and to enjoy the time you can spend together with your seatmate; the vista is improving by the minute. You realize that you'll soon be able to observe the whole park and are surprised to see your children waving at you as they ap-

proach the roller coaster, which makes you glad you're still in touch and know they're all right.

Exit Signs

Leaving Construction Zone. Plateau ahead. When your children are no longer living at home and have gained financial independence, you will find that your family remodeling is complete and that you've reached a new season of parenthood. Entering this new season can be a gradual process, taking place over several months or years, or it can happen overnight when your adult child makes the decision that she can pay her own way in life and live on her own. Becoming financially independent and living away from home has no relationship to your child's age, as ending markers of other seasons have. Instead, your adult child's getting married, having a baby, getting a choice job, and being ready to be responsible for her own livelihood are your tickets to parental independence . . . your passport to becoming a Plateau Parent.

Plateau Parent

CHILD'S MIDDLE-AGE YEARS

We live in the present, we dream of the future, and we learn eternal truths from the past.
—MADAME CHIANG KAI-SHEK

PLATEAU PARENTS ARE THE lighthouses, the beacons, of the family, perched atop a plateau on the mountain of parenthood that you've been climbing for over two decades. You've now completed the remodeling of your family, enabling your children to feel comfortable returning to the empty nest as self-sufficient and responsible adults who have created an independent life of their own.

You're ready for a time of rest and relaxation, a time to finally say that the first circle of parenthood, parenting children, is officially over and the second circle, parenting adults, is officially in gear. You can now bask in the glow of your fully grown children, the "fruits" of all your previous parenthood labors. The remodeled family, whatever its shape and size, is the central magnet pulling you as Plateau Parents in one direction or another on your mountaintop perch.

In this season of parenthood, your adult children determine what your family tapestry will look like, feel like—whether it will now include significant others, spouses, grandchildren. This is the one truth that has remained constant throughout parenthood: Your children constantly redefine your lives. Therefore your children determine your rebirth through grandparenthood, how you define old age, and how you answer the call of freedom that beckons you to enjoy life while you can. Today's Plateau Parents start fresh careers, take up a new sport, pour themselves into traveling, or commit to volunteer work, whether they're grandparents or not, as they flourish in the remodeled life that they began fashioning when they were first released from parenting children.

FOUR GENERATIONS—you the parents, your aged parents, your adult children, and your grandchildren—form the complicated tapestry of family in this season of parenthood. Penny, the mother of a thirty-year-old in a Circles group for parents of young adults, said that when she was in this season, she started to understand why her parents had cried so hard at her wedding. And she even recognized the reasons that *their* friends, who didn't even really know her, cried, too, as they witnessed this beginning of a new circle of life, growing and diverging from theirs, just as they had begun their lives with their own partners a generation ago.

Our friend Felicity also understood: "When one of my twins had twins, I became nostalgic and started to sound like my mother, telling my daughter, 'I remember when you were just. . . ,' bombarding her with stories of days gone by."

Part of Plateau Parents' new habit of repeating their parents' words of wisdom is fueled by this new appreciation of parenthood, as reporter Cokie Roberts discussed in her book, *We Are Our Mothers' Daughters.* One story she related about a trip she took with her sister to her aunt's home demonstrated this point. On entering the airport, her sister heard herself being paged:

"It was my mother, already ensconced at my aunt's, suggesting we ride a shuttle bus instead of driving; she was worried about us traveling at night. Now, we were both in our forties at the time. But my sister and I were both also mothers of children who had left home. We knew exactly what our mother was doing, because we did it ourselves. Motherhood is forever."

This is a poignant season, one that offers a new perspective of the continuity of parenthood. Parents now see just what their own parents experienced as they themselves became "grown up." As Donna, the mother of a forty-eight-year-old daughter who had just had her third child, reported in an interview: "Now I understand why my parents were so overjoyed when their grandchildren were born." Many parents can't wait to be part of another circle, to take on the responsibility of showering another generation of their family with the legacy of love that they've received from their parents and grandparents. It gives them renewed purpose like no other experience in life.

Senator John Ashcroft of Missouri proved that he has felt the power of his grandchild's pull on his soul when he told a crowd of twelve hundred at the Greater Kansas City Chamber of Commerce annual dinner in 1998 that he was going to work to ensure that Kansas City continue to be a great city because his toddler-age grandchild was growing up there. Through his grandchild, Senator Ashcroft was embracing his chance to relive his own and his child's childhood. He was gaining a new spirit through grandparenthood, professionally and personally.

In this plateau season of parenthood, parents who aren't grandparents find that their lives follow a mature path of independence they had never expected. Because their own parents were grandparents, they have no models for being a Plateau Parent without grandchildren. Now they have to create their own road maps of the rest of their lives without a time-tested, hand-me-down copy to use because their children remain childless. Some Plateau Parents told us that they felt cheated when they couldn't continue the family traditions that their parents and grandparents kept alive with their grandchildren. However, when parents felt uncomfortable being mothers and fathers themselves, they said they were relieved that they weren't expected to reprise, through their grandchildren's growing stages, the seasons of parenthood they had experienced for the past twenty-five years or more.

Whether or not they have grandchildren, Plateau Parents are even more dramatically aware of the circular nature of life if they need to care for the oldest generation in their families. Though illness and aging may physically slow them down, too, the Plateau Parents we interviewed told us that they relished life even more when they knew, from witnessing their aged parents' declining health and death, just how precious and capricious life was.

It is precisely how you think about your world from this plateau position that determines what your "old age" will be like: full of promise of new adventures with children and grandchildren and new depths of discovery about work, friendship, and community, or just a short run down the other side of the mountain. Plateau Parents are learning from both generations, their adult children and their aged parents, how to live and how to grow old and how to die—which makes life on a plateau a transformative and provocative season of parenthood.

Members of our Circles groups who had reached this plateau admitted to being awed by the mystery of what had happened to their family: everyone had changed once again. Their young adult children had become mature adults who had grown comfortable in their own circle with their own children. And now their parents were becoming helpless "children" dependent on their care. This is a profoundly riveting season for parents who may have never quite gotten used to the idea that they are grown-ups themselves.

ANSWERING FREEDOM'S CALL

. . . I am amazed at my increased energy and vigor of mind; at my strength to meet situations of all kinds; and at my disposition to love and appreciate everything . . . all at once the whole world has turned good to me.—HORACE FLETCHER

Answering freedom's call is the core challenge for Plateau Parents. Now is the developmentally appropriate, predictable season in which they can fully revel in the freedom from the demands of being financially responsible for their adult children, though their offspring may have long left the nest. Plateau Parents have now adjusted to having a remodeled family, one without the day-to-day responsibilities of parenthood.

These parents in our Circles groups told us that they felt as if they now had permission to expand or change their careers, accept a transfer to another city, move to the Sunbelt, improve their golf game, take swing dance lessons, take on community service projects, build dream homes, go on luxury cruises. They believed they no longer had anyone who needed them to be there for them, physically or financially, and they relished their new independence. They may have just begun to "get a life," as the saying goes, after having given up their previous one "for the kids."

But in fact, "the kids" are now beginning to act more like their parents, being concerned about where their Plateau Parents are all the time, whether they're taking care of themselves, if they're enjoying life. Their adult children need to know that their lighthouses are still on shore and being maintained, even as they themselves drift farther away. As Ian, one of our interviewees, remarked: "I can't make a move without having to report in to my kids. And if my wife and I want to take a vacation, we even have to check in every day so that they won't worry. When my wife had to have minor surgery, our daughter went ballistic because we didn't call and tell her what was going on, even though she was a thousand miles away."

Another reason that adult children begin to take a special interest in their parents' lives in this season of parenthood is that they now begin to need them again to care for the grandchildren. Some Plateau Parents we interviewed welcomed the fact that their adult children expected them to baby-sit and help them feed and clothe their children. Their being needed again led them back down the mountain toward the past seasons of parenthood that they had grown, in hindsight, to glorify. They were enamored with the possibility of caring for a new generation, getting more opportunities to relive the first circle of parenthood, but making this go-round better for their grandchildren than it was for their children.

Others told us that they were thrilled to briefly revisit past seasons of parenthood through their grandchildren, eager to stop by to play "when they could." Grandparenthood was like stopping by their old neighborhood. It was fun and nostalgic and reminded them of the reason they now enjoyed living on a more quiet and orderly plateau.

Still others suffered cognitive dissonance—conflicting emotions that felt off-key—during this season of parenthood because their grandchildren's transforming them into grandparents upset the structure of the remodeled, independent family life they had worked so hard to build. Mike, one of our Circles group members, commented: "We had planned to go out to a movie one Saturday night, but the kids called and wanted us to baby-sit for the grandkids. My wife, Cindy, told them we could, but I hit the ceiling. Who's running our lives now, us or our children? I asked her."

Cindy told us that she feared that not being on constant call to help with the grandkids would make her a bad mother, would mean that she was somehow not fulfilling her duty. This feeling was left over from days gone by when she and Mike not only paid for all of the food, clothing, and shelter for their children, but were also committed to "be there" to meet all of their children's needs. Mike and Cindy hadn't made the transition from being their children's caregivers to being their adult children's consultants and mentors. This couple found themselves responding to their adult children as if they were still in the first circle of parenthood, parenting children, when they needed to behave as caring, independent Plateau Parents.

BEING ASKED TO BECOME full-time baby-sitters for grandchildren prompts some Plateau Parents to lie awake at night, worrying: My children won't love me if I tell them no; my husband will kill me if I say yes; what'll I do when I have to give my grandchild back and can't have her every day? The good news is that for some grandparents, full-time baby-sitting for grandchildren fits their personality and temperament and fulfills their Plateau Parent goals. They think that running around after their grandchild will keep them young and fit; give their life new meaning; take them back to those wonderful days of yesteryear when they had little ones who needed them; and bring them closer to their own children.

As these examples illustrate, when adult children have children, the degree of their renewed dependence on their Plateau Parents can strengthen or damage parent-child relationships, enrich or derail the marriages of Plateau Parents, and improve or strain everyone's mental well-being. Once again their children are defining their lives, now through their grandchildren. If you'd planned on a certain kind of freedom when the "kids were grown," you may now feel that you want to be reborn as grandparents on your own terms, in your own inimitable way. So what's the bottom line regarding grandparents' "obligation" to their grandchildren in this season of parenthood?

In the first circle of parenthood, children forced parents to take on the obligation of keeping them safe and secure until they were able to do so independently. As Family Remodelers, young adult children demanded that their parents provide them with a safety net as they took their maiden flight from the nest. Now, independent adults hope their parents will be their consultants and mentors, the identity they started developing during the previous season. In every season, the obligation to their children that parents feel best springs from their love and devotion. And the obligation that their children have had to their parents throughout their lives now starts to break through the surface as it prepares to flower when parents become Rebounders.

Plateau Parents' decision about becoming full-time baby-sitters, therefore, is most healthy when it is rooted in mutual love, respect, and caring, the seeds of which were first planted in the Family Manager season. The younger generation—adult children—is best advised to consider their parents' needs and priorities as they ask their parents to make this decision, as well as others. Plateau Parents have the right to categorically deny or enthusiastically offer their services to care for their grandchildren on a part-time or full-time basis, as well as float loans, take their extended family on vacations, and share weekly golf games and shopping trips. But one of the great privileges of being a Plateau Parent that their adult children ideally give them is being able to answer freedom's call as they see fit.

THE SANDWICH GENERATION: FREEDOM WITH STRINGS ATTACHED

Although Plateau Parents may be experiencing a sense of relief over relinquishing responsibility for their children's and grandchildren's basic needs, their own parents will eventually need assistance with the very basics of life—food, shelter, clothing, care—that they just finished providing for their children. Plateau Parents' own tools of self-reliance, independence, and responsibility must now be tapped to address the problems of their aging parents. The role reversal begins as the oldest generation of parents becomes dependent on their children because they are incapable of taking care of themselves.

So then what happens to answering freedom's call? The models for taking care of aging parents come directly from the example that your *own* parents set in taking care of *their* parents. If you never witnessed that kind of caregiving or if what you witnessed was a nightmare, this experience can magnify the emotional turmoil in your lives, as our Circles groups of Plateau Parents discussed.

Phoebe was one of the most outspoken group members. She told us that her grandparents had all died before she was born, so she was unaware of the time and patience needed to be an advocate for an aging parent. When her mother broke her hip and needed surgery, she figured that her mother would be home in a few days and back to her busy routine as a bank teller within a few weeks. Reality hit her hard when the doctor called her to explain that her mother wouldn't be able to drive for six weeks. Because her father had moved across the country after her parents' divorce many years earlier, and Phoebe was an only child, she was suddenly plopped into a new relationship with her mom—as her caregiver. She was clueless about how to redefine their relationship or stop the flood of resentment that was building up inside of her over the fact that her world was being turned upside down by this new responsibility. In fact, she had never even thought about how difficult it would be to make this transition, because she had never been close to anyone who had . . . and had been lucky enough to never have to do so herself before now.

On the other hand, some Plateau Parents in our Circles groups vividly recalled that as children they tagged along with their parents on trips to the hospital to see their grandparents when the eldest generation had a heart attack, contracted pneumonia, or had a stroke. Although they understood how much time it took out of their parents' days and nights to be their own parents' advocates, these Plateau Parents said that they never understood why their parents were so upset by these health problems when the doctors were so reassuring about their grandparents' chances for a full recovery. Now, however, they identified with their parents' emotional turmoil. On top of their fears concerning the medical problems their parents were battling, these Plateau Parents were anxious about needing to take care of their parents, who had always been the ones who took care of them.

They reported feeling a sense of melancholy over their new, unsettling relationship: their parents had become their children, and they had become their parents' parents. This was a monumental spiritual shift in identity for Plateau Parents, just as it was for their parents before them, although these Plateau Parents didn't realize it years ago. Nicole, one of our Circles group participants, revealed that she found herself in another mourning period in this season of parenthood, just as she had finally recovered from grieving over her empty nest. Her father had always been so sharp and eager to hop in the car to go on errands for her or play cards "with the boys." But that man seemed to have disappeared. In his place was a father who forgot who she was, one who shouldn't drive, his doctor said, or he'd surely wind up as lost as a runaway puppy.

Not only was Nicole losing the helpful, vigorous father she had always known, as his dementia worsened, but she was also losing every moment of free time she had after coming home from her new job that demanded more than twelve-hour days. She worried about her father's ability to make his own meals and wash his own clothes; so these became daily chores for Nicole, as did chats with his doctor to try to regulate his medicine. She didn't know how she would ever have a moment to herself again, she told us, something she had come to treasure after her kids were grown. In fact, she admitted that she had reneged on her promise to her daughter to baby-sit for her three-year-old grandson on her day off, because she now had to take her father to his doctor's appointments or the supermarket on her free day.

Roger empathized with Nicole as she tearfully told her story of being pulled in so many directions. He had never expected his mother to wind up with kidney failure, he said, let alone think that he would ever need to become an expert on dialysis. But such was his fate. He knew that he would have to drive his mother to dialysis three times a week and monitor her progress every day. He had promised his dad that he would take care of her, as his father lay on his deathbed just two years earlier. Now he felt that he *had* to be there for his mother; after all, she'd always been there when he needed her. Although he and his wife, Marjorie, had planned to take a two-month trip across the country now that their children were grown and on their own, their trip had quickly become just wishful thinking.

As they coped with the changes in their lives, these Plateau Parents learned that their freedom was, therefore, all relative, literally and figuratively. It wasn't a birthright of this season of parenthood. Therein lies the challenge, the conflict. As is true in every other season of parenthood, Plateau Parents face the predictable, universal, and inevitable challenges of prioritizing their lives: listening to their own inner voice that tells them what they want to do with their lives, as well as the heartfelt message that compels them to take care of the needs of those with whom they feel the deepest human connection—their parents and children and, now, their grandchildren.

All human beings spend parenthood adapting to this basic human need to forge one's individual identity while being responsible for helping their offspring give birth to theirs. Now Plateau Parents have an additional test of their skills of self-reliance, independence, and personal responsibility: helping their parents move comfortably into the final season of their lives and their grandchildren blossom into their first stages of childhood.

Today, the possibility of living longer impacts Plateau Parents in profound ways. They may be able to decide for themselves when they want to "be there" for their children and grandchildren—take family trips, accompany them on doctors' visits, baby-sit, celebrate milestones, and attend school functions. However, Plateau Parents won't have the freedom to make their own decisions about filling their "free time" when their parents have taken it away by needing them to take care of them.

Plateau Parents who are being called upon to care for their aged parents may be forced to do double duty, as Valerie discovered: "I was really caught in the middle. My daughter's baby was due at the same time that my mother was gravely ill in a hospital in Mesa, Arizona. I didn't know which way to turn. I stayed home with my daughter for two weeks until she had her baby and then flew off to Arizona to be with my mother. She died the day after I arrived. I'm still upset that I wasn't with my mother for the final two weeks of her life."

Valerie's example demonstrates the difficulty that Plateau Parents face in juggling a life rife with loved ones needing them, a life that often necessitates letting freedom's call ring . . . unanswered. In order for parents to respond to freedom's call in this season, their relationships with their adult children and their aging parents need to be strong, and communication about the importance of Plateau Parents' maintaining their independence needs to be open. The work of previous seasons of parenthood now proves to be critical to everyone's healthy and peaceful coexistence.

REBIRTH THROUGH GRANDCHILDREN

Everything else you grow out of, but you never recover from childhood.—BERYL BAINBRIDGE

Plateau Parents relive the first circle of parenthood again and again and again through the growing stages of each of their grandchildren. They miraculously become three and eight and ten and fifteen along with the youngest generation. And they receive another blessing from the gift of grandchildren, as members of our Circles group of Plateau Parents tearfully shared: seeing their own lives come full circle by watching their own children blossom into parents.

"You'd think that I would get used to it," Mary Ann, a four-time grandmother, remarked in one of our interviews. "The whole experience has been a process of reliving my entire life as a parent again. Watching my son, Don, and daughter-in-law, Judy, respond to their infant, their faces mimicking mine, is absolutely mind-blowing. It reminds me of all the mistakes I made with my son when he was a child, of all of the times I screamed at him when I shouldn't have.

"Don and Judy are much better parents than my husband and I were. It touches me more than any other experience in my life. It leaves me speechless, in awe of the power that our children have over us, even after they have supposedly grown up."

Joan, another of the many grandparents we interviewed, found that reaching this plateau of parenthood was life changing:

"I was so caught up in being independent from my parents that I didn't want any help from them when my children, Blaine and Blakely, were born," she remarked. "And they just pushed and pushed, criticizing my every move. So when I became a grandmother, I was careful. I didn't butt into the details of Blaine and his wife, Dana's, affairs. But oh boy, did I love their baby!

"And a miracle . . . the most amazing miracle happened. Blaine and I suddenly reached a new peace in our relationship. He told me that he saw me through new eyes, just as I saw him. I swear, just talking about it makes my heart swell. I consider this my greatest spiritual achievement, not repeating the mistakes I think my parents made with me so I can now be close to my son."

Many Plateau Parents told us that they were closer to their adult children as a result of their new identity as grandma or grandpa.

"It's funny," noted Nina, one of our Circles group grandmothers, "but when my grandchildren were born, I became a friend to my daughter. Before that, I was just her mother."

This shift isn't hard to predict for those who remember being Sponges in Season Two when they were beginning parenthood and starting to relate differently to *their* parents. Depending on whether adult children's relationships with their parents are close or distant, the younger generation holds the cards to a smooth or troublesome rebirth through grandchildren for parents.

Therefore it's essential for Plateau Parents to be aware of the leftover aches and pains from old wounds that they inflicted on their own children, wounds that haven't healed and are carried into this season of everyone's lives. Their adult children will remember how critical their parents were of their grades, clothes, and friends, as Dorothy told us she so vividly recalled after her first baby was born. "I couldn't stand going over to my parents' house with Austin for fear that my mother would tell me that I hadn't dressed him right or was feeding him too much or too little."

Other adult children told us that memories of being spanked when they were young drove them to keep their own children from spending time at their grandparents. They had vowed never to strike their child but knew that their mother and father believed that if you "spare the rod, you'll spoil the child." Their parents' disapproval of their behavior as children was destined to be repeated with their own children, these parents feared. It was easier to deprive their Plateau Parents of a relationship with their grandchildren in order to avoid conflict.

IF GRANDCHILDREN DON'T GRACE parents' lives in this season, they probably never will. In this case, parents must face the truth about never experiencing childhood again, another process of grief and of accepting disappointment if they had been anticipating the reprise of the first circle of parenthood.

As Steve, a Circles group father, remarked, "I never consciously focused on any of my three kids ever marrying. But now that they are forty-two, forty-five, and forty-nine, I don't think that I'll ever get any in-laws or grandchildren. I never planned on having any, but I am constantly fighting with myself over whether or not I'm sad or relieved. I do feel somehow responsible for not pushing our children to have children; but my wife tells me that I'm crazy. She says it's their lives, and I don't have any control over what they do."

Steve demonstrates the oft spoken societal expectation of Plateau Parents: Something is missing in their lives if they cannot brag about their grandkids. Their children are now seen as the generation to ultimately carry on the family name; give birth to their legacy, the next generation; and allow Plateau Parents to live on in perpetuity through their grandchildren.

Without grandchildren in their lives, Plateau Parents' relationship with their adult children is unique because they are sharing the same lifestyle— one without reliving the first circle of parenthood. However, Plateau Parents will develop through adulthood differently from their children because these same children will always primarily define their parents' lives, just as they have from their births forward. Now their adult children's lives won't be defined predominantly by a new generation but will be driven by those factors that define the lives of people who aren't parents: careers, social alliances, volunteerism, avocations, and leisure activities.

REDEFINING OLD AGE

We are always the same age inside.—GERTRUDE STEIN

It is impossible to talk about redefining old age in this season of parenthood without referring to the relationships that Plateau Parents have with their adult children and with their aged parents. From their ringside seat on the plateau of parenthood, these parents experience an optical illusion: what used to be "old" has now fast-forwarded about twenty years, and what used to be "young" has been rewound about twenty years!

Events in their children's lives are Plateau Parents' markers, lines on the growth chart of their lives. Watching their children progress through young adulthood—getting married, having children, buying a house, having a career—are things that Plateau Parents remember doing just "yesterday." Each marker reminds Plateau Parents of their advancing age. Their awareness of the circular nature of parenthood heralds a sense of completeness of the first circle of parenthood. They can now officially acknowledge that their children are adults, not young adults; and they therefore must reconcile what that means to them as it relates to their own aging.

Fifty years ago "old age" meant that when you turned sixty-five you were ready for retirement and unable to make long-term plans for fear of the physical deterioration that was waiting just around the corner. Current medical technology has extended the years during which people can enjoy healthy lives. In addition, it has given women the opportunity to delay having children until later in life. Therefore today's Plateau Parents, whose children are, generally speaking, about twenty-five to forty-nine years of age, can be anywhere from forty-five to ninety years of age.

Depending on their health and outlook on life, these Plateau Parents may feel and look either "old" or "young." According to Sharon R. Kaufman in *The Ageless Self,* older Americans "do not perceive meaning in aging itself, rather they perceive meaning in being themselves in old age. Many researchers have noted that mental health depends upon ensuring a continuous sense of self across the adult life span."

Because their grandchildren may provide Plateau Parents another chance at reliving the stages of childhood for a second, third, or even tenth time, many grandparents feel transported back in time to a youthful vigor they had long since forgotten. They are able to maintain a sense of continuity and meaning in their identity as mothers and fathers that help them cope with change in their own physical and financial status. Many Plateau Parents told us that one of their primary goals was to try to "stay young," just to prove that they are still the same energetic "Mom" or "Dad" that their children knew and loved.

Plateau Parent interviewees prided themselves on teaching their children and grandchildren that they were the pioneers of a new breed of "old-sters" who were redefining old age as a time of life to be relished, not the end of all possibilities of growing and learning. Many are competing in se-nior golf matches, tennis tournaments, and races to keep fit and enjoy ac-tive lives. They are starting businesses, buying second homes, and traveling the world with their children and grandchildren, finally feeling they have the financial wherewithal to have a little fun, to live out their dreams, to answer freedom's call, to celebrate their good fortune of their remodeled family. Some didn't even want to be called "Grandma" or "Grandpa" because that pushed them more firmly into the coffin of "being old" or because that was the name they called *their* own grandmothers or grandfathers.

For those whose parents had passed away, being the oldest generation in the family motivated them to live their dreams . . . today. These Plateau Parents told us that they felt Father Time breathing down their neck, ad-monishing them to make each day count. Their aged parents' illness or death had taught them that they would never know how long they had left to enjoy life, regardless of their chronological age. "Carpe diem" became their mantra.

On the other hand, we heard more than a modicum of fear in the hearts of Plateau Parents who were now the oldest living generation of the family. They moved to the top rung of the ladder with the frightening knowledge that they were next in line to fall off. This realization places a heavy bur-den on Plateau Parents. They begin to think in terms of the "last" of things: the last roof they'll put on this house, the last chance they'll have to travel to Europe, the last time they'll move. Seeing themselves as the next generation in line to "go" gives them a clearer view of the finality of their own lives as they sit perched on their plateau. This kind of "doomsday" perspective can forecast the end of Plateau Parents' lives before they're emotionally ready.

Their possibilities for exploring spiritual growth, new friendships, and education, as well as business ventures and volunteer opportunities, *before* they reach the last season of parenthood is defined by who is dependent on whom. If Plateau Parents have the luxury of solid, loving relationships with their independent adult children, as well as with their own aged par-ents, and if their own health is intact, "old age," as it has traditionally been defined, is but a future destination.

"DANGEROUS LIAISONS"

Plateau Parents who have these gifts may feel invigorated by starting a new life with a new partner. Beginning new relationships with the opposite sex can be one prickly subject between parents and their adult children during this season of parenthood, we discovered from our interviews. Those who had lost their spouses to divorce or death said that finding their second or third true love made their adult children either grateful or suspicious, depending on the relationship between the two generations.

In cases in which their adult children were grateful for their parent's new companion, Plateau Parents' relationships with their adult children remained strong. Some of our Circles group Plateau Parents reported that their adult children were pleased that their parents had loving companionship that freed them from being responsible for their parents' happiness. Other Plateau Parents, however, reported that their adult children were suspicious of their parents' new love interest because they saw this intruder as being out for one of two things—robbing them either of their mom or dad or of their inheritance—or both.

Taylor, one of our Circles group members, could relate well to those Plateau Parents who complained about the distrustful noises they were hearing from their adult children when they started dating again. When she began spending a lot of time in her next-door neighbor Emile's apartment, her children started going crazy. What do you need a new boyfriend for, anyway? they kept asking her. Taylor had it made, she told us: a nice nest egg that she and her second husband had wisely invested; loving grandchildren who lavished her with attention, even when they were away at college; and a doting daughter and son. Her adult children had already lost their father and one stepfather through her mismatched marriages and subsequent divorces. Now that they had all of their mother's attention again, they'd gotten closer to her than ever before.

They feared they would lose their bond with their mother to her new fling, Emile, if they didn't step in and prevent her from making another mistake, Taylor explained. They also knew that their mother's money wouldn't last forever. Not only had they counted on inheriting her money, but if this new gold-digger, as they called their mother's boyfriend, got wind of how much was in her trust, they feared that all their mother had saved might be wiped out, making her dependent on them. Taylor refused to listen to her adult children as they begged her to at least consider a prenuptial agreement that protected her assets; the more time she spent with Emile, the stronger their resentment of this perceived intruder grew. Taylor told us that she eventually stopped seeing Emile when he kept badgering her to get married. "I don't need to complicate my life again," she had told her adoring children, much to their relief.

Just as parents can try to put the kibosh on teenagers' romances that they think are "trouble" by establishing dictums about who they can and can't date or how "serious" they want them to get in a romance at a certain age, adult children often try to dissuade their Plateau Parents from what they perceive as "dangerous liaisons." Though the younger generation may influence their parents' feelings about their new true loves, Plateau Parents are best advised to follow their heart, taking the responsibility for their own happiness and independence and being grateful for the comfort and companionship as they live out their lives. In addition, however, Plateau Parents need to understand and validate their adult children's feelings, just as their now adult children needed to respect their parents' feelings when they were teenagers, years ago.

Plateau Parents can reduce their offspring's fear that they are losing their parents, that they are being hoodwinked by lascivious paramours, or that their "missing" parents are being displaced. They can defuse the potential for conflict between generations by reassuring their adult children that any new loves won't change their relationship or endanger their financial stability, even though they may spend less time with their family because of their new romance.

Sherry's Baby: On the Road or on Call?

"I was too concerned about making sure that the kids and the house were perfect in front of my mom and dad," Sherry, a mother of eight children ranging in age from thirty to forty-eight and eleven grandchildren, remarked at one of our Circles group meetings. "What's important in life is not the Steuben glassware. It's that the children and the grandchildren are all okay. That's what I have realized at the ripe old age of sixty-eight."

It was a blustery night for the group to get out in, but all of the couples had braved the cold. "To talk about our kids?" Sherry questioned. "Of course, we would go anywhere in any weather to be able to talk about our kids!"

Everyone agreed with Sherry. That night's meeting was a bittersweet dis-

cussion of the changes in these couples' lives since "the kids" were grown. Sherry dominated the conversation by explaining how dumbfounded she was by the experience of being a grandparent.

"You feel like raising children was what you were supposed to do," she commented "It's just like a miracle to see the job being passed onto your children. You get a sense of all that you have accomplished by seeing them parent their own children."

But it's still odd, she continued, to be the one in the position of having adult children and now grandchildren. "My father and mother were physically consumed, worn out, when they were my age. They were even thinking about retirement. But instead of being exhausted like they were, I just feel like I'm starting over, starting a new life."

Sherry laughed about how different the role reversals felt. "My kids now want to know my schedule, when I'm going to be out of town and when I'm working. I was always the one asking them those questions. My husband, Enrico, wants to downsize to a smaller house, but the kids don't want us to. They want us to refinish the basement as a playroom for their kids! They're starting to get nostalgic on us, wanting us to keep the old house and their rooms, and we're ready to move on.

"It's really weird. We were thinking of finally getting that little beach house we had always dreamed of on Hilton Head, but our children say that it's not fair. We wouldn't be close enough to see the grandchildren if we moved that far away. I think that they're right; we always told them that their family is their most priceless possession. I guess they really listened."

Sherry admitted that just when she was planning to add more hours to her job selling real estate, along came one of her daughter's weddings to plan and another daughter's due date with her second child in just a few weeks. In addition, her own mother was getting so confused and disoriented, dementia they called it, that it wasn't safe for her to drive or to handle her own finances. Sherry had become her mother's chauffeur to the doctor and her banking adviser, as well as her daily confidante.

"I guess my turn to have fun will have to wait for old age!" Sherry said, laughing.

Sherry's experiences rang true with the others in her Circles group because they reflected how parents must adjust to the changes in their children's lives when they become parents. Becoming a grandparent was so different for Sherry because it meant being needed, being on call, and being closer to her children than she had been in decades, all from this new perspective. Moreover, it was her children who wanted her close— what a switch from their adolescent days!

The freedom that Sherry had thought would be hers had never materialized, much as it hadn't for most Plateau Parents we interviewed. Instead, grandparenthood provided a continuous link to her family and maintained the continuity of her primary identity: mother.

For Sherry and the millions of parents like her who are simultaneously caring for children, grandchildren, and aged parents, seeing people on both sides of her life who were depending on her made her aware of her new position in the family. We advised Sherry that in order to adjust to life on the plateau, she would have to work at preserving the freedom she now had; it's too easy to fall into the routine of being perpetually on call.

We suggested that Sherry find an assisted living arrangement for her mother and father and direct her energies to making that space comfortable for them. In the meantime, we helped her accept the fact that she could not always be with her mother, so she needed to make sure that someone was available to take her mother when she needed to go to the doctor or on other important errands. Her good friends and adult children encouraged her to take care of herself, too; over time, she realized that those who loved her were right.

Sherry thought it was odd that her mother wasn't the one telling her to "take life easier, to let the kids help her more," as she had always done when Sherry's children were younger. Instead, now it was her adult *children* and good friends who took on the role of consultant.

Though she wished that she had more control over the things that happened to her in her life, Sherry realized she could make choices that would give her a sense of her own definition of what "growing older" was, instead of thinking that her fate was sealed by others around her. She feared getting as worn down as her own father and mother when they were her age. They were her only models of how to parent grown kids who have families of their own, models that hadn't taught her how to grow old gracefully.

So it was up to her, we suggested, to create a new model that would teach her children that this season of parenthood could be rewarding. She needed to avoid being pulled in so many directions that she got exhausted and couldn't enjoy the fruits of her past labors. Learning to accept her life and to focus her attention on the little joys of parenthood and grandparent-hood helped Sherry achieve the peace of mind she craved.

Elaine and Bill's Spoilers: Separate Agendas

A retired teacher outfitted in a red, white, and blue sweatsuit and a toothy smile, Elaine jumped in line to talk to us after our weekend workshop on grandparenthood. Her deeply lined face glowed with pride as she waxed poetic about her eight-month-old granddaughter, Parker. Spoiling a grandchild with teddy bears and toys was now her new job, which helped assuage her guilt at having always been in class, grading papers, or meeting with students when her now thirty-year-old daughter, Heather, a professional ballerina, was growing up.

Still fit and trim from her weekly dance lessons, Elaine found being a grandmother special, too, because it brought back so many precious memories of prancing around in matching tutus with her darling little girl. She swelled with emotion each time she held Parker, her first grandchild, imagining the dances they would do together without the constant stress of her being on call night and day as "Mom."

However, one problem kept bothering her. She didn't want Parker to call her "Grandma" because she still thought of her late mother, Mildred, as Grandma. Mildred had always referred to Elaine and her husband, Bill, as "the kids," which now seemed like a ridiculous name for them. It was confusing for Elaine now . . . all of these changes in the family over so many generations.

Playing with Parker made her miss having her mother around to talk to, as well as long for the experience of being the mother of a little girl again herself. It also made her feel closer to her mother, even though she had passed away several years earlier. She now understood why Mildred had loved coming over just to hold and kiss Heather when Heather was a baby. She had loved little children, Elaine mused, and wasn't sure how to handle big ones. Despite the fact that it brought back so many bittersweet memories, caring for Parker made Elaine feel relieved to finally be needed again by a child. She loved little children as much as her mother had.

Heather also loved having Elaine over to visit. But she was quick to point out to her mom, whenever she criticized the fact that Heather never wore a coat and drank too little milk, that she was a fully grown woman who could take care of herself, a fact that never could quite sink in for Elaine. Once her baby, always her baby, Elaine had liked to say. Even though Heather didn't want her mother to fuss over her as she used to, she secretly did want Elaine to shower that kind of attention on Parker. So she put up with having to be "babied" herself.

On the other hand, Bill's parents, Rosemary and her late husband, Al, had never seemed to relish that "being needed" feeling of parenthood. Al was hardly ever home when Bill was young, Bill remembered. He loved taking hunting or fishing trips for weeks at a time. When Heather was little, Elaine would often come over to Rosemary's alone because Bill was away for the weekend with his dad. If Al ever did come over to Elaine and Bill's, he would leave quickly because he was "too tired" to stay.

After thirty-five years of marriage to Bill, Elaine suddenly saw him becoming just the kind of grandfather that his father was. Bill seemed ready to return to his workshop not long after he arrived at Heather's. He adored Parker, of course, but claimed that he was too old to put up with Parker's crankiness once the newness of the visit wore off.

Feeling this way reminded him of his years as a teacher, a part of his life that he'd been glad to put behind him. For the first time in his life, at age sixty-eight, Bill was looking forward to doing exactly what he wanted to do, not what anyone else wanted him to do. Having paid for all of Heather's dance training and for her extravagant wedding, he was ready to spoil himself.

This dream was short-lived, we later learned, because Rosemary, who was still trying to live in her own home at the age of ninety, took a serious fall on an icy sidewalk, breaking her hip, pelvis, and three vertebrae. As an only child, Bill knew that he was now responsible for seeing that his mother got the best care possible. Her independent life—and his—looked like history.

Both Elaine and Bill had separate agendas in this season of parenthood; Elaine's included being a mother and a grandmother, but Bill's identity wasn't attached to being a father and grandfather. Their freedom seemed precious to them now, but they wanted to be able to enjoy it in different ways. Once more the couple was forced to change their routine because their family commitments came first. Their overriding goal was to preserve their own day-to-day agendas as long as possible, a goal that was rendered unattainable by the unfortunate turn of events with Bill's mother.

Bill admitted that he had no models of caregiving to follow in this season of parenthood. His frustration with his granddaughter, daughter, and mother stemmed from his feeling as if they had robbed him of his freedom by wanting him to spend time with them, just when he had gotten out of his work-related and parental prison, he said.

We helped Bill understand that his mother, granddaughter, and daughter were pulling on his heart because they needed him in new and different ways. By fighting the urge to run away from them, he could help heal his old wound that was the result of feeling deserted by his father during his own childhood. In Bill's case, the process of mending that gap left by his parents would eventually feel good but now was uncomfortable.

Bill couldn't accept that taking care of his mother and being a caring grandparent and a supportive dad was turning into a full-time job. He admitted that he felt guilty that he wasn't as involved as he could be, just as he did when Heather was a baby, a feeling that created much stress for him. He was dumbfounded that his family had once again become so time-consuming, but gradually he understood that being needed could lead to personal fulfillment—if he learned to reframe the situation.

Margo and Pascal, Control Freaks: Unresolved Crises

"I heard that when your son marries, you gain a daughter; and when your daughter marries, you gain a son. But not when your son-in-law steals your daughter away," Margo stated matter-of-factly in our interview over lunch. Her husband, Pascal, nodded in agreement.

"Celebrating your sixty-third birthday without your daughter at the party is not my idea of a good time," Margo continued, referring to the party that their son, Leo, gave for her. "But it wasn't our idea to be dumped. It was hers. So I'm just trying to make the best of it. We don't know what we did wrong. We always tried to be the best parents we could be. We have our best years ahead of us, and she is just killing us by pushing us away."

We discovered that the pain of Margo and Pascal's broken relationship with their forty-year-old daughter, Yvette, had made this season of parenthood miserable. It colored everything they did. It had all started when she was a teenager and began dating a boy her parents hated. He was of a different religion, and they found out that he and Yvette were having sex, two things Margo and Pascal were dead set against. Yvette had always been very strong willed and when they confronted her about these issues, the war was on. She told them that they were too strict, too old-fashioned in their rules, and as soon as she could, she was moving out.

When Yvette turned eighteen, she was gone. She moved in with Max, her latest boyfriend; they eventually married and had a daughter. Margo would call Yvette, and they could talk for a while, but their conversations always ended in a shouting match. She and Pascal hated Max and wished Yvette would leave him, bring her daughter, and come back home. Then maybe she could find a decent man to marry.

"We want to go see our granddaughter, Chelsea, but we feel like we are always saying or doing the wrong thing. All we want from Yvette is for her to do the right thing, to apologize and make amends. She tells us that we are trying to run her life, break up her marriage, and take Chelsea away from her father. So what if we try to give her advice; is that such a crime? Now Yvette never calls us. We're close to our son, Leo, but even he can't talk to his older sister. Leo needs us all of the time; we're constantly giving him money here and there, and he follows our advice.

"We threw him a big wedding last year, and we buy him and his wife little things to get started in their new house, just like we wished our parents had done for us. But our daughter will take nothing from us, needs nothing. We feel like 'Honor your father and mother' is a sacred commandment. We are her elders, her parents, and she should respect us no matter what.

"In most ways, we just go about our business. Now that the kids are grown, we travel a lot. But Yvette couldn't care less. Somehow, this family feud is like a cloud hanging over our old age. Our parents had such close relationships with brothers and sisters and us that I can't understand how this happened in our family."

When we interviewed this couple, our hearts went out to them, for Margo and Pascal were oblivious to the ways to help heal their deep family wounds. They were sitting on a plateau in this season of parenthood, wanting to feel good about the prospect of beginning new relationships with their granddaughter, Chelsea. But they had never begun a new relationship with their daughter, Yvette, and their son-in-law, Max—a new *adult* relationship.

Margo and Pascal had always expected Yvette to be obedient, to behave, and to conform to the dream they had for her. It was the theme of their parenthood. But she had never obliged them in her younger years and was always the rebel. Now that she was married and a mother, she and

Max were building their own family, making their own decisions, taking control over their own destiny, without Margo and Pascal.

To them, Yvette's behavior was a direct rejection of them and of everything they stood for. The world was black and white to them, and the only right way to live in it was according to their rules. This absolute way of maintaining order and control in their world had worked for them in raising their son, Leo. He had always followed their rules, and now he called every day, sometimes twice a day, just as Margo had done with her own mother. So why didn't Yvette? They didn't yet understand that their insistence on complete obedience from their children had affected both of their children: it had prevented Leo from moving out of childhood into adulthood, and it had driven Yvette away from them.

As we interviewed families whose children were devoted to their parents in this season of parenthood, one thread woven throughout their lives became obvious: The parents who were most successful in this season had limited their roles in their adult children's lives; they made a point of keeping some distance between themselves and their children, offering them invitations, and letting their children come to them.

Margo and Pascal illustrate a basic universal truth: Parents will always think of their children as *children.* But when they continue to *treat* them as children after they are adults, their adult children will remain as dependent on their parents as they were as children. Margo and Pascal were stuck as Family Remodelers, mourning the empty spot in their nest that their daughter had left. They couldn't have been more miserable or angry, because they couldn't bring themselves to accept Yvette's need to be independent.

Stella, a sixty-five-year-old woman in one of our Circles groups, was also suffering from what she perceived to be the loss of her children:

"I had to make myself not call my kids every day. When I couldn't stand it any longer, I traveled to Chicago where my son and daughter lived, and we had a meeting of the minds. I told them that I missed them, that I wanted them to be close to me, even though they didn't have any children to help bind us together. How to be a parent to adults, I didn't know. How they could be good adult children, they didn't know.

"But I was grateful that we could talk about it. We had a strong enough relationship after they got out of college and weren't dependent on me for money that we could communicate out of love, not need. I realized that we really didn't need to be a family in order to survive economically, but we needed to be a family to survive emotionally. It was the best trip of my life, and it set the tone of open communication and of understanding the commitment we had to each other that I know I can count on for the rest of my life."

W E SHARED STELLA'S STORY with Margo and Pascal, whose parenthood had been colored by an authoritarian message—"I am the parent, and because of that, I'm in control; you must do as I say because I'm your parent!" For them to change that message now would take work.

But to afford them any hope of a mature relationship with their daughter for the rest of their lives, Margo and Pascal would need to acknowledge the fact that Yvette was doing what she was developmentally supposed to do: becoming economically and psychologically independent from them. We urged them to see that they were in mourning over the loss of the past relationship that was based on parenting a child. When parents can work through the stages of grief—denial, anger, depression, bargaining, and acceptance—they will find that a new life awaits them as independent parents, independent adults who can appreciate the mutual respect that comes from serving as their children's consultants, not their dictators.

Dottie's Drama: Who's Having a Heart Attack?

"It couldn't be happening," said Dottie, a sixty-one-year-old mother of a thirty-year-old unmarried daughter who was in the Peace Corps. This was her first thought when the hospital called her about her eighty-five-year-old mother, Frieda, who had felt chest pains and was in the emergency room eight hundred miles away. By the time Dottie reached her mother, she was comfortable but clearly in medical trouble.

For someone else, Dottie explained, that might not be so unusual. But her mother was never in trouble. Her mother was always in control. Dottie told us that her "mother thought that God had put her on earth as his agent to be in charge of the world."

Seeing her mother lying there in her hospital bed hooked up to all those wires and tubes was more than she could take. There had never been a day in Dottie's life when her mother didn't have a piece of advice, a quote from the Bible before Sunday dinner, a correction to make on the stock market, a health tip or two for her. Dottie and her older brothers, J.J. and Austin, were the most important reasons their mother got up in the morning.

Now Dottie was her mother's primary caretaker . . . by default. Her brother J.J. was too freaked out about his mother to be of any help, and Austin's daughter had just had a baby and he and his wife couldn't leave her side. Because her brothers were older than she was and Dottie's father had died when she was just a baby, her mother had doted on Dottie after Austin and J.J. had gone away to college. Dottie had always felt dependent on Frieda, because she had such a controlling personality.

But now the tables were turned. Now she was the one in charge. She knew nothing about medical care of heart attack patients. The only person she had always turned to in a crisis this big was the one person who was causing it—her mother.

Dottie's mother had never taught her children how to cope with an event like this. In fact, she'd refuse even to talk about creating a will, a living will, or a plan of action to follow if she became seriously ill. Now she was unable to make those decisions, too sick to participate in her own care. Dottie knew that being so helpless must be making her mother crazy. She knew that the one thing she would want her to do was get the facts from the doctor and help her fight the good fight for her life as she had always done herself.

Being responsible for getting her mother the best care possible meant that Dottie would have to break her ties of dependency on her strong mother. We pointed out to her that now it was her turn to take control, a job for which she was prepared by having been her mother's apt pupil for sixty years. As a mother herself, Dottie had gotten lots of practice in managing a family with her own daughter, even though her mother always had a suggestion about how to prepare meals, what classes her granddaughter should take in school, and the best spots for family vacations. Her strong presence would always be a part of Dottie, we explained to her, so she needn't feel alone and vulnerable without her mother by her side as she helped her through her illness.

Oddly enough, by their absences her brothers helped Dottie cope by making her become more assertive. For the first time she insisted that they be a part of the caregiving team for their mother, because she knew how much it would mean to her recovery to know that her three kids were all there by her side. They had never been very close before, Dottie said, because there had never been a need for them to work together and support each other. Having gone to different colleges and lived in separate cities, their paths seldom crossed, much to her mother's chagrin. Now Dottie understood what her mother had meant when she said, "Family is your most priceless possession. You'll need each other someday and be glad there's three of you."

Having never been the one her brothers listened to in the family, Dottie was surprised that they came to the hospital, met with the doctors, and helped her devise a plan about what to do about this unforeseen turn of events in their family, all at her urging. J.J. even said that she suddenly reminded them of her mother as she took over control of her caregiving operation.

Dottie had been a strong mother and had marched her way through her daughter's ear infections, tonsillitis, broken arm, and appendectomy. She now understood that those coping skills she had so easily used as a mother of her daughter could now be helpful to her again. Her mantra became "I can handle this; I'm a strong person; I've been through bad stuff before; my strong faith will help me through this crisis." Whether Dottie's mother survived her heart attack or not, she now realized that she was the new CEO of her family, at least for the moment. Though she never thought she'd have the job, her brothers and she found that Dottie's being in charge now was both comfortable and comforting to all.

George's Generation Ends: Disappointment Over a Son

"I am so proud of my wife, Barb," George remarked at one of our Circles groups. "She's still going strong doing the puppet shows that she's produced for preschools for forty years. My only regret is that our son, Beau, never had children. He just turned forty-five, and I just turned seventy-five. We had been pressuring him to settle down and get married, but he always had excuses. Then, ten years ago, he sat us down and told us that he wouldn't be having kids or even be getting married, for that matter, because he's gay. I don't mind telling you, that announcement hit us like a ton of bricks.

Barb and I reacted to the news so differently: She's still embarrassed about it and can't talk about him anymore in front of her friends without crying. Not only does she feel mortified by who he turned out to be, but she says it's cruel of him to not give her any grandchildren with whom she can do her shows and stuff. She keeps looking for somebody or something to blame, instead of just accepting him for who he is, like I do.

"Thinking that Beau is the last generation of our family I'll see alive,

however, makes me a little weak in the knees," George admitted. "He used to tell us that he was too selfish to have kids, but now I think that his being gay is the real reason. This is all a little easier for me to take than for Barb, because the son of a friend of mine also 'came out of the closet' recently.

"His son had gone through bouts of depression that kept him from holding a steady job, just like Beau. Through some lean years as a literary agent, Beau has needed a little help, financially, which Barb didn't mind giving until he confessed that he was gay. Since then, it's been hard for her to have anything to do with him. I've also struggled with Beau's financial dependence on us. I'd always thought that maybe it was a mistake to help him, that he should make it on his own. I've been supporting myself since I was eighteen, when I put myself through college. But it's a different world these days, I tell my wife, and Beau has a lot of problems to face.

"Barb and I fight about this all the time. She says that we should cut him off, that he needs to be able to handle his own life, and that it breaks her heart to even see him now. His living at home off and on, when he's short on cash, is a nightmare. But I can't cut the apron strings. After all, he has no one but us to help him. He's an only child; he's all we have. I can't bear to turn him away. Barb says that he's ungrateful and takes advantage of us, that he's an 'entitlement' kid, as she calls him. He does act like he's entitled to everything we have.

"Without any grandkids, my wife and I had hoped to do some fancy traveling after Beau was grown. Now we're afraid to spend the money—he's got expensive tastes, still has bouts of depression, and we hate to spend what little inheritance he has. What will he do when we're gone?"

George and his wife, Barb, were matter-of-fact about this season of parenthood. No, Beau's life had not turned out the way they had hoped. George felt sorry for his son and continued to be overprotective and treat him just as he did when Beau was ten—asking him whether he remembered to wear his coat, what he had for dinner, if he'd taken his vitamins, was he being safe. The way he treated Beau seemed to maintain his childish self-absorption and dependency. Although Barb often complained bitterly about Beau's dependence and his sexual orientation, she admitted that she felt responsible, somehow, for the "mess" that his life was in, as she termed it. Her inability to solve his problems frustrated her and made her angry with him.

We suggested that George and Barb work together to help Beau become independent and help Barb accept that she wasn't to blame for the fact that Beau was gay or suffering emotionally. George and Barb began attending a support group for families of gays and lesbians, a positive move toward their unconditional acceptance of their son, sexuality and all. We helped them confront the two issues they were struggling with: establishing trust and respect in their relationship with Beau.

In this season of parenthood, George and Barb needed a game plan to chart the course for the remainder of their lives and help Beau chart his, building a bridge of trust and respect between them. We presented them with some options for enjoying the economic freedom they could have while they were both healthy. Without a young child for whom they were responsible, they were free to come and go as they pleased, particularly since George was a salesman who traveled and Barb could do her shows whenever she wanted. Beau's pull on their lives was the result of their inability to give up feeling responsible for him and push him out of the nest. Because he didn't have some of the typical grown-up tags that they would have liked him to have—spouse, children, financial independence—it had been hard for them to think of him as an adult. So the old patterns remained.

Beau's frequent visits to the family nest and nest egg demonstrated that he was in an old, comfortable role of being a dependent little boy. So, George and Barb needed to help Beau become capable of managing his own finances, as well as understand theirs by involving him in their estate planning. Talking about these serious subjects made George and Barb uncomfortable at first, something most Circles parents also told us. But as they worked with a responsible financial planner, Beau began to feel important and needed, and George and Barb felt relieved. They were helping him become more responsible and feel accepted, no apron strings attached.

IN OUR CIRCLES GROUPS of Plateau Parents, money was a looming issue, raising pithy questions that had life-altering consequences: Were "the kids" entitled to Mom and Dad's inheritance? Was it selfish to take that cruise instead of contributing to the adult children's bank accounts? Should we put a new roof on the house or start a college fund for our grandchildren?

Money matters are more critical in today's Plateau Parents' lives than in previous generations because they are expected to live longer than their parents. Therefore, their health care will be more expensive, as will costs for nursing homes or assisted living centers. Minding their retirement funds so that their children won't be burdened with these expenses is a major concern of Plateau Parents. If they've been fortunate enough to put together an estate package that will leave something for their children, who gets what becomes an issue.

"Being of sound mind, I blew my kid's inheritance in Las Vegas" read a bumper sticker one of our Circles group parents proudly displayed. But this mind-set also conjured up much guilt among those who had devoted their lives to their children and hated to spend their inheritance on themselves. These Plateau Parents had become accustomed to sacrificing for their children and couldn't imagine indulging themselves if they could give pleasure to their offspring.

Opening financial discussions with their children remained a stumbling block for most of our Circles groups' Plateau Parents. They claimed that in the hustle and bustle of their children's lives, there never seemed to be a time or an opportunity. Harold, one of our Circles group Plateau Parents, put it this way: "I kept wanting to tell my daughter and son-in-law about our investment portfolio, but they were always talking about the baby and their jobs. So my wife, Caroline, and I invited them to lunch in town and just came right out and told them about our financial arrangements. I'd gotten on the computer and had built this estate plan that listed everything: stocks, bonds, savings accounts, insurance policies, including nursing home and burial insurance." Harold went on to say that before lunch was over, their daughter was crying, not wanting to face the reality that it was time to consider her parents' plans for the last phase of their lives. But their daughter and son-in-law seemed relieved to know that Harold and Caroline were financially secure and that they had taken care of their affairs so they wouldn't be a burden to their children.

Harold's example of confronting these issues in a straightforward manner is a constructive way of giving Plateau Parents' children the long view of their parents' financial status. If conflicts are to arise over money matters, as they surely will, it's better to address and ideally resolve them before moving on to the next season of parenthood.

Rano Ends the Rebellion:
Father and Son Make Their Peace

Rano, a fifty-five-year-old father of two adult sons, approached us after a Circles group to tell us about the year before the death of his ninety-three-

year-old father, Antonio. He spoke in a near whisper as he described the re-
lationship between Antonio and himself, one built on anger and distrust,
stemming from his own rebellious adolescence. Rano described this last
phase of Antonio's life as one of profound enlightenment as he began to truly
appreciate the fragility of life through the death of his father:

"I was still rebelling," he admitted, "until the time that my dad finally
needed me. Then I found that I wanted to be there, wanted to help him. It
was weird. I was so into proving how tough and independent I was up until
that time. I was the quintessential baby boomer, you know, drugs, sex, and
rock 'n' roll. I burned my draft card and lived in Canada until the war in
'Nam ended, and I don't think Dad ever forgave me for that. He was a World
War Two vet and believed it was a man's duty to 'serve his country with
honor,' as he always said.

"When I was in Canada, I thought I didn't need my square old dad.
All he'd given me was a hard time, and I didn't want any more of that. So
I stayed away from him. After I moved back to the States, I got a job as far
away from home as I could and stayed there. I'd send a card on his birth-
day and Father's Day, and maybe I'd call once in a while, but he'd end up
lecturing me about what an ungrateful son I was. Man, I swore I'd never
treat my sons like that. But when Dad's doctor called from the hospital
and told me that he'd been admitted with terminal cancer, my wife, Ka-
rina, and I flew back 'home' to help him. I knew deep inside that he
needed me, and I decided that I really needed him as well. I needed to tell
him that I was sorry, that I finally understood that all he ever wanted was
to take care of me, help me be the best person I could be, and protect me
from harm."

Rano continued to explain that taking care of his father, as his health
slowly declined, helped him understand what sacrifices his father had
made for him: worrying about him when he was out late, repairing the
damage he did to the car, bailing him out of the many scrapes he got into.
Now Rano had to take a leave of absence from his job as an advertising
copywriter because he simply couldn't make the client deadlines long-
distance.

He did so willingly, hoping that his father would have done as much or
more for him. His parents had divorced twenty years earlier; he rarely saw
his mother and knew that, as an only child, taking care of his dad was pri-
marily his responsibility. But he welcomed the chance to mend the fences
that he knew had been broken over time.

We could see from Rano's face that this final season of his father's parent-hood was a difficult but meaningful one for him. Antonio had always wanted to get closer to his son, and he was able to tell Rano how happy he was that they were finally doing so, albeit at the end of his life. Taking care of Antonio in this last phase of his father's life reminded Rano of how important he had felt being needed by and taking care of his sons when they were young children.

Luckily for both of them, Rano was also moved by his father's suffering to see the importance of giving up being the "rebellious child" in this relationship and becoming the "responsible adult," an identity he now wished he could have assumed many years ago. Taking care of his father had helped Rano become mature enough now to be able to acknowledge his mistakes. By not only telling, but also showing, his dad how much he loved him and needed his love all through the years, he and his father would have the relationship that they had missed out on in the past decades.

Rano told us that during the year before his father's death, they had been able to talk about their beliefs and different views of the world. Antonio had been forced by his illness to take stock of his own life and decide what was really important: control or a relationship with his only son. By keeping an open mind, he was able to listen to Rano's story of youthful rebellion against what he believed to be an unjust war and corrupt politics and his desire to make the world a better place. Rano was also able to see Antonio's patriotic picture of life, duty, and commitment. They found that their beliefs weren't as far apart as they had thought, and although they regretted not having shared them with each other before, they were glad they were finally able to do so.

Rano was able for the first time to introduce his sons to their grandfather so they could know and understand this link to their past. He was proud of his boys and knew Antonio would like them, as well as Karina. Many tears were shed as Rano kept his long vigils with Antonio, wishing to replace their past wasted years with a life they could share. He had learned one important lesson from the past: Staying close to his grown sons could help all of them avoid repeating the regret he was now feeling.

Pamela, the Revolving Door

Pamela says that she didn't intentionally end up in a job that forced her to travel nine months out of the year. But after two divorces and three soured romances, this seventy-four-year-old whose children were fifty, forty-six, and forty-eight knew only how to keep living life on the go. After all, now her children didn't really need her, she told us. In fact, neither did her grandchildren. She was finally free—free of a man, free of children, free to explore the world.

Her children had been at odds with each other since childhood, and traveling was one way Pamela could avoid getting caught up in their squabbles. She found her grandchildren much easier to be with than her children, she reported to our Circles group, which was why she had just taken her twenty-three-year-old granddaughter on a safari in Africa, her latest adventure. Taking her grandchildren with her on trips was not only fun and kept her feeling young, but it was also a way that she could really get to know them without spending much time with her children.

"This time of life is not about rocking in a rocking chair, like it is for some of my friends," she explained. If she could still work, then that's what she wanted to do. Some of her friends were into charity work. Too much politics, she said. Besides, her youngest grandchildren, who were twelve and thirteen, were so proud of all of her travels. She would bring them exotic gifts from around the world, and they would eat them up. What other grandma was going to do that?

"Why sit around and wait to get sick and die?" was her famous line. This gutsy, in-control lady had been the same way as a child, she told us. If anyone dared her to do anything, she did it faster and bigger than the dare. She came by this no-nonsense attitude naturally.

"Nothing ever got past my mother, who was a real pistol," she told us, and she and her brother had always admired her spunkiness. When she died several years earlier, it made a lasting impact on her friends and family, inspiring them to reach for their dreams. Pamela hoped she was passing on this same legacy to her children, grandchildren, and great-grandchildren.

"If I stop traveling, what kind of role model will I be for my family?" Pamela asked us. "My parents are both gone, but I know that they would be proud of me for working so hard. Besides, I have to travel to see my grandkids because my children are all scattered across the country. This family is constantly at war with each other, so I have to be like a State Department shuttle diplomat to get to see anybody. Nobody comes to Grandma's anymore."

"If not now, when?" That was Pamela's mantra to motivate her to plan more time in her life to interact with her children and grandchildren. They all had busy lives of their own, sometimes too busy even to eat together on those rare occasions when Grandma visited on holidays. Pamela had fond memories of family dinners when her children were young many years ago, even though they often turned into bickering bashes. Now her children would rather do anything than get together at one place and break bread. "What did I do wrong?" she asked us. "Why don't they get along?"

As we learned more about the different personalities of each of Pamela's children, we shared our view that making her children close to each other was neither Pamela's responsibility nor under her control. We also reminded her that if she wanted to be close to them, it couldn't be just on *her* terms. She would have to be more available to fit her life around their agenda.

As she looked back over her life, Pamela felt that she must have failed somewhere since she wasn't the matriarch her own mother had been. Her children didn't revolve around her as she and her brother had around their mother. We learned that one of her sons was dependent on her for his livelihood, however, which was both good news and bad news for her.

He happened to be the one with whom she was the closest after her last divorce. He also was the one who was most like she was . . . with extravagant tastes and a love for travel. Like her son, she had a problem budgeting her finances. She was so in debt that she couldn't ever imagine getting out. Her son borrowed from her; she borrowed from her daughter; and her daughter screamed at her to stop this madness. Who was the grown-up and who was the child? her daughter would ask her mom.

It was a worthwhile question to examine, we admitted to Pamela. She had refused to take a mature position on her son's financial state because she would have felt hypocritical doing so, since she couldn't handle her own affairs. We suggested that both receive guidance from a professional financial counselor and a family therapist who could help them address the responsibility they were shirking and, in the process, gain a more fulfilling relationship based on mutual respect, not mutual dependency. They decided to give it a try, after which both she and her son agreed that "Neither a borrower nor a lender be," would have to apply from now on if they were to survive financially and become self-sufficient adults.

Pamela's ability to relate to her children and grandchildren was based not on her living the life of someone with great material wealth, we explained, but on her feeling connected emotionally and spiritually to them all. But she had no road map for how a family works when it's spread out all over the country and likes it that way. Her mission: Find a way to weave the family threads together to give her peace of mind and change her attitude about what constituted a good role model for her children from a workaholic to a doting grandmother. She also needed to realize that her family might be different from the one in which she grew up, but that it could still be nurturing for everyone.

Because her children were scattered hither and yon, Pamela continued her shuttle diplomacy, staying with each one for a short while so that she could get to know them better as adults. We urged her to pay close attention to the family traditions that her adult children had developed with their children in order to begin the process of weaving a new family fabric. Pamela didn't like it that her children weren't close to each other but reminded herself that this was a situation over which she had no control. By resolving to no longer get involved in their squabbles with each other, something that she had done since they were little children, Pamela started to enjoy her visits and was beginning to like the adults her children had become. She got the impression now that they actually enjoyed her visits more, too. As her grandchildren started calling to invite her to come to their birthday parties and soccer games, Pamela became hooked on reliving the "good old days" of her children's youth through grandparenthood.

Instead of bringing the family together at Grandma's—as she had envisioned—she was bringing Grandma to her family, rotating her visits on holidays and birthdays. In addition Pamela decided to follow our advice about prioritizing her family by making a career shift, even at her tender age, and becoming a travel agent. In this new career she knew that she could work anywhere in the country with e-mail and on-line access to everything she needed.

As she spent more time in her own home, however, she discovered that her adult children would ask if they could come to Grandma's over the summer to show *their* children where they grew up, something they couldn't ever do before because their mother was almost never there. Because her adult children now wanted their children to learn about their family's roots, they redefined Pamela as the matriarch of the household, just as her mother was. Now she had a road map for being a Plateau Parent that provided her with the best of both worlds: the freedom to travel to her children when she wanted as well as a home base her family could flock to when they needed to roost.

As the second circle of parenthood ends, fortunate are the Plateau Parents whose adult children treasure the sense of family that their parents have worked so hard for over two decades to build. From this perspective there comes a desire to be close to their Plateau Parents and to thank them for putting up with their rowdiness, particularly as they experience their own Volcano Dweller season. This gratitude will become a life raft for Plateau Parents when they enter the third circle of parenthood. It's only then that they will truly be able to reap the dividends of the emotional bank account they have been investing in for their entire lives.

Self-Discoveries of Plateau Parents

Your pocket guide to the truth revealed in the Plateau Parent season of parenthood.

- ➤ **Free at last, free at last . . .** Your children are off on their own, riding their roller coaster, having a good time, and making the best of their independence. As you ride the Ferris wheel of this season, you're exhilarated by your sense of freedom from the long years of parenthood.

- ➤ **Children are good; grandchildren are the best.** From your perch high above it all, the view is wonderful. But something is missing: the patter of little feet around the house, the smell of baby powder, the tinkling laughter of children. The gift of grandchildren fills that void and lets you go around the circle of your soul once again.

- ➤ **Why am I feeling so creaky?** From atop the Ferris wheel of this season of parenthood, you can see the entire vista of your parenthood: where you've been with your now grown children and where you're headed in the future. As you wave and try to talk to your children as you see them fly by on their roller coaster, you remember how it felt to maneuver those curves and catch your breath on the plunges. Now that you've been off the roller-coaster ride for a number of years, it looks like so much fun again. But you're grateful that being a grandparent isn't a full-time job like being a parent—you don't have the same kind of energy.

> **Being on top is scary and lonely.** As much as you want to stay steady, you feel yourself rocking as you realize that the winds of change are strong at the top. As the wheel starts to move again, you'll find that your parenthood skills will be needed in taking care of your own parents.

Exit Signs

Leaving the Plateau. Slow down: Dead end ahead. As you head down off the plateau, you begin to realize that this will be your last trip around Parenthood Park. You've been transformed into seven different identities by your adventures: Celebrity or Roadie, Sponge, Family Manager, Travel Agent, Volcano Dweller, Family Remodeler, and Plateau Parent. You've climbed the ladder to the top rung, after your parents vacated that spot, and now you can look back on where you've been and all of these identities, these personas, that your children have imposed on you. Your circle is almost complete as you watch your grandchildren and maybe great-grandchildren make their journey around the circles of their souls. The past seven seasons of parenthood have seen the seeds of independence, self-sufficiency, and responsibility flourish for over fifty years in fertile beds of unconditional love and mutual respect between you and your children. And as your ability to live independently fades, it's time for your children to take care of you . . . as you took care of them.

Being Parented by Children

Rebounder

CHILD'S GOLDEN YEARS

The one who thinks over his experiences most, and weaves them into systematic relations with each other, will be the one with the best memory.—WILLIAM JAMES

YOUR DAUGHTER DRIVES YOU to the doctor. Your son helps you pay the bills. Your granddaughter brings over the groceries. Your grandson calls just to see if you're okay . . . every day. When you begin to need your adult children and grandchildren to take care of you in these ways, you've left the Plateau Parent season behind and have entered the Rebounder season of parenthood.

You may be a Rebounder for a short time, just for the final days of your life, if you're struck by an acute illness or suffer a debilitating or critical physical injury. Or you may be a Rebounder for many years, as you more gradually lose your ability to be an independent player in the game of parenthood. During this last season, however, all parents inevitably and predictably become Rebounders who try to bounce back from health problems as they struggle to remain independent and adjust to the need for care during the tarnishing of the golden years.

In basketball, rebounders love to jump for the ball after a player tries to score. They are right under the basket, on the ready, eager to make the

267

next play. In parenthood, Rebounders do the same as they wait expectantly for a sign that they are needed, wanted, special: a request for advice by their granddaughter, an invitation to go to lunch or a movie with their son, or a gift for their birthday from their great-granddaughter. If they consider themselves members of a successful family, they will be honored, revered, and respected as they are still seen and see themselves as the team leader—the family matriarch or patriarch—despite their limited playing time during this final season.

Regardless of your chronological age—usually between seventy and one hundred years of age—as a Rebounder you can still be vital, can still contribute to the family, when you have a team of children, grandchildren, and great-grandchildren who understand your value. Then the Rebounder years will be peaceful and rewarding. You'll become the heroes you always dreamed of being and will pass on the legacy of love and caring that you hoped and prayed would be yours. Whether or not this will be a season filled with love and compassion, familiar faces, and gentle words depends on how your adult children—who are now the Plateau Parents that you used to be—include you in their day-to-day lives.

PARENTS IN OUR CIRCLES groups who were in this season of parenthood fell into three categories of Rebounders, depending on their personal style of playing the game of parenthood that they had been practicing since childhood: the Proud Independents, the Humble Submissives, and the Aged Sages. The Proud Independents balked at any assistance but the most fashionable of canes and resisted the idea of moving out of their house or accepting any kind of "helping hand" from the younger generation, just as they resisted their parents' helping them get dressed and do homework, for example, throughout childhood. They sought to prove to their children, grandchildren, and great-grandchildren that they were still the fully capable players they used to be and believed they still were.

On the other hand, the Humble Submissives in this season sported a different attitude from their more feisty counterparts, an attitude characterized by regret for inconveniencing their adult children, which led them to also believe that they weren't getting the help they needed and wanted. By admitting that they needed and wanted help, but not asking for it, they took on the persona of the whining children they used to be themselves: the children who never seemed to get enough attention.

The third category of Rebounders, the Aged Sages, combined the best qualities of Proud Independents and Humble Submissives. These Rebounders strove to maintain their independence but were willing to ask for help and to recognize that they were fortunate to get it. They were also sufficiently humble in making requests of their children rather than making demands and whining when their needs weren't immediately met. These Aged Sages were typically the peacemakers in their childhood years. Spending time with their family was rewarding to them because they loved each other's company. They were truly unselfish team players, happiest doing for others and working together for the good of the entire family.

A LL THAT HAS COME before prepares Rebounders for this last passage of their lives, even their passage through death. The power that the end of parenthood holds depends on how Rebounders were built, season by season, by the impact of their children on them during their children's childhood and their children's adulthood. Parents reflect in this season on how much their children are and have been their focal point, how much of their identity as parents has determined who they are and how their lives were spent.

In this final season of parenthood, as in every season, it is the interaction—the teamwork, coordinated play, and number of assists—among the generations that determines parents' peace of mind, the security of their souls, the meaning at the core of their being.

MAKING NICE

Until you make peace with who you are, you'll never be content with what you have.—DORIS MORTMAN

When parents become Rebounders, they complete the fundamental change in their relationship with their children that has been slowly taking place since the Family Remodeling season: adult children need their parents less and less, while their parents come to need *them* more and more. Initially the need for parents and their children to separate and then reconnect at an adult level is mostly psychological; but as parents become Rebounders, their psychological connection with their adult children remains constant and the physical need to be connected increases.

Rebounders need to maintain the connection between the generations to keep their identity as mother and father intact. Research has also proven that this connection improves Rebounders' health, according to Dean Ornish, author of *Love and Survival: The Scientific Basis for the Healing Power of Intimacy:* in a Harvard University study, 126 healthy graduates in the 1950s were asked about the tenor of their relationships with their parents. In a follow-up survey thirty-five years later, 91 percent of those who had reported not being close with their mothers were experiencing major health problems, such as heart disease, high blood pressure, duodenal ulcers, and alcoholism. Among those who had earlier reported feeling close to their mothers, the figure was 45 percent.

Those Rebounders whom we interviewed who appeared to make their main concern pleasing their children, grandchildren, and great-grandchildren found that "making nice" encouraged their family to give them the support they desired, as well as the best chances for optimum health and longevity. You can "catch more flies with honey than with vinegar," was the battle cry of one Aged Sage Rebounder whom we interviewed:

"When I stopped complaining that my daughter never called or my sons never came to see me, I suddenly became more popular. I had to learn not to push my grandchildren into taking care of me. Instead I asked them about their lives and didn't complain about mine. Like magic, they then started coming to family night at the retirement center where I live, showing off their children's report cards and pictures of their latest vacation. They even remembered to include me on the invitation list for my grandchildren's and great-grandchildren's birthday parties."

Another Aged Sage, seventy-eight-year-old Kate, also illustrates this point: Kate told us that she listened intently to her fifty-seven-year-old daughter, Bonnie, for her opinion about the car that Bonnie insisted she buy. She realized that Bonnie was more in the know than she was about what was the safest, most affordable, and, above all, the most "in" car because she had just bought a new car for her own daughter, a senior in high school.

She didn't mind driving her big, fifteen-year-old car; but Bonnie insisted that she drive one that was smaller, more compact, complete with air bags and the latest safety features. Although Kate had bought her own cars for over forty years, she liked the idea that she was coming to rely on Bonnie's advice now. Kate felt as if all of her motherly efforts to teach Bonnie to be a responsible, capable, caring woman were paying off, she told us. In short, "making nice" was a productive way for this Aged Sage to feel victorious in the game of parenthood.

Humble Submissive Rebounders, on the other hand, still remember when *they* held the job of consultant to their adult children as Plateau Parents. But now that the players have different positions and their *children* are Plateau Parents, many told us that they felt useless because their children no longer turned to them for advice about friends, spouses, and business and personal problems as they used to. These Rebounders, who now feel as if they just "sit on the bench," need to be needed just as they did in the Family Remodeler season. So they do what they can to "make nice" to their adult children so they will keep them in the game and make them think that their lives are still valuable to the family.

Rebounders try as hard as they can to avoid laying guilt trips on their children when their offspring don't meet their expectations, notes Jane, a Humble Submissive in one of our Circles groups who was recovering from hip replacement surgery: "Leila, my seventy-year-old daughter, is always the last one who calls after my physical therapy appointments that my son is kind enough to take me to each week. Now it hurts me so badly that she never even asks how my hip is, even if she calls a few days after my therapy. She seems to be too busy to think much about her poor old mother, and I hate to bother her. So I just call her when I feel good enough to not complain about all of my problems. She's always telling me not to whine so much. I wish I could have my great-grandchildren over to play, just like I used to with my grandchildren when they were young. Let's see, that'd be about thirty years ago. Shoot, time's getting away from me!"

Morris felt the same way as Jane. He hated to spend the weekends in his retirement home. Everyone was invited to their kids' houses for Friday night dinner, Saturday lunch, or Sunday brunch but him. This Humble Submissive would drop gentle hints to his kids that weekends were like a ghost town at the home, not trying to force his way into his son's and daughter's busy lives, but silently hoping they'd just figure out on their own how lonely he was and bring him to one of their houses to watch a game on television even one weekend a month. Sometimes he would ask them to pick up some laxative, vitamins, and juice for him, hoping they wouldn't feel he was imposing on them and praying that a dinner invitation might come when they saw his empty refrigerator after dropping off their purchases.

Being an imposition was a crime worse than death for Fiona, one Proud

Independent we interviewed. She had lived in her house for over fifty years, seventeen of them all by herself since her husband had died. Although the time had long passed for her to move out of her bungalow, which was falling down around her, according to her two daughters, Fiona kept putting off the time for discussing that event. Maybe next summer, she'd tell the children, thanking them for their offer to help with home repairs so they could put the house on the market but refusing even to entertain the thought of moving to one of those "jail cell" apartments in the senior citizen center near the condominium of one of her daughters.

Fiona also told her children that she thought it was nice of them to think of her welfare by suggesting that she quit her volunteer hours at the hospital three blocks from her home; they told her that they feared for her life when she had to climb the stairs in her house, let alone cross the busy intersection to get to the hospital. She was grateful for their concern but had her own agenda: to prove just how fully capable she was of living her life as independently as she had since she was a feisty teen over seventy years ago.

A S GRANDPARENTS OF OLDER grandchildren who themselves are having children, Rebounders now have a whole new generation to "make nice" to. Once again they find that they must reinvent themselves in this season as they take on a new identity: great-grandparent. Another circle of little people exploring their world and demanding to be noticed gives great-grandparents reason to pause and reflect on the underlying truth of parenthood: Children define their parents' lives.

Adult children, their children, and their children's children have the powerful upper hand in this game, as usual, because they are now the Rebounders' reason for getting up in the morning, to get suited up and ready to play, even if other team members are now miles away. For example, getting a daughter's letter from her vacation or a postcard written by a five-year-old grandson can make being alive worthwhile for a Rebounder. Again, the attention from her offspring is a sign to the Rebounder that she has been a good parent or grandparent. But some parents, particularly the Humble Submissives, worry about seeming too needy for attention in this season:

"So I won't outstay my welcome, we only stay three days when we go see my daughter's family to celebrate each holiday together. And they only live one hundred miles away," remarked one of our grandparent interviewees. "We just don't want to bother anyone or get anything messed up, not on our account. We just don't want to be in the way."

Whether they want to be or not, an increasing number of Rebounders will be "in the way" of their Plateau Parents' lives as the baby boomer generation continues to age. In 1998 one baby boomer was turning fifty every eight seconds, and more of those boomers will be making it to the Rebounder season. By the year 2050 there will be thirty-six Rebounders who are over age sixty-five who may need to be cared for by their Plateau Parents, compared with six Rebounders who were in the same season of parenthood in 1900. The medical, political, and social advances that are putting a young spin on old age are teaching everyone that boomer Rebounders are becoming an ever increasing force to be reckoned with, particularly in the lives of their Plateau Parent adult children.

The media have generally portrayed Rebounders as Humble Submissives who are perpetually crabby, unsatisfied, and bothersome "old people." We predict that this stereotyping of Rebounders will inevitably change when the boomers start to become Rebounders because of the reciprocal nature of "making nice." As increasing numbers of baby boomer Rebounders need the Plateau Parent generation to take care of them, their influence on the national stereotyping of aging will begin to make life nicer for the oldest generation of Americans.

FINAL ACCOUNTING

The true appreciation of life's puzzles and pains is not in the living, but in the accounting.—JACQUELYN MITCHARD

Time. This last season of parenthood revolves around how much time is left on the Big Clock in the game of life. Is there time to heal all the old childhood wounds? Is there time to patch up old holes in conversations with grandchildren? Is there time to relate to another generation? Time is either Rebounders' enemy or friend, or a little of both, because it is, once again, how you interpret the hourglass of your life (half-full or half-empty) that determines how you function in this season.

As Rebounders, you have a say in the quality of the legacy you will leave. You take stock of all aspects of this season of parenthood—who will inherit the family treasures in your homes, all of your personal belongings, and any financial fortune you have amassed. Everything is seen in the light of what you have left to give to your family while you're alive, as well as what you have to leave that will benefit your family after you're gone. All of these decisions revolve around the factor of time—and health—and how these resources are best utilized in the last season of parenthood.

Rebounders tell us that they worry: Am I close to my children? Are my children close to each other? Are they able to appreciate what I did all these years so that I wouldn't be a burden to them now? Will my children keep our faith? Will my children think about my grandchildren and great-grandchildren financially or squander their inheritance? Should I simply have fun playing now and not be concerned about whether anyone else benefits from my life's hard work?

While reflecting on their family's lives, many Circles groups of parents in this season told us that they uncovered old wounds: "I only have one regret," ninety-five-year-old great-grandmother Bertha told us with tear-filled eyes. "My mother never told me that she loved me."

Bertha admitted that it surprised her to hear herself say those words because it proved to her that even after "all these years," her pain remained. It wasn't that her mother didn't love her, she continued. She just never *told* her that she did. Bertha said that she told *her* children every day how much she loved them because she hadn't had that gift given to her. She never pushed them to do anything for her, she shared, but did ask for help when she needed it. All of her friends thought that her children were saints. Bertha agreed.

"Making nice" worked for everyone in her family because now her family expressed their love for her. Bertha said that their doing so was her biggest accomplishment. Even her great-grandchildren told her how much they loved her, she related to us proudly. All this Aged Sage Rebounder had to do was call her family when she was feeling left out of the game during this season of parenthood. And they were only too happy to remind her that they needed her "assists": her love, her attention, her quick wit, her special touch. Although they all lived out of town, Bertha's family wrote weekly notes, sent her gifts on holidays, and, along with their parents and grandparents, celebrated her ninetieth birthday with her at a big party they threw.

Many parents we interviewed were not as fortunate as Bertha to have caring children and grandchildren. Most of these Rebounders fell into the Humble Submissive category and were angry and bitter toward everyone. Their regrets about their family colored their view of their lives: "I wish my children called more. Then I'd be happy"; "If only they came to see me more, I wouldn't be so lonely"; "I wish my children would let me spend more time with them and the grandkids."

These Humble Submissives had no one to play with, felt out of the game and permanently on the bench, leaving deep and painful scars on everyone. For those who still hoped to reconcile their regrets, the fear of the circle of their soul closing before they were at peace with themselves was real.

IT IS THE CUMULATIVE interest of parenthood that now reveals itself. The account has been open for at least fifty years now. How it has been managed through all of the previous seven seasons—Celebrity, Sponge, Family Manager, Travel Agent, Volcano Dweller, Family Remodeler, and Plateau Parent—and how conflicts have or have not been resolved in each, determine where the family fits into parents' final accounting.

"All of my goals have been met; I've accomplished what I set out to do," commented a Proud Independent named Marvin in one of our Circles groups. "I now see how lucky I am because I have nothing to prove to any-one anymore."

When he retired two years earlier at age eighty, Marvin's fifty-five-year-old son was made the CEO of the family insurance business. "I was my son's mentor until he took over the business, but now that's done," he said. "You cannot have two bosses, so I have to be careful and not second-guess his decisions. I know he likes for me to be around when *he* wants me to, and I like to be whatever help I can. I've been around forever. I inherited the business from my father, who came to America on a boat when he was fifteen years old. The newcomers in the company don't have any idea how much sweat went into making it what it is today. I like to tell them stories from the old days when we were just starting."

Part of parents' final accounting means getting to a comfort zone such as Marvin has, a place in which a Rebounder is content with who he is. Also a Proud Independent, eighty-eight-year-old Dodi talked about feeling good about inviting her sixty-year-old daughter, Kari, to stay at her house when Kari moved to town; but she also shed no tears when she left. Kari was still the disorganized, easily distracted child she used to be, according to her mother:

"I have come to accept the fact that Kari is not going to do things the way I want her to do them. I finally don't feel responsible for her decisions, right or wrong." Dodi was comforted by her final and absolute resignation of needing to be in control of her daughter's life.

ADULT CHILDREN PLAY a role in ensuring that this season of parenthood is comfortable for their parents when they assist them with this life-in-review process. When their relationships are built on love, mutual respect, and trust, they listen patiently to their parents' stories of yesteryear; encourage their parents to enjoy life now; and support their interest in spirituality and religion that is comforting to both generations as Rebounders' lives draw to a close.

This season may signal the first time that parents feel the desire or pull to make peace with the fact that they may not be around for many more years. But how do they reconcile such a thing? Our Circles groups of Rebounders drew upon their experiences with the passing of their own parents to chart their course in navigating these treacherous waters. Their own parents' views about death—whether they thought of it as a natural part of their lives, as a dreaded inevitability, or as a transition to a better place, for example—impacted Rebounders' own perspective about the end of life. In addition, when they were able to help their parents with their final accounting as well as witness their parents' final days, making peace with their own life's end was already a familiar, and therefore a more comfortable, process.

In the same vein, Rebounders' histories with their own parents motivated them to either repeat or change the way they informed their own children about their finances, burial arrangements, living wills, family keepsakes, and insurance policies. Wanting to share these seemingly morbid matters appeared odd to some of their Plateau Parent children, out of character or scary, particularly when they had never talked with their parents about such adult topics before or witnessed their grandparents' ease in doing so. Some Rebounders told us that they tried to introduce these subjects in the context of "when I'm gone," but their children, who were in denial about their parents' advancing age, quickly hushed this upsetting subject.

Although their adult children may resist the notion that their Rebounder parents now need them to be responsible for carrying on the family traditions and rituals, they may feel even more uncomfortable trying to accept the fact that their parents have made their "final" plans. The bottom line? Plateau Parent children are forced to face the fact that they are now or will become their parents' parents, the most traumatic emotional transition of their lives, because they have spent their entire lives being their parents' children, even as adults. Plateau Parents don't know how to take on this new identity, although they may have been shown the way by their parents, just as their parents don't have clear directions for their journey as a Rebounder, other than the models their own parents have been.

Eighty-two-year-old Claudia told us that her daughter, Ann Marie, would explode into tears whenever she would bring up the subject of her last wishes—wanting to be cremated and have her ashes sprinkled in her rose garden. Claudia was frustrated by her daughter's refusal even to listen to her plans, she told us, because Claudia felt a certain sense of peace in thinking about spending eternity among her beautiful roses. Claudia's acceptance of the finality of her life was an important key to opening doors to her comfort and security. Sharing her vision of not only how she wanted to be treated in her final days, but also how her daughter would carry on without her, was critical to ensuring that both generations appreciated the time they had together in this final season of parenthood.

As a means to this end, Claudia decided to detail her wishes in a notebook in which she also tucked information about her insurance policies, an advance directive, a safety deposit box key, her will, and her estate plan. She put these things in a large manila envelope and gave it to her daughter for her to read in private. "I'm still doing things to try to please my daughter after all these years," she admitted. "I hate to see her upset. As the old saying goes, 'A mother is only as happy as her least happy child.' "

A S IN EVERY OTHER SEASON, parents' responses to their children create the most riveting memories for both generations. If Rebounders' memories of their critical parents create guilt-inducing pictures of old people who never seemed satisfied with the way their adult children treated them, they are faced with a decision—to repeat or to change this negative legacy their parents left them. Depending on their response to the memories, therefore, Rebounders can be drawn closer to their families or pushed away from them.

If Rebounders can adopt a perspective of seeing their adult children's care as necessary and nurturing, they can feel a sense of gratitude toward their children for their care and support that is unmatched in any other season. Findings from two major polls conducted for the American Associ-ation of Retired Persons (AARP) shed light on this issue. According to the surveys, ". . . more than a third of elderly parents say their grown children have failed to help them in a time of need in the past five years. But when asked the same question, only 16 percent of adult children agreed. In an-other finding, 67 percent of older parents said that they didn't need ser-vices to enable them to be independent."

In interpreting these data, Constance Swank, AARP's director of re-search, said: "If you don't perceive you need help, you are less likely to perceive you are getting it."

The old adage "Perception is reality" holds true for Rebounders as they do their final accounting. In their final season, Rebounders are deter-mining whether they will leave this world with the same kind of "stats" their parents had. Their reminiscing about days gone by is an important tool through which they can interpret all of the identities, changes, losses, separations, and agendas that they have lived through during every season of parenthood. Reconciling one's life feels purposeful, as parents actually teach their adult children, grandchildren, and great-grandchildren lessons about aging and parenthood while seeing how many points they have ac-crued over their lifetime.

HELP! WHO'S IN CHARGE?

The last of the human freedoms—to choose one's attitude in
any given set of circumstances, to choose one's own way.
—VICTOR FRANKL

The essence of this season of parenthood lies in that provocative subject that has been a source of conflict throughout parents' lives: control. As Re-bounders, parents need to feel emotionally and psychologically in charge of their own lives, even while they may not be physically able to make their formerly routine parenthood moves—doing their own laundry, going shopping, keeping house.

Again, as in every other season of parenthood, children hold the key to unlocking the important door of self-respect for their parents. When they listen to their parents' wishes and follow their directions, the old patterns of parent/child relationships still feel intact. Now, however, these adult children are caring for their parents in ways that remind them of caring for their own young children—encouraging their parents' independence, self-reliance, and responsibility for their own lives, as is reasonably safe.

This universal and predictable aging process that eventually makes "children" out of all of us is frightening to Proud Independent Rebounders. It causes a gradual loss of control over their time in the game of life, a loss that some say makes them feel as if they are losing their minds, not to mention their ability to make their own decisions. Marge, an eighty-three-year-old Proud Independent member of our Circles group, knew firsthand how control could be a sticky issue. Although she had twisted her ankle as well as broken her hip in the past year, she said that she just couldn't wait until she could walk again without assistance:

"I may go slow, but I'm still going to walk without a metal cage in front of me," she told us. "After all, what would my great-grandchildren think if their great-grandma was hobbling around? My mother always told me when she was my age that nice ladies don't hobble around! My children drive me crazy, though. They want me to use a walker all the time."

The Proud Independents like Marge whom we interviewed had daily conflicts with their adult children and neighbors over issues of autonomy and quality of life. These Rebounders who insist on maintaining their independence, even when it is dangerous to do so, are stuck in the quicksand of still wanting to parent their adult children and not be parented by them. They make the necessary transitions in this season of parenthood difficult for all generations.

Cyrus, one Proud Independent eighty-year-old father of two grown sons whom we interviewed, resented others wanting to take charge of his life. He had started his own real estate agency in his neighborhood fifty years ago after working for ten years as a real estate agent for another company. Now his sons and granddaughters wanted him to retire so they could take over the business.

"Who are they to tell me to leave my empire after all these years?" Cy shouted. "I'm doing fine! I grew up in this neighborhood and played in the park down the street where I like to take my lunch now. I can take care of myself and do what I want. What do they have up their sleeve, putting me out to pasture? They don't want to have to worry about me! They want all of my money, and they don't really care if I live or die!"

Proud Independents want never to be at the mercy of their children, or of anyone else, for that matter, according to those we interviewed. They rebel against their adult children's intervention in their lives, against their telling them where they could live, what they should eat, how much money they have and could spend, and when they should get the mental and physical care they need.

Ironically, then, parents are now reaping what they sowed. By their example, Proud Independent Rebounders have taught their children to be in control of their own lives. So their adult children try to dictate what their parents do, as a natural consequence of the modeling they had. How parents react to this necessary evil determines whether this season deteriorates into a battle of wills.

As with the Proud Independents, the Humble Submissive Rebounders we interviewed generally didn't have a good relationship with their children, because they didn't ask for what they needed and wanted and then complained when they didn't get it. These helpless "children" stayed in the background, waiting for invitations and any displays of caring and love, much as they did as young children. The most cherished moments in their lives were getting an invitation to join the "kids" for dinner or to share in the grandkids' social events, such as soccer tournaments and ballet recitals. Both kinds of Rebounders counted the outstretched arms of their adult children as indicators that the continuity of their identity as mother or father was still there, even as they were being slowly transformed back to their childhood selves.

During their decades of parenthood, Aged Sages had a different perspective about life than their Proud Independent and Humble Submissive counterparts. Taking the long view of the essence of parenthood—making meaningful and lasting connections between parents and their children—was critical to their intellectual, spiritual, emotional, and physical health. This long view enabled them to adapt to the inevitable changes in life and provided them with ample emotional support, which led to their happiness and well-being, as well as to longevity, according to recent research.

A pioneering study at the University of Southern California in Los Angeles found that "a close, affectionate relationship with middle-aged children prolongs survival for the elderly," according to a report in *USA Today*. In fact, the article noted that "loving ties with middle-aged kids do more to lengthen life than any functional support."

" 'Most people realize healthy family relationships are a good thing, but many haven't realized that this is so important [that] it can affect their survival,' says study leader Haitao Wang." One finding: "Even after taking into account practical support from offspring, those who felt above-average closeness with their children were 40% less likely to die over the thirteen years than those below-average in closeness with their kids."

The connections made with family through the first and second circles of parenthood allow Rebounders to now feel immortal, to be fully alive, forever through their offspring and *their* offspring's unending circles. When Rebounders see that these spiritual connections to life on earth that their family have provided give meaning to their own lives in their final days, and link them to a universal circle, they start to believe that some larger, more powerful force must be in charge of their destiny—not just themselves, their doctors, or their children. Many Rebounders in our Circles groups asked rhetorically: What other explanation do we have for feeling so in touch with the larger family of all human beings?

Watching them reach out to a higher power for comfort and a sense of purpose and direction makes a lasting positive impression on their adult children, who grow closer to their parents when they share a common spiritual bond in both an earthly and ethereal sense, Rebounders reported. If their adult children's own spiritual awareness is untapped, however, they might think that their parents have "gone off the deep end" or have "lost it," as one Rebounder put it whose adult children were aghast when she started to explore her religious roots for the first time in her life. These adult children of Rebounders might be frightened by realizing that they ultimately are losing control over what happens to their parents, just as they were fearful when they had to adjust to the fact that they ultimately had no control over their children's lives.

Comfort for Clara: Staying Independent

At Clara's eightieth birthday party, she bragged about her one-year-old great-granddaughter, Melinda, with enormous pride. Melinda was the new light in the lives of her thirty-year-old grandson, Grant, and his wife, Shari. Clara saw her fifty-six-year-old daughter, Cindy, and son-in-law, Albert, doing everything they could for their grandchild, just as she and her husband, Donald, also eighty, had done for Grant. Her daughter, grandson, and now great-granddaughter gave her a reason for living that she had previously found in her career as a pioneering female lawyer.

On her seventy-fifth birthday, Clara retired from her life as a partner in the pressure cooker of the law firm that still had her name on the door. She had started working at the firm as a clerk fifty-five years earlier and had taken some time off when Donald had a serious bout of pneumonia. After he recovered, she decided that maybe it was a good time to stop pushing herself so hard. Retirement seemed like such a good idea as she thought about all the things she would like to finally do, such as travel, learn how to play golf, and relish the priceless experience of playing with her great-granddaughter.

Clara thought that her great-granddaughter might afford her one last try to influence a new little person. But the times had changed so much since she was a mother that she found herself absolutely in awe of the equipment and conveniences that Shari used to care for her daughter. When she and Donald visited Shari and Grant on their farm twenty miles out of town, they would retreat to the bedroom each night at about eight P.M. Clara realized that she was tired, unable to fight the bedtime battles or clean the house and plan schedules for Melinda as she had done when caring for Grant whenever Cindy and Albert went out of town. It was clear now that everybody else had a role in caring for Melinda but her. Clara wondered if her inability to help care for Melinda was a sign that she'd soon need someone to help take care of her.

However, she was determined that no one was going to have to pay money to take care of her! Therefore she bought nursing home insurance for Donald and her, so that Cindy and Al's energy could be devoted solely to grandparenting Melinda. She and Donald still wanted to live in their own home, as they had for fifty years, so it scared her when she wasn't able to do everything she used to do without feeling as if she had been run over by a truck. But she knew that she shouldn't complain. Every week she attended a funeral for someone she used to work with, or his or her mom or dad. She was glad that she had saved and wisely invested over the years, since this would ensure her independence.

Unfortunately, she did feel as though she were becoming a nuisance to her daughter in one way. Clara's increasing problems with hearing and seeing upset Cindy, who would nag her when her hearing aid would squeal or wasn't working well, or when she wouldn't wear her glasses because they hurt her nose. These conflicts were making her feel as if she were the child instead of the parent. Memories of those years when Cindy was an obedient daughter who consulted her about raising her son seemed as if they came from someone else's life.

Clara remembered being the same kind of dutiful daughter Cindy had been. She found herself filling her time alone reminiscing about her child-hood growing up on a farm in the Midwest. As a child, whenever she felt alone and unimportant, her mother would tell her that everything would be okay. Clara now wished that she could have her mother here to comfort her whenever she felt lonely, which was happening more and more often. She se-cretly liked having Cindy worry about her, a feeling that she didn't dare tell Cindy about because it would ruin her independent image!

We discovered in our interviews that in this season of parenthood there seems to be a caste system in place. Those on top are the ones whose chil-dren slather them with attention, gifts, food, and visits. As if they are at summer camp, parents told us they felt the best when they were "made nice over," worried about, but not told what to do or issued ultimatums, particularly if others could see that they were the recipients of their adult children's "no strings attached" care packages. This is important informa-tion for all generations to tuck away as they consider their personal "love" inventories. For parents of adult children who are now Plateau Parents themselves, every day is an opportunity to seize a moment to care, which was Clara's reason for retiring and focusing on her family. Her agenda was simple: Be there for the kids and be able to give and receive their love and adoration. She told us she regretted that she had worked so hard and for so many hours when her children were younger; now she wanted to make up for lost time through her children, grandchildren, and great-grandchildren.

We suggested that her challenge now would be to adjust from being a Proud Independent to being an Aged Sage grandma and great-grandma, as well as mom. She admitted that it made her feel good inside that her chil-dren worried about her, nagged her about her hearing aid and the like. Clara finally realized that she didn't need the title of "lawyer" to feel proud of who she was. She just needed her family's love.

Her mom and dad had been the focus of her life as they reached this season, she realized with a shudder. Knowing how much it had meant to them when she became their caretaker motivated her to let her daughter fuss over her. It was the normal course of events, Clara told us matter-of-factly. It was the way the world worked.

Once Clara decided that this role reversal was "normal," she and her daughter benefited from each other's efforts. Doing so helped Clara put a positive spin on being an Aged Sage in this final season. Why fight it? she asked. She had done everything the right way: bought insurance, retired gracefully, saved wisely, and taught her kids to navigate on their own.

The only thing left to do was make peace with the fact that being a good enough parent was enough of a lifetime résumé. As she saw the generations age, Clara understood that time marches on, regardless of our opinion about it. With her pragmatic attitude and belief that the circles around her would still spin beautifully without her, Clara was at peace.

Steve's Crash Course: Unreconciled Family Feuds

Like a cat with nine lives, seventy-eight-year-old Steve had been at death's door several times in the past few months, according to his son, Gardner. He was unbelievable, "like an Energizer bunny," Gardner joked, shaking his head.

His humorous comments about Steve's still being alive hid the underlying crisis brewing inside Gardner. The family was at extreme odds with each other. Gardner wasn't talking to his sister, Annette; Gardner's son was on the outs with his stepmother, Gina, the second of Gardner's wives. Steve had always thought that their children were both wrong for not being able to reconcile their differences with the family. It made life so complicated that Steve could hardly keep the family feuds straight, as innocent relatives started to take sides. When his children would come to visit him, Steve would ask one about the other, hoping to hear some good news.

"Remember, we don't speak to each other, Gardner told Steve, referring to his sister, Annette. Gardner corrected himself in his discussion with us by explaining that they spoke only when their father was about to give them something from his estate. But by now Steve actually had little left to his name. His children had cleaned out their house after he and his wife, Joan, had moved to an assisted living center just six months earlier, leaving only a few pieces of furniture and some paintings that even they did not want. He didn't fight their greed; it was easier just to go along with whatever they wanted in order to avoid a fight.

That was, of course, the pattern of his whole life. His children had run all over him as they were growing up, and now, things were no different. They had always made him feel as though they were entitled to everything that he and his wife had. That was never as much as the other families seemed to have, but he told us that they did okay; and what they did have, they sacrificed to get for the sake of their children.

Every time his children fought about what he should eat or what medicines he should take, he got sweaty and wobbly, literally weak in the knees. He knew that all they wanted was his money, but he was helpless to do anything about that. After all, they had gone through most of it when they were young! Now he knew that he was getting weaker and weaker, he told us in a bedside chat. He had no patience for their unsavory discourse.

Annette and Gardner needed to begin acting like parents of young children who decide just how much information their toddler or preschooler can handle before telling them all the sordid details of their adult problems. Although their father could intellectually understand the turn of events in his life—the feuds based on jealousy, sibling rivalry, greed, and control—he couldn't handle them emotionally. He was disturbed by the fact that although he had become a Rebounder who seemed to be in the spotlight much of the time, he was not a hero to his children.

Steve wanted to be remembered for being a good person, for loving his children and being adored by them, not for being someone in the middle of a knock-down, drag-out drama. He also resented being seen only as a source of "things," rather than as a fountain from which his children could nurture their souls.

The bickering and backbiting nature of his children's ways and their greedy coveting of what little he had left were shattering his dreams. Things were no different from the days when his children would claw at each other at the kitchen table and living room couch, he realized with regret. Because of their feuding, he decided not to put them in charge of his living trust. He would rather that his friend Nate, a lawyer at the bank he frequented, be the person who handled his affairs after he was gone. He needed to know that he could trust that person, that he or she would represent his best interest, and he didn't want to bother Joan with all of the details of their finances. It made him sad to feel that his children weren't trustworthy enough for the job.

They didn't understand who their father was, Steve told us. Instead they treated him simply as someone who was dispensable, someone whose purpose in life had been served and could now be thrown away. He knew that they didn't respect him, and it hurt him to know that he had been of such little importance in their lives. He certainly didn't feel appreciated, and as he looked back on his life, he began to realize why. He had never been a participant in his children's lives and had never provided a model from which they could have learned about communication, empathy, and caring for others. So now he was paying for it, he decided.

Steve told us that it was hard for him to concentrate on his own "exit strategy" while he worried about what would happen to his house and what remained of his possessions when he was gone. Would his children take care of them? They had sold almost everything that he had given them or they had taken from him and his wife. He was bound and determined to retain some sense of control over his own life. He saw his children as not having any time for him now, just as he hadn't had time for his parents, who had basically ignored him while he was growing up.

Instead of fighting the tide that was making it difficult to die gracefully, Steve had to work on his own internal patches of ice on which he and any of his family could slip and fall at any moment. Because he was so consumed with the turmoil caused by his children's feuds, he hadn't taken the time to forgive himself or his children for the mistakes they had made and the suffering they had all endured. He was as much at fault as they were, he now realized. He was reaping what he had sown.

"If I had to do my life over again," he noted, "I would have invested more in my children's thoughts and feelings, not just in the material things they needed and demanded."

We suggested to Steve that he apologize for his past transgressions. He needed to tell his children that he loved them and to forgive himself, rather than beat himself up for living his life as he did. By doing so, he could reinforce in his children the lesson that they had just taught him. Even in the last days of his life, his children's pull on his heart and soul was the most powerful force he would ever feel, if he allowed himself to feel it. It is a risk, as Steve had discovered, to shut yourself off from it.

The downside of choosing not to get drenched with the sweet and savory flavors of parenthood during his lifetime came to haunt Steve like a nightmare. He loved his children so much that he wanted to do what he could to help prevent them from making the mistakes he and his own parents had made. We were proud of the courage he displayed and were impressed by the energy he mustered before he died to tell his son and daughter to invest their time and love where they would reap the highest interest in return: in their children.

Ruth's Uprising: The Battle for Independence

Ruth, an eighty-seven-year-old participant in one of our retirement center Circles groups, knew how to speak her mind. "No, I will not move out!" was her first reaction when her three children, sixty-four- and sixty-one-year-old daughters and a fifty-nine-year-old son, insisted that she leave her home of thirty-six years and move to a distant city and live with her oldest daughter.

She explained that she was perfectly capable of living by herself and just wanted her children to stop nagging her about how they thought she needed somebody around all the time. Being on her own was exactly what she wanted after her husband, Myron, died fifteen years ago. Myron had been quite the talker; at first she found the quiet almost too loud. But she adjusted to the silence in the house and found she needed it after a long day of volunteering at school.

When we questioned her about her volunteer job, Ruth told us proudly, "I still walk to the neighborhood school to tutor and then walk back home every day, just like I've done for fifty years, ever since my children went to school there."

Volunteering kept Ruth connected to the best part of her life, she explained. To her, working in the same place that held her fondest memories was a lifesaver; but to her children, it was a recipe for disaster. They worried that she could get hit by a car crossing the street because she was unsteady on her feet and easily got confused about where she was going.

Ruth couldn't understand what had happened to make her children such worriers. When they were younger, they were so happy that she was a part of their school, tutoring in reading and helping the kids who had trouble with spelling and writing. Now it seemed as if they thought that she wasn't smart enough anymore . . . just because she was a little older. It hurt her feelings so much to see that her own children had so little respect for the work that she had done for so long.

It shouldn't have been surprising, though, that they didn't understand the value of commitment, she admitted. Her son had held a job no more than one or two years before he got itchy and wanted to move on. It was the same with one of her daughters. She sold insurance but had changed companies about ten times in the past several years.

"I nagged them incessantly about having a better work ethic, like their father had," she admitted. "What is wrong with them? Where did I fail?" she asked us, clearly agonizing over her motherhood.

None of her children had stayed married or had any children of their own. That was also upsetting to Ruth, she confided. Her children had never known what it was like to care about someone other than themselves, she told us. And now they were acting like rebellious teenagers by picking on her.

Ruth's story exemplifies the conflict that Rebounders face as they waver between being Proud Independents and Humble Submissives in their attempt to remain in control of their lives. Now that her daughter wanted Ruth to move in with her, she hated to hurt her daughter's feelings by refusing her generous offer, demonstrating her ambivalence about playing the part of a Humble Submissive: whatever she did, either she or her daughter would be upset.

Also being a Proud Independent, Ruth felt that her daughter's bossing her around was stifling, and she blamed herself for never teaching her that people don't like to be treated as if they have no say-so over their lives. Besides, Ruth admitted to us, her daughter wouldn't listen to her advice anyway, which sounded to us as if her daughter were destined to be a Proud Independent someday, too, just like her mother.

Ruth told us that she had always been sort of a loner, which was one reason that she hated seeing her children alone. She hadn't been a joiner in school, a part of a clique, or even into the neighborhood bridge club or school PTA. It seemed that now that she was older, her tendency to want to keep her own company was even stronger. In fact, she wished that everyone would just leave her alone, especially since all her children did was criticize her life, in her view. And all she did was give them back the same medicine.

"I am old enough to do what I want to do," she told our group. "I don't know why my kids think they know what's better for me than I do. They act like they're in charge of my life. It's my life! I don't want to cause any fights between all of us, though. They're all the family I have left."

We pointed out to Ruth that she had a lot to gain from putting a new frame around parenthood as an Aged Sage Rebounder. We helped her understand that her adult children were concerned about keeping her safe because they loved her. They wanted to keep her out of any danger or discomfort that might jeopardize her well-being.

Ruth was also concerned about her children's ability to be successful adults. She needed to see that she could still help them learn to manage their own lives, lessons that they were demonstrating they needed, by starting to manage hers differently. As we talked, Ruth began to see how allowing her children to help her with such things as finding a companion who could walk with her to and from school could help them feel more responsible and nurture their sense of helpfulness.

In addition, she started to hold her tongue, as we advised, whenever she felt like criticizing her children's work habits. Instead of spending more years being a resentful nag without the results she wanted, she began to ask her children about their lives and chose to "make nice" as a means of helping her children become the adults that she needed for them to be, in order for her to feel at peace. We knew that it would take time for this family to change their pattern of behaving with each other. As Ruth started paying more attention to maintaining her own independent life and supporting her children's, we were confident they would all realize their common goal: independence for everyone.

Melancholy Colleen: Abandonment

A retired sales clerk who had just celebrated her seventy-first birthday, Colleen introduced herself at a Circles group by telling us her story. Her husband had died just two years ago. A year earlier she had been diagnosed with a brain tumor that had just been successfully removed not two months before her husband died. It had been a hellish few years for Colleen. She said that she felt she deserved some happiness after suffering the loss of her ability to walk and talk as she used to because of the brain damage and then losing her husband of thirty-five years on top of that.

Colleen was angry with God for doing this to her. Formerly a deeply religious woman, she could not make any sense of what had happened to her. How could God take away her husband and her health all in the same year? She had also been forced into early retirement from her job of thirty-two years right before she got the tumor and was quickly replaced by a younger version of herself.

Now her children, forty-nine-year-old twins, Megan and Susan, had to help her financially, as well as medically, with taking her to the doctor and helping her remember to take her medicine. Her doctor informed her that she couldn't drive because her reflexes weren't quick enough. So what was she to do? She told us that she felt she had been abandoned by everyone: first her kids grew up; then her husband left her; and now she had to rely on her children just to pay the rent.

As Colleen looked at her life, she saw nothing but failure. She was re-minded of what her mother's life had been like in the years before she died, "desperately alone and poor as a church mouse," as she put it. Fortunately she'd recently acquired a new boyfriend, Garrett. Knowing that Garrett was by her side reassured her that she would not be following completely in her mother's footsteps; at least she would not be alone.

A predictable equation ran through the stories in our interviews during this season of parenthood. The attitude of each person in this season equaled her response to the ups and downs of her life to date. Colleen was a product of how she had coped with all of the changes in her life over the years and how she interpreted them. They could have made her stronger, crazier, or worn out, just as they could all of us.

Because she looked at much of her recent past as a series of inexplica-ble failures, her thoughts led her to believe that she'd been defeated and victimized by the normal changes in health and circumstances that all families experience, as well as the less common tragedies that she had confronted in the past few years. She felt as if she had been targeted, sin-gled out, and that made her bitter.

In addition, she had never adjusted to her children being independent, self-sufficient adults. Now they saw their mother's unhappiness eating away at her health. Their coping skills far outweighed their mother's. In fact, because of their own faith, they found themselves encouraging her to also find strength in her faith instead of turning her back on it. Colleen's own father, we learned, had been a minister all of his life, as had his grand-father; so a strong religious faith had always been a part of her family.

It wasn't too late, we encouraged her, to continue to develop her spiri-tual growth. Her personal accounting ledger had measured only what she had accomplished financially. We encouraged her to start a new column for understanding what mattered in life spiritually.

Being old and sick is probably everyone's worst fear. A person in this condition might feel disconnected from memories of the time during which she was "capable." But instead of thinking of herself as "old and sick," we helped Colleen see that deep inside she was still Colleen—the same lov-ing mother and grandmother she had always been. She needed to accept the changes that had happened to her as opportunities for growing and learning about life, not disasters. She now had the freedom to decide how to optimize her days.

We suggested that she think about her children's assistance with gratitude and feel lucky that they could help support her. Megan and Susan needed to know that their efforts were appreciated, because they were having their own battles accepting their mother as dependent on them. But they were thrilled with the fact that she had a new man in her life to care about and to care for her.

As a Humble Submissive Rebounder, Colleen had a tendency to feel sorry for herself that would never win her any friends or her grown children's affection, both of which she desperately needed in order to feel at peace deep within her. Instead we encouraged her to apply a new framework to her expectations of her life, a framework that would help her look at the remaining years one day at a time, a slower, new way to approach life that fit her abilities now. Instead of regretting what wasn't hers, Colleen tried to be thankful for what she had and who she wanted to become: an Aged Sage.

Lisa's Legacy: Great-Grandchildren Keep Her Connected

Although her husband, Denny, and she had been a prominent community volunteer team in their hometown, Lisa told her Circles group that she was never lonely after Denny passed away. "What's the point of staying home moping around?" she answered us when we asked her if she ever got tired running around from charity event to charity event all by herself. "I'll have lots of time to rest later. Besides, no one's there!"

So at seventy-nine years of age, this Aged Sage Rebounder kept up the pace she had followed for decades, even taking her grandchildren and great-grandchildren to Disney World, her trusty walker leading the way.

"Every year for my birthday, we must take a trip," she told us. "Now I let the great-grandchildren choose where, as long as their parents can come along to help me keep up with them."

Traveling together helped Lisa feel confident that they would stay a family; although they all lived in the same city, everyone was so busy running around with work, school, and other activities that she had to wait to see them according to their schedule, she told us.

Lisa kept busy volunteering on committees for the local art gallery gala and local diabetes fund-raising drive. But her fifty-five- and fifty-eight-year-old sons and their wives; her twenty-six-, twenty-nine-, and thirty-one-year-old grandchildren; and her three-, five-, nine-, and eleven-year-old great-grandchildren provided the core of her life, the compass that gave di-rection to her soul.

She had intentionally trained her daughters-in-law to follow in her civic footsteps, which led her granddaughters to do the same. That meant Lisa was asked to baby-sit the dogs and her youngest great-grandchild nearly twice a week. Nothing pleased her more than to talk to her great-grandchildren about when she was a child, when their daddies and grand-dads were little, or when the house she lived in was brand new, not sixty years old.

Lisa knew that this was her last shot at "raising" little ones. Although her oldest great-grandson was eleven, she didn't want to count on being there to see another generation. So she made it a point to remind them of what was important to her and to shower them with so many cookies, funny stories, and candy that they wouldn't ever be able to forget her.

Speaking her mind was one of Lisa's strengths. But she had long since given up telling her kids what to do. In fact, she started to rely more on them than they did on her, unlike the turn of events with her own parents when they were her age.

She told us that her parents had never shared their financial situation with her. So when they passed away, all of the responsibilities for sorting through their fiscal morass fell on her shoulders . . . and fell hard. She didn't want her children to be in the same situation she had been in once she could no longer manage on her own. Therefore, making sure that her fi-nances were in order and that her children knew where everything valuable was in her house became her priorities.

Legacy leaving. That was the name of the parenthood game that Lisa, an Aged Sage Rebounder was playing. We complimented Lisa on her remark-able ability to adapt to all of the course changes that her life's journey had taken. She prided herself on letting her sons and their wives live their own lives, and she had worked hard to avoid trying to control her grandchil-dren's lives. We also credited her "making nice" with her children and grandchildren as the cause of the good relationship she now enjoyed with her family.

Lisa was a private person, so it was unusual when she broke one family tradition and shared her financial situation with her family. Because of the frustration that she had suffered in sorting through her parents' estate, she was brave enough to sit her boys down and tell them about her financial status. Without a previous model or any personal experience in this area, she worried that this was a risky move. She wasn't used to sharing her private affairs with anyone, even her sons, and she wasn't sure how they would take this final accounting of her life.

Her sons were able to advise her wisely, however, and her involving them in her finances took away her fear that she would repeat what she considered to be her parents' mistakes. As we helped her cope with her "exit strategy," as she called it, we encouraged Lisa to continue to take control of the things she could control: what she thought about her life and her ability to give her family the positive memories that they would have of her after she was gone. Little did she know how talented she was at being a Rebounder.

Dan's Exit: Planning for the End

Everything is in order, noted Dan, referring to his will, his estate planning, and his medical directive about not bringing him back when his "number is up," as he put it. Dan had practiced law for seventy-five years and was clear about one thing: Nothing was going to catch him unprepared. He even had his funeral all planned out down to the pallbearers, and he knew just where his small fortune was going. Now that he was unable to get out of bed, at the tender age of ninety-nine, his big goal was to make it to the century mark, even if he was in this sorry state.

He had talked with his children, Nora and Dana, who were both trustees of his estate, as well as lawyers in his firm, about keeping him comfortable and at home. He was resigned to his fate, he told us, and had no regrets. His daughters tried to follow all of his wishes, even listening to the same lectures he had given them for nearly seventy-five years about the importance of family and the fact that one's "good name" was his most important possession.

The one gift that Dan really needed was to be reassured that his integrity was still intact, although being dependent on his children and grandchildren upset him primarily because he believed that he was being a burden to them. That was the last thing he had ever wanted, having been a fiercely Proud Independent all of his life.

"I used to travel around the world, going from meeting to meeting," he would tell us. "Now I just lie here. I can hardly even move without someone's help!"

Nora and Dana, as well as his caregivers, repeatedly showered him with

pep talks about how well he was doing, even though they knew he was get-
ting weaker each day. They became a team, managing his life's affairs in
consultation with him. For example, when he voiced concern about his wife,
Madeline, who had been diagnosed with Alzheimer's five years earlier, they
all promised that she would be taken care of as well as possible. She was in
the nursing home not far from his apartment. For hours on end he would
discuss Madeline's care with Nora and Dana, having them vow they would
never let her be alone at the end of her life and would talk to her every day
as they talked to him, reassuring her that everything would be okay even
though she no longer knew who they were.

Dan also wanted Nora and Dana to know how much he appreciated
their visits each week and how much he respected them as professionals as
well as daughters. He always repeated his praise as, tears streaming down
the girls' faces, they smothered their father with kisses in payment for his
compliments. Dan loved knowing that they loved him, and he told one of his
caregivers that of all his accomplishments, they were his best.

When he thought of all the big moments in his life, all the important cases
that he had won in his long, storied legal career, Dan always concluded
that being victorious in the case of having two loving daughters was his
most prestigious. For him, knowing that his daughters would carry on his
legacy of commitment to learning and loving was repayment enough for the
monetary gifts he was making to them. They smothered their father with
adoration, which was exactly what he needed and wanted as an Aged Sage
Rebounder. He had done the same to them when they were born, so
thrilled to have two healthy babies that he took out an ad in his church
newsletter thanking God for the gifts that he had been given.

He was more than happy to give up control over his wealth and his
health to his daughters, because he trusted them implicitly to do the right
thing for him in what he felt was his last year. That in itself helped him
feel more comfortable. He knew that between them and the good Lord,
he'd be fine.

His daughters alternated coming over when the doctor visited with him
at his home each week. He was an old family friend who told Nora and
Dana to keep their father comfortable because there was nothing else they
could do. Dan consulted with Nora and Dana on everything. He asked
them whether he should take a certain medicine, and he was still alert
enough to know whether he was following doctor's orders. Dan was still a

believer in "the doctor knows best," but his children would be the checks and balances to his doctor's advice. His peace of mind made him grateful for the love that had made his life complete. As with all his investments, the deposits of love and caring he had made in his life were paying big dividends now.

He wasn't afraid of dying, he said one day to one of his caregivers, because he felt as though his time on earth were done, that he "had played his last tune," as he told it. Nora and Dana decided that they would help their father with his dying, just as he had helped them through life, all these years. They asked him each day when they visited if he had any good-byes he wanted to say. Until the end, they were making sure that their father knew he was a hero in their eyes. It was all he had ever hoped to be.

Hank's Think Tank: The "Old Folk's Home"

Hank believed that he didn't really have a choice. His wife, Grace, had become so ill that they had to move from their apartment to an assisted living center on the other side of the city, where somebody other than she could take care of their meals and her medical needs. The move would have been fine, but Hank's buddies all lived back at the apartment complex, he told us. Hank didn't want to move; after visiting the retirement center, he told us that it was so full of old people that he couldn't imagine living there. He didn't think of himself as old, although at ninety he was, as the numbers certainly suggested.

Hank and Grace had lived in their apartment for twenty years, and he liked all of his young, independent neighbors who averaged about seventy-five years of age. He didn't want to have to make new friends, especially with old "geezers" who were always complaining about their aches and pains, he admitted candidly. Besides, their apartment was so close to where their children and grandchildren lived that they often just popped in to say hello.

But Grace didn't share his point of view. She wasn't as attached to the apartment or to their neighbors. She was now preoccupied with her medical problems and had difficulty even considering their options. Grace knew that she needed more medical assistance than she would get if they stayed in the apartment, and now she felt so sick most of the time that she didn't really want to be seen by anybody.

As a retired bank president, Hank was in his element as the unofficial chairman of the board at the apartment complex in which they had lived.

But at home he had always done what his wife had wanted, even when they were first married, he recalled. She had always run the show; even to the extent of giving him the little bottle of vitamins when they bought that popular brand that comes with a large bottle and a small bottle. He could fill his up with vitamins from her big bottle when he ran out, she had always assured him. Having acquiesced to the way she wanted to organize their world, he knew his destiny was to move . . . so they packed off to the assisted living center.

This season of parenthood was like any other season for Hank. He was always accepting of his lot in life and went easily with the flow. A few years after their move, Grace passed away; but Hank stayed in the retirement center, although he still dreamed of his good life back at the old apartment. He hated the food in the center—he'd enjoyed his wife's home cooking for sixty-two years—and he was so lonesome without Grace. It was hard for him to adjust to living alone in the center, but he had thought that being with his family would ease some of the isolation he felt.

He was so lost, so indecisive, now that Grace was gone. In the banking world he had charted his own course; but at home Grace was his compass. Their children did come to see him now, but not as often as they used to when Grace was alive. Hank began to wonder if he wasn't getting a taste of his own medicine since he had left the home front up to Grace and had spent so much time at his office. He loved his kids and thought they loved him, but he was worried that they didn't want to be around him as much now because he always cried at some time during their visit. He missed Grace so much, even though her failing health had made their last few months together difficult, and he couldn't imagine living alone for much longer. And at times he was inconsolable over the fact that she was gone.

Hank hinted that if his children wanted, he would be glad to move in with them. He knew that he needed to get out of the center, because it reminded him too much of Grace. He didn't even mind the idea of having to adapt to the change of moving: He'd do anything to get closer to his children and grandchildren, to be the father and grandfather he had always hoped to be. He remembered when not many people lived to be ninety, and Hank was proud that he still thought of himself as young. Not so many people are able to live good lives at this age, he mused, even though he was struggling to keep from giving up because he was so lonely.

His strongest link to his family was with his sixty-one-year-old son, who was also a banker. He had asked him to help manage his money so that he would have enough to take care of himself after the medical expenses for Grace were paid. Hank found that the occasional talks with his son over finances gave him great pleasure, and he yearned for even the simplest signs that he was still important to his family: getting calls from his grandson to discuss the baseball scores, getting to tell family stories to his great-grandkids, being invited to go to the bank with his son. He hoped that he wouldn't become a burden to his kids and lose the only family ties he had. For Hank, who was in good health, remaining connected to his family became his main agenda.

When his children were growing up, Hank was so busy with his job that he was never into being even a part-time Family Manager or Travel Agent. As a Volcano Dweller when his kids were teens, he tried to steer clear of falling debris. After he retired from his position at the bank, being a Plateau Parent began to change his relationship with his children. His oldest son was now a vice president of a large bank chain, and Hank loved to talk banking with him. Grace's declining health had helped him refocus on their grandchildren and allowed Hank to finally pour some of his energy into parenthood. He may have seemed "old" to his kids, but to his friends, who numbered in the dozens, he was a spring chicken.

For the last thirty years Hank had grown to love telling his children and grandchildren about the past, which for him became more positive than the present. We helped Hank understand that even without much control over his world, he had much for which he could be grateful—an occasional meal at one of his children's homes, good conversation with his son, and watching a baseball game on television with his grandson and great-grandson from time to time.

His children defined his life in this season as they always had. They made him happy when they included him in their family activities. For Hank, "making nice" with his family was his ticket to feeling good about being a father, a goal that all dads, be they presidents or painters in their "other" life outside of home, long to reach. However, this goal is less attainable for fathers, such as Hank, who observed from the poolside rather than plunging into the water of parenthood. In this season, Rebounders learn the truth about the axioms "What goes around, comes around"; "You reap what you sow"; and "You get what you give."

When parents wait until the Rebounder season to strive to make connections—bond—with their offspring, they will be left wanting, their emotional tanks never being filled, as Hank experienced. As noted in the Celebrity season of parenthood, fathers begin their journey on a path that is peripheral to the one their pregnant wives are taking as they physically transform themselves into Celebrity mothers, leaving them to be their Roadies. Over the course of a lifetime, many fathers are then transformed into ciphers—loving but strange, often distracted, as Roger Rosenblatt said in a *Time* magazine essay. He wrote:

"Years ago, when I was preparing to interview President-elect Ronald Reagan, I read that his son Michael complained that his father had never attended any of his college football games. I also read that Reagan had made the same complaint about *his* father, an alcoholic for whom he had felt deep, painful yearnings. So in our interview, I asked Reagan if he ever recognized his father in himself. It was the only time when his mask of affability fell, and we were very quiet for a minute."

Rosenblatt's interview with Reagan resonates the dilemma many Rebounders face: How do they turn themselves into Aged Sages if they have been a "strange, often distracted" family man, particularly when they were simply following in their father's footsteps in assuming this identity that our culture has traditionally fostered and genetics naturally supported? As Hank struggled with this classic Rebounder dilemma of fatherhood, he needed to understand that the process of becoming an Aged Sage starts at the beginning of parenthood rather than at the end. Therefore Hank, like all Humble Submissives, as well as Proud Independent Rebounders, was now faced with making the best of the relationship he had: inviting his children and grandchildren to visit him, reveling in the occasional dinner and evening with his family, asking for pictures of the great-grandchildren, trying to make friends at the retirement center, and being proud that his children had grown up to be independent and self-sufficient.

His children, grandchildren, and great-grandchildren still needed him to love them, however, to be Dad, Grandpa, Great-Grandpa. Rosenblatt explains: "Fathers are softer in this era, more temperate, and hands-on, like mothers. Still, they remain very big deals. The children of my baby-boom friends look up to their kinder, gentler dads with no less awe than I did to mine."

When their parents' physical and mental health begins to fail, thinking that their "mom" or "dad" is just old and tired, or a little worn out, gives adult children the permission to avoid their own adjustments to this inevitable season in their parents' lives and the whole experience of dying itself. This season of parenthood reminds adult children of the old adage "You can only control what you do with whatever hand you're dealt in life."

By helping their parents feel as much in control as possible of the decisions that are made around death and dying, adult children are giving them the precious gift that their parents gave them—helping them be as self-reliant, independent, and responsible, as much in control of their own destinies, as is humanly possible. Adult children can control parents' comfort during their passage through the dying process by getting them the best medical attention, providing emotional support, and ensuring their dignity. In dying, just as in living, parents' responses to their care will reinforce the value of their relationship with their children.

A parent's death is the final play that ends the active career of a Rebounder in the game of life. Through her passage to death, a parent teaches her children what they need to know about living: her true confessions about their lives and her hopes and dreams for her family, the details that she would take care of if she could again plot her game plan for living, as well as for dying. A parent teaches her adult children that reconciling the past is a necessary step in moving on to the future in life and death.

Self-Discoveries of Rebounders

Your pocket guide to the truth revealed in the Rebounder season of parenthood.

> ➤ **So now the ride is over.** Now that you've gotten off the Ferris wheel, you either want to go around again or are relieved that it's over, depending on whether it was a rocky or smooth ride. Either way, you realize that your day at the park is almost history as you wend your way to the Exit signs.

> ➤ **Look! Your kids are getting on the ride you just left.** When you see your kids getting on the same ride you were on, you wave and feel so good that they're following your lead. They got on the roller coaster after you rode it and then hopped on the Ferris wheel. You want to get close enough to tell them exactly what to expect, how it'll feel, and what to do if they get scared when the ride gets shaky, just as you yearned to do when you saw them on the roller coaster. Waiting for them to catch your eye and pay attention to you is frustrating, so you make every effort to make yourself be seen and heard.

➤ **What an incredible park!** You've spent almost your entire adulthood at Parenthood Park, and the most important memories of your adult life were born within its boundaries. You wonder how you can leave a place that has become so much a part of you and if you will be able to stay just long enough to watch your children, grandchildren, and great-grandchildren as they enjoy their ride. In the meantime, you get a thrill from seeing them having such a good time on the Ferris wheel, just as you did, and keep telling yourself that they will be able to find their way out of the park someday without you. After changing your identity so many times, you have one final transformation left—leaving the park with the knowledge that you have used your time in the park to the fullest. That is the only way you can leave the park in peace.

➤ **I hope somebody's around to help us get out of the park.** As you make your exit, you just hope you can remember where you saw the Exit signs and parking lot from your panoramic view atop the Ferris wheel. You want your children and their children to be around to help you, but you're not sure when or if they'll come to your aid. At this point in your life, you realize that you must have faith in yourself, that you'll eventually find your way home, just as your parents did before you, and theirs did before them.

And the Circle Continues . . .

Life is eternal:
and love is immortal;
and death is only a horizon;
and a horizon is nothing save the limit of our sight.
—ROSSITER RAYMOND

DOESN'T IT SEEM PROPHETIC, and certainly universal, that parents begin life as they end it, being dependent on someone else and in need of care themselves? So the end of the path is really the beginning. As parenthood comes to a close for one generation, their children pass on to future generations of children what they have learned from their parents. Without children, adults' stories end with themselves. With the birth of a child, every child, the continuous saga of the seasons of parenthood begins anew.

Starting a
Circles Group

Philosophy is perfectly right in saying that life must be understood backward. But then one forgets the other clause—that it must be lived forward.—SØREN KIERKEGAARD

IF YOU WOULD LIKE to start a Circles group with your own friends at home or in the workplace, here are some guidelines. The only requirement is that the members of your group all share at least one of the same seasons of parenthood as they address the ways their children have redefined their lives by their growth and development in that season. Common questions we were asked by those wanting to start their own Circles group included these:

➤ **Why are Circles groups helpful?** By sharing information about themselves as parents in every season of parenthood, mothers and fathers discover that they are all on the same path, all traveling on the same road, navigating the same terrain. They also admit—out loud— the truth about being parents: It is the identity that gives the most meaning and purpose to their lives throughout their lifetime.

➤ **What would you recommend as the maximum size of the group?** A Circles group can be as small as two or three people or it can be as large as twenty, but we recommend seven to ten. One group expected six mothers to show up, but only three came. Those three met anyway and had a riveting three-hour chat over many cups of coffee. A group is too large when it limits the comfort members feel in participating, a factor that is also influenced by the personalities of the people involved.

➤ **How can you recruit members for Circles groups?** Neighbors, co-workers, relatives, fellow parents of children's classmates, fellow PTA or PTO members, childbirth education class constituents, and friends are all potential candidates for Circles group membership, with one caveat: Each member of a particular Circles group must have at least one child in the same developmental stage as fellow members. We met with a Parents of Triplets Club, in which the members were all parents of toddlers and preschoolers. Although the group wasn't organized as a Circles group per se, it became one as we talked about the Family Manager season of parenthood instead of how to toilet train and discipline their children, for example. So groups already in existence can become a Circles group if members already share the common thread of their children's developmental stages.

➤ **How often and for how long should Circles groups meet?** Circles groups can be scheduled weekly, twice monthly, or monthly, as group members' calendars allow. Some members found the groups so cathartic that they decided to meet once a week as a way to get group therapy without the price tag. We found it easier to keep a regular day—the second Tuesday of the month, for example—to help everyone plan their lives around their Circles group. In some cases, particularly with Sponges, Family Managers, and Volcano Dwellers, the intensity of the season turned their Circles groups into life rafts. The groups we organized met for approximately two hours; yours can be longer or shorter, over a lunch hour or even part of a weekend retreat. Be prepared: in many of our Circles groups, no one wanted to go home!

CIRCLES GROUPS' SAMPLE QUESTIONS

Following are some discussion questions to get the ball rolling. These questions can be posed and answered in present or past tense depending on the particular point at which parents find themselves during each season of parenthood.

CELEBRITY

1. At what point during your pregnancy did you first think of yourself as a mother?
2. What aspect of being pregnant made you think of yourself as a mother?
3. What changes have you experienced in your relationship with your own parents since becoming pregnant?
4. What impact did your parents have on you as you were growing up that is influencing you as you go through your pregnancy?
5. How much does your parents' opinion influence your ideas and beliefs about parenthood?
6. How do you think pregnancy has changed you as a person?
7. As you anticipate the birth of your child, what thoughts and feelings do you experience most frequently?
8. How has pregnancy changed your relationship with your spouse? How much has it impacted other relationships in your life?
9. How long do you plan to stay home after your child is born?
10. What is your biggest fear about the physical changes of being pregnant? How have you coped with these physical changes? How has your spouse coped?

SPONGE

1. How do you feel about all of the attention you're getting as a new mom or dad?
2. How has being a "mom" or "dad" changed how you feel about the old "you"?
3. What is the most surprising emotion you're feeling during this year?
4. What was/is the difference in how you feel now compared with how you felt when you were pregnant?
5. How differently do you feel about being a mom or dad than you thought you would feel?
6. What is the biggest surprise about being a mom or dad of a two-month-, three-month-, six-month-, nine-month-old?
7. What word would you use to describe how you feel about your life with a one-year-old, nearly one-year-old, six-month-old?

8. How has the relationship with your work, parents, friends, and partner changed during the first year of your baby's life?

9. What differences occurred in your relationship with your own parents when your first child was born? your second child was born? your third child was born?

10. How do you feel that your life has changed compared with your spouse's?

11. What is your reaction to the jobs of cook, butler, maid, and hero—the life of a parent in the first year?

12. How have your priorities changed since you became a mom or dad?

13. How much "free time" do you have now, and how do you want to spend that time?

FAMILY MANAGER

1. What was your biggest challenge once your children started walking?

2. How did your life change once your baby turned a year old?

3. What happened to the "honeymoon" feeling? Did it leave before now?

4. How does working outside the home affect being a Family Manager? Not working outside the home?

5. How is the relationship with your parents changing now?

6. What do you remember about your life before your child was born?

7. How do you feel about being a "police officer"? How differently do you feel you have to behave now that you have a child for whom you are modeling "being good"?

8. How much "free time" do you have now, and how do you want to spend that time?

9. How does having a two-, three-, four-, or five-year-old make you feel about yourself?

10. How do you feel having a preschooler has affected your sense of "getting things done" and being organized?

11. Describe your main accomplishment each day as a parent of preschoolers.

TRAVEL AGENT

1. Describe the impact your parents had on you as you were growing up that influences how your raise your children.

2. How does your parents' opinion now influence how you raise your children?

3. How has having a child in school all day changed your life?

4. Who needs a report card most, you or your child? Whom do you need a report card from?

5. Who's in control of your life, you or your children? When did you begin to feel this way?

6. Did you feel differently as a parent when your child learned to read? Started receiving letter grades?

7. If you worked full-time outside your home, in what ways did you take charge of your child's itinerary when he was six, eight, ten? How does his day care provider/baby-sitter impact your child—your family?

8. As your child's world widens, how does that affect you?

9. In what ways did you experience the "separation blues" with your first, second, third, or fourth child?

10. What effect does your six- to eleven-year-old have on your working or not working outside the home?

11. When each of your children entered formal school—kindergarten— how did your life change?

12. When did you come to realize who your child was—problem learner, ice hockey star, math whiz?

13. What was your favorite year of elementary school? Why?

14. What is your fondest childhood memory of your elementary school years?

VOLCANO DWELLER

1. What was the biggest change in your life after your children became teenagers?

2. What was your own adolescence like?

3. How does having teens impact your memories of your relationship with your parents when you were a teen?

4. How does your teenager differ from the teen who you were at this stage of childhood? How do these differences affect your feelings toward your teenager?

5. What issues surrounding adolescence affect your marriage?

6. What surprises you about your feelings toward your adolescent?

7. What effect do your adolescents have on your working outside the home?

8. What issues surrounding money have been brought to the surface because of your adolescent?

9. Do you wait up at night for your teenager to come home, or do you go to sleep while he is still out?
10. How often do you feel pangs of this being a "countdown" phase . . . until your teen leaves home?
11. How do you know that you are doing a good job raising your teenager?
12. How did you react when you found out your child was gay?

FAMILY REMODELER

1. How did you feel when you realized that your child would be moving out of your home and may not live there again?
2. Given that you may feel some grief at the prospect of having an empty nest, what are you doing (or did you do) to compensate?
3. What influence does your relationship with your own parents have on your view of the "empty nest"?
4. If this is your second (or third or fourth) child to leave, how is the experience different from that with your first child? What if this is your last child to leave?
5. How did your finances and living arrangements change as a result of your child's leaving the nest?
6. How did you redefine yourself given that your child was no longer physically at home?
7. What did the empty nest do to your relationship with your spouse, your friends, and your family?
8. How did you retain ties with your child once she left home? Communication? Finances? Spiritual? Physical? Emotional?
9. How did your life change once your child was gone: work schedule, cooking, travel, "fun," household chores?
10. Do you feel that you still have a "child" or that your "child" is an adult? Describe the reasons for your answer.
11. How did your parents handle the "empty nest"?
12. How do your children remind you of your own young adulthood?

PLATEAU PARENT

1. What is the greatest impact that having grandchildren—or not having them—has had on you?
2. Describe your rebirth through grandparenthood.
3. Describe your sense of freedom that you have now that you are parenting an "adult child."

4. When do your grandchildren and children make you the happiest? The most upset?

5. How old do you feel because of the age of your children?

6. How do you try to meet your children's expectations of you? How do they try to meet yours?

7. How has your relationship with your children changed since they had children?

8. How has your relationship with your parents changed since they began to need more care?

9. How do your grandchildren remind you of your children and your children remind you of you?

10. How do your grandchildren treat you differently from the way your children did?

11. Do your grandchildren treat you the way they treat their own parents?

12. Do your children talk to you more or less often or differently since they had children? Why?

13. In what ways do you feel needed by your grandchildren?

14. What do your grandchildren expect from you?

15. Why do you like to talk about your family?

16. How do your grandchildren remind you of your own childhood?

17. How do you feel about needing to take care of your own parents?

REBOUNDER

1. What is the greatest impact that great-grandchildren have had on you?

2. How old do you feel inside? Older than your age or younger? Why do you feel that age?

3. How has aging affected your relationship with your own children? Your grandchildren?

4. What have you done to get your life in order in case something should happen to you?

5. What is the most important legacy you would like to leave your family?

6. What kind of help and support from your children and grandchildren are you receiving? In your opinion, is it what you want or need?

7. When you need help, how do you ask your children for it?

8. How do you feel about needing your children to take care of you?

9. How do you feel when your children start telling you what you need to do, where you need to live, and when you need to do things? What do you do about those feelings?

10. How has moving out of your home affected you? your family?

11. What are your main interests now that you have great-grandchildren?

12. What are your most predominant memories of parenthood?

13. What regrets do you have about being a parent?

14. In what ways do you try to "make nice" to your children and they try to "make nice" to you? Have you always done those things? Why or why not?

15. If you could change one thing about your family, what would it be? Why?

16. Describe your view of how being a parent defined who you have been during your life.

17. What memories of your own childhood do you often recall?

Notes

I keep six honest serving men (They taught me all I knew); Their names are What and Why and When and How and Where and Who.—RUDYARD KIPLING

INTRODUCTION

1. Berry, Carmen Renee, and Traeder, Tamara, *Girlfriends,* Berkley, Calif., Wildcat Canyon Press, 1995.
2. Canfield, Jack; Hansen, Mark Victor; Hawthorne, Jennifer Read; and Shimoff, Marci, *Chicken Soup for the Mother's Soul,* Deerfield Beach, Fla., Health Communications, 1997.
3. Edelman, Marian Wright, *The Measure of Our Success,* Boston, Beacon Press, 1992.
4. Galinsky, Ellen, *The Six Stages of Parenthood,* New York, Addison-Wesley Publishing, 1981, 1987.
5. Hedrix, Harville, Ph.D., and Hunt, Helen, M.A., *Giving the Love That Heals,* New York, Pocket Books, 1997.
6. Lindbergh, Anne Morrow, *Gift from the Sea,* New York, Pantheon Books, 1995.
7. Mitchard, Jacquelyn, *The Rest of Us,* New York, Viking, 1997.
8. Moore, Thomas, *Care of the Soul,* New York, HarperPerennial, 1994.
9. Munsch, Robert, *Love You Forever,* Ontario, Canada, A Firefly Book, 1986.
10. Nagel, Greta, Ph.D., *The Tao of Parenting,* New York, A Plume Book, 1998.
11. Peterson, Karen S., "Celebrating the Bond between Fathers and Sons," *USA Today,* April 2, 1996, quoting Hanson, Bill, *Father and Son,* New York, Bright Books, 1996.
12. Schoen, Elin, *Reflections on Parental Development,* New York, Doubleday, 1995.
13. Sheehy, Gail, *New Passages,* New York, Random House, 1995.
14. Meryl Streep, "The Meryl Streep Nobody Knows," by Liz Smith, *Good Housekeeping,* September 1998.
15. Spock, Benjamin M., M.D., *A Better World for Our Children,* Bethesda, Md., National Press Books, 1994.
16. Viorst, Judith, *Necessary Losses,* New York, Fawcett Gold Medal, 1986.

311

SEASON ONE

1. Barron, James Douglas, *She's Having a Baby—And I'm Having a Breakdown*, New York, Quill, William Morrow, 1998.
2. Benedek, Therese, M.D., and Anthony E. James, M.D., eds., *Parenthood, Its Psychology and Psychopathology*, Boston, Little, Brown & Company, 1970.
3. Coles, Robert, *Erik H. Erikson; The Growth of His Work*, Boston, Little, Brown & Company, 1970.
4. Eisenberg, Arlene; Murkoff, Heidi E.; and Hathaway, Sandee E., B.S.N., *What to Expect When You're Expecting*, New York, Workman Publishing, 1984.
5. Erikson, Erik, *The Life Cycle Completed*, New York, W. W. Norton & Company, 1982.
6. ———, *Identity and the Life Cycle*, New York, W. W. Norton & Company, 1959, 1980.
7. Jodie Foster as quoted in "Babies, It's You," by Anne-Marie O'Neill, *People*, September 21, 1998.
8. Jennifer Louden as quoted in "I'm Not Crazy, I'm Pregnant," by Paula Spencer, *Baby Talk*, April 1998.
9. Mussen, Paul Henry; Conger, John Janeway; Kagan, Jerome; and Huston, Aletha Carol, *Child Development and Personality, Sixth Edition*, New York, Harper & Row Publishers, 1984.
10. Longman, Phillip J., "The Cost of Children," *U.S. News & World Report*, March 30, 1998.
11. Stone, Elizabeth, as quoted in *The Quotable Woman*, Philadelphia, Running Press, 1991.

SEASON TWO

1. Gillian Anderson, Leeza Gibbons, Rosie O'Donnell, Jane Seymour, Jaclyn Smith, Keely Shaye Smith, "Baby Talk," by Deborah Norville, *McCall's*, August 1998.
2. Blauvelt, Harry, "Mickelson Eyes Further Addition," *USA Today*, August 12, 1999.
3. Coopersmith, Stanley, *The Antecedents of Self-Esteem*, Palo Alto, Calif., Consulting Psychologists Press, 1981.
4. Eisenberg, Arlene; Murkoff, Heidi E.; and Hathaway, Sandee E., B.S.N., *What to Expect the First Year*, New York, Workman Publishing, 1989.
5. Sarah Ferguson and Catherine Hicks as quoted in "My Favorite Mother's Day," *Family Life*, May 1998.
6. Helen Hunt as quoted in "Helen's Hunt for Happiness," by Joe Dziemianowicz, *McCall's*, July 1998.

7. Krasnow, Iris, *Surrendering to Motherhood,* New York, Hyperion, 1997.
8. Lisa Kudrow and Elle Macpherson as quoted in "Babies, It's You," by Anne-Marie O'Neill, *People,* September 21, 1998.
9. Lamott, Anne, *Operating Instructions,* New York, Fawcett Columbine, 1993.
10. Leach, Penelope, *Babyhood,* New York, Alfred A. Knopf, 1995.
11. McClure, Vimala, *The Tao of Motherhood,* Novato, Calif., New World Library, 1997.
12. Madonna as quoted in "Stargazing," by David Eugene Freze, *Kansas City Star,* March 4, 1998.
13. Mickelson, Phil, "Putt Daddy," *People,* July 12, 1999.
14. Mussen, Paul Henry; Conger, John Janeway; Kagan, Jerome; and Huston, Aletha Carol, *Child Development and Personality, Sixth Edition,* New York, Harper & Row Publishers, 1984.
15. Rosie O'Donnell as quoted in "Rosie's Devotion," by Joanna Powell, *Good Housekeeping,* June 1998.
16. Ornish, Dean, M.D., *Love and Survival,* New York, HarperCollins, 1998.
17. Peterson, Karen S., "Supermom: A Demanding Role, But Fun," *USA Today,* November 30, 1998.
18. Roiphe, Anne, *Fruitful,* New York, Penguin Books, 1996.
19. Saavedra, Beth Wilson, *Meditations for New Mothers,* New York, Workman Publishing, 1992.
20. Connie Smith as quoted in "Connie Smith Returns Refreshed After Taking 20 Years to Be a Mom," by Brian Mansfield, *USA Today,* December 2, 1998.
21. Stoddard, Alexandra, *Mothers: A Celebration,* New York, Avon Books, 1996.
22. "Survey Says . . ." *Baby Talk,* September 1998.
23. Robin Williams as quoted in "What Really Makes Life Fun," by Dotson Rader, *Parade,* September 20, 1998.

SEASON THREE

1. Alter, Jonathan, "It's 4:00 p.m. Do You Know Where Your Children Are?" *Newsweek,* April 27, 1998.
2. Clarke, Jean Illsley, and Dawson, Connie, *Growing Up Again,* San Francisco, Harper & Row Publishers, 1989.
3. Cline, Foster, M.D., and Fay, Jim, *Parenting with Love and Logic,* Colorado Springs, Colo., Pinon Press, 1990.
4. Covey, Stephen R., *The 7 Habits of Highly Effective Families,* New York, Golden Books, 1997.
5. Eisenberg, Arlene; Murkoff, Heidi E.; and Hathaway, Sandee E., B.S.N., *What to Expect: The Toddler Years,* New York, Workman Publishing, 1994.
6. Kelly, Marguerite, and Parsons, Elia, *The Mother's Almanac, Revised,* New York, Doubleday, 1992.

7. Tim McGraw as quoted in "Hunky Tonk" by Jeremy Helligar and Lorna Grisby, *People*, April 27, 1998.

8. Mussen, Paul Henry; Conger, John Janeway; Kagan, Jerome; and Huston, Aletha Carol, *Child Development and Personality, Sixth Edition*, New York, Harper & Row Publishers, 1984.

9. Meg Ryan as quoted in "Marvelous Meg" by Alanna Nash, *Good Housekeeping*, July 1998.

10. Rene Russo as quoted in "Rene Russo's Long Road to Happiness," by Bernard Weinraub, *Redbook*, August 1998.

11. Smiley, Jane, "Mothers Should," *The New York Times Magazine*, April 5, 1998.

12. Ben Stein as quoted in "The Dad Perspective: Prose from Two Who Know," by Bob Minzesheimer, *USA Today*, June 11, 1998.

13. Meryl Streep as quoted in "Mery Streep's One True Role," by Andy Seiler, *USA Today*, September 9, 1998.

14. Andrea Thompson as quoted in "Arresting Officer," by Nick Charles and Monica Rizzo, *People*, April 27, 1998.

15. Unell, Barbara C., and Wyckoff, Jerry L., Ph.D., *20 Teachable Virtues*, New York, Perigee Press, 1995.

16. Wyckoff, Jerry L., Ph.D., and Unell, Barbara C., *Discipline Without Shouting or Spanking*, Minneapolis, Minn., Meadowbrook Press, 1984.

SEASON FOUR

1. Becker, Debbie, "Inkster: Major Accomplishment," *USA Today*, June 28, 1999.

2. Glenn, H. Stephen, and Nelson, Jane, Ed.D., *Raising Self-Reliant Children in a Self-Indulgent World*, Rocklin, Calif., Prima Publishing, 1988.

3. Hochschild, Arlie Russell, *The Time Bind*, New York, Metropolitan Books, 1997.

4. Kabat-Zinn, Myla and Jon, *Everyday Blessings*, New York, Hyperion, 1997.

5. Miller, Alice, *The Drama of the Gifted Child*, New York, Basic Books, 1981.

6. Mussen, Paul Henry; Conger, John Janeway; Kagan, Jerome; and Huston, Aletha Carol, *Child Development and Personality, Sixth Edition*, New York, Harper & Row Publishers, 1984.

7. Price, Susan Crites, and Price, Tom, *The Working Parents Help Book*, Princeton, N.J., Peterson's, 1996.

8. Deborah Pryce, "For Ohio Lawmaker, Ill Child Puts Politics in Its Place," Jill Lawrence, *USA Today*, November 17, 1998.

9. Randy Quaid, "Ryan's Express," Karen S. Schneider, *People*, December 21, 1998.

10. Robinson, Holly, "My Day as a 10-Year-Old," *Ladies' Home Journal,* September 1997.

11. St. James, Elaine, *Simplify Your Life with Kids,* Kansas City, Mo., Andrews & McMeel, 1997.

12. Wyckoff, Jerry L., Ph.D., and Unell, Barbara C., *How to Discipline Your Six-to-Twelve-Year-Old . . . Without Losing Your Mind,* New York, Doubleday, 1991.

SEASON FIVE

1. Barrish, I. J., Ph.D., and Barrish, Harriet H., Ph.D. *Surviving and Enjoying Your Adolescent,* Kansas City, Mo., Westport Publishers, 1989.

2. Bassoff, Evelyn, Ph.D., *Mothers and Daughters: Loving and Letting Go,* New York, New American Library, 1988.

3. Cline, Foster, M.D., and Fay, Jim, *Parenting with Love and Logic,* Colorado Springs, Colo., Pinon Press, 1990.

4. Elias, Marilyn, "Teen-age Girls Say Mom's Become a Pal." *USA Today,* December 14, 1998.

5. Kesler, Jay, *Emotionally Healthy Teenagers,* Nashville, Tenn., 1998.

6. Lieber, Phyllis; Murphy, Gloria S.; and Schwartz, Annette Merkur, *Stop Treating Me Like a Child,* New York, MJF Books, 1994.

7. Nelsen, Jane, Ed.D., and Lott, Lynn, *I'm on Your Side,* Rocklin, Calif., Prima Publishing, 1991.

8. Pipher, Mary, Ph.D., *Reviving Ophelia,* New York, Ballantine Books, 1994.

9. Wolf, Anthony E., Ph.D., *Get Out of My Life,* New York, Noonday Press, 1991.

SEASON SIX

1. Bee, Helen L., *The Journey of Adulthood,* New York, Macmillan Publishing Company, 1992.

2. Coburn, Karen Levin, and Treeger, Madge Lawrence, *Letting Go,* New York, HarperPerennial, 1997.

3. Hudson, Federic M., *The Adult Years,* San Francisco, Josey-Bass Publishers, 1991.

4. ———, and McLean, Pamela D. *Life Launch, Second Edition,* Santa Barbara, Calif., Hudson Institute Press, 1996.

5. Moran, Victoria, *Shelter for the Spirit,* New York, HarperCollins, 1997.

6. Scott, Tom, " 'Letting Go' of Our Children Isn't Easy," *The Sun Newspapers,* May 20, 1998.

7. Stevens-Long, Judith, *Adult Life,* Palo Alto, Calif., Mayfield Publishing Company, 1984.

8. Sullivan, Patricia, "Empty Nest Syndrome: Starting a New Phase of Life," *Our Children,* June/July 1998.
9. Viorst, Judith, *Necessary Losses,* New York, Fawcett Gold Medal, 1986.

SEASON SEVEN

1. Bee, Helen L., *The Journey of Adulthood,* New York, Macmillan Publishing Company, 1992.
2. Hudson, Federic M., *The Adult Years,* San Francisco, Josey-Bass Publishers, 1991.
3. Kaufman, Sharon R., *The Ageless Self,* Madison, Wisc., University of Wisconsin Press, 1986.
4. Pogrebin, Letty Cottin, *Getting Over Getting Older,* New York, Little, Brown & Company, 1996.
5. Roberts, Cokie, *We Are Our Mother's Daughters,* New York, William Morrow & Company, 1998.
6. Stevens-Long, Judith, *Adult Life,* Palo Alto, Calif., Mayfield Publishing Company, 1984.
7. Sheehy, Gail, *New Passages,* New York, Random House, 1995.
8. Wilson, Craig, "Some Thoughts While Waiting for 50 to Arrive," *USA Today,* September 24, 1998.

SEASON EIGHT

1. Albom, Mitch, *Tuesdays with Morrie,* New York, Doubleday, 1997.
2. Bee, Helen L., *The Journey of Adulthood,* New York, Macmillan Publishing Company, 1992.
3. Edelman, Hope, *Motherless Daughters,* New York, Delta, 1994.
4. Elias, Marilyn, "Love Your Parents—Save Their Lives," *USA Today,* November 18, 1999.
5. Friday, Nancy, *My Mother My Self,* New York, Delta, 1977.
6. Fumia, Molly, *Safe Passage,* Berkeley, Calif., Conari Press, 1992.
7. Hudson, Federic M., *The Adult Years,* San Francisco, Josey-Bass Publishers, 1991.
8. Kaufman, Sharon R., *The Ageless Self,* Madison, Wisc., University of Wisconsin Press, 1986.
9. Kennedy, Alexandra, *Losing a Parent,* San Francisco, Harper, 1991.
10. Linkletter, Art, *Old Age Is Not for Sissies,* New York, Penguin Books, 1988.
11. Peterson, Karen S., "36% of Seniors Say Their Kids Don't Help," *USA Today,* January 28, 1999.
12. Rosenblatt, Roger, "The Greatest Dad in the World," *Time,* June 21, 1999.
13. Schiff, Harriet Sarnoff, *How Did I Become My Parent's Parent?"* New York, Penguin Books, 1996.

Bibliography

One may not have written it well enough for others to know, but you're in love with truth when you discover it at the point of a pencil. That, in and by itself, is one of the few rare pleasures in life.—NORMAN MAILER

Albom, Mitch, *Tuesdays with Morrie*, New York, Doubleday, 1997.

Bardwick, Judith M., *Psychology of Women*, New York, Harper & Row, Publishers, 1971.

Barrish, I. J., Ph.D., and Barrish, Harriet H., Ph.D. *Surviving and Enjoying Your Adolescent*, Kansas City, Mo., Westport Publishers, 1989.

Barron, James Douglas, *She's Having a Baby—And I'm Having a Breakdown*, New York, Quill, William Morrow, 1998.

Bassoff, Evelyn, Ph.D., *Mothers and Daughters: Loving and Letting Go*, New York, New American Library, 1988.

Bee, Helen L., *The Journey of Adulthood*, New York, Macmillan Publishing Company, 1992.

Benedek, Therese, M.D., and Anthony E. James, M.D., eds., *Parenthood, Its Psychology and Psychopathology*, Boston, Little, Brown & Company, 1970.

Berry, Carmen Renee, and Traeder, Tamara, *Girlfriends*, Berkeley, Calif., Wildcat Canyon Press, 1995.

Blauvelt, Harry, "Mickelson Eyes Further Addition," *USA Today*, August 12, 1999.

Brown, Lyn Mikel, and Gilligan, Carol, *Meeting at the Crossroads*, Cambridge, Mass., Harvard University Press, 1992.

Canfield, Jack; Hansen, Mark Victor; Hawthorne, Jennifer Read; and Shimoff, Marci, *Chicken Soup for the Mother's Soul*, Deerfield Beach, Fla., Health Communications, 1997.

Caron, Ann F., Ed.D., *Strong Mothers—Strong Sons*, New York, Henry Holt & Company, 1994.

Chodorow, Nancy, *The Reproduction of Mothering*, Berkeley, Calif., University of California Press, 1978.

Clarke, Jean Illsley, and Dawson, Connie, *Growing Up Again*, San Francisco, Harper & Row Publishers, 1989.

Cline, Foster, M.D., and Fay, Jim, *Parenting with Love and Logic,* Colorado Springs, Colo., Pinon Press, 1990.

———, *Parenting Teens with Love and Logic,* Colorado Springs, Colo., Pinon Press, 1992.

Coburn, Karen Levin, and Treeger, Madge Lawrence, *Letting Go,* New York, HarperPerennial, 1997.

Cole, Thomas R., *The Journey of Life,* Cambridge, England, Cambridge University Press, 1992.

———, and Gadow, Sally A., *What Does It Mean to Grow Old?* Durham, N.C., Duke University Press, 1986.

———, and Winkler, Mary, *The Oxford Book of Aging,* New York, Oxford University Press, 1994.

Coles, Robert, *Erik H. Erikson; The Growth of His Work,* Boston, Little, Brown & Company, 1970.

Coopersmith, Stanley, *The Antecedents of Self-Esteem,* Palo Alto, Calif., Consulting Psychologists Press, 1981.

Covey, Stephen R., *The 7 Habits of Highly Effective Families,* New York, Golden Books, 1997.

Deborah Pryce, "For Ohio Lawmaker, Ill Child Puts Politics in Its Place, Jill Lawrence, *USA Today,* November 17, 1998.

Edelman, Hope, *Motherless Daughters,* New York, Delta, 1994.

Edelman, Marian Wright, *The Measure of Our Success,* Boston, Beacon Press, 1992.

Eisenberg, Arlene; Murkoff, Heidi E.; and Hathaway, Sandee E., B.S.N., *What to Expect When You're Expecting,* New York, Workman Publishing, 1984.

———, *What to Expect: The Toddler Years,* New York, Workman Publishing, 1994.

———, *What to Expect the First Year,* New York, Workman Publishing, 1989.

Erikson, Erik, *The Life Cycle Completed,* New York, W. W. Norton & Company, 1982.

———, *Identity and the Life Cycle,* New York, W. W. Norton & Company, 1959, 1980.

Friday, Nancy, *My Mother My Self,* New York, Delta, 1977.

Fumia, Molly, *Safe Passage,* Berkeley, Calif., Conari Press, 1992.

Galinsky, Ellen, *The Six Stages of Parenthood,* New York, Addison-Wesley Publishing, 1981, 1987.

Gilligan, Carol, *In a Different Voice,* Cambridge, Mass., Harvard University Press, 1982, 1993.

Glenn, H. Stephen, and Nelson, Jane, Ed.D., *Raising Self-Reliant Children in a Self-Indulgent World,* Rocklin, Calif., Prima Publishers, 1988.

Gottlieb, Annie, *Do You Believe in Magic?* New York, Times Books, 1987.

Guttman, David, *Reclaimed Powers*, New York, Basic Books, 1987.

Harris, Judith Rich, *The Nurture Assumption*, New York, Free Press, 1998.

Hedrix, Harville, Ph.D., and Hunt, Helen, M.A., *Giving the Love That Heals*, New York, Pocket Books, 1997.

Hewlett, Sylvia Ann; Ilchman, Alice S.; Sweeney, John J., *Family and Work*, Cambridge, Mass., Ballinger Publishing Company, 1986.

Hochschild, Arlie Russell, *The Time Bind*, New York, Metropolitan Books, 1997.

Hudson, Federic M., *The Adult Years*, San Francisco, Jossey-Bass Publishers, 1991.

————, and McLean, Pamela D., *Life Launch, Second Edition*, Santa Barbara, Calif., Hudson Institute Press, 1996.

Hulbert, Kathleen Day, and Schuster, Diane Tickton, eds., *Women's Lives Through Time*, San Francisco, Jossey-Bass Publishers, 1993.

Kabat-Zinn, Myla and Jon, *Everyday Blessings*, New York, Hyperion, 1997.

Kaufman, Sharon R., *The Ageless Self*, Madison, Wisc., University of Wisconsin Press, 1986.

Kelly, Marguerite, and Parsons, Elia, *The Mother's Almanac, Revised*, New York, Doubleday, 1992.

Kennedy, Alexandra, *Losing a Parent*, San Francisco, Harper, 1991.

Kesler, Jay, *Emotionally Healthy Teenagers*, Nashville, Tenn., 1998.

Krasnow, Iris, *Surrendering to Motherhood*, New York, Hyperion, 1997.

Lamott, Anne, *Operating Instructions*, New York, Fawcett Columbine, 1993.

Leach, Penelope, *Babyhood*, New York, Alfred A. Knopf, 1995.

Lerner, Harriet, Ph.D., *The Mother Dance*, New York, HarperCollins, 1998.

Levinson, Daniel J., *The Seasons of a Man's Life*, New York, Ballantine Books, 1986.

Lidz, Theodore, *The Person; His and Her Development Throughout the Life Cycle*, New York, Basic Books, 1968, 1976.

Lieber, Phyllis; Murphy, Gloria S.; and Schwartz, Annette Merkur, *Stop Treating Me Like a Child*, New York, MJF Books, 1994.

Lindbergh, Anne Morrow, *Gift from the Sea*, New York, Pantheon Books, 1995.

Linkletter, Art, *Old Age Is Not for Sissies*, New York, Penguin Books, 1988.

Maslow, Abraham H., *Toward a Psychology of Being*, New York, Van Nostrand Reinhold, 1968.

May, Rollo, *Existential Psychology*, New York, Random House, 1960.

McClure, Vimala, *The Tao of Motherhood*, Novato, Calif., New World Library, 1997.

McGrath, Ellen, *When Feeling Bad Is Good*, New York, Henry Holt & Company, 1992.

Miller, Alice, *The Drama of the Gifted Child*, New York, Basic Books, 1981.

Miller, Jean Baker, *Toward a New Psychology of Women*, Boston, Beacon Press, 1976, 1986.

Mitchard, Jacquelyn, *The Rest of Us*, New York, Viking, 1997.

Moore, Thomas, *Care of the Soul*, New York, HarperPerennial, 1994.

Moran, Victoria, *Shelter for the Spirit*, New York, HarperCollins, 1997.

Munsch, Robert, *Love You Forever*, Ontario, Canada, A Firefly Book, 1986.

Mussen, Paul Henry; Conger, John Janeway; Kagan, Jerome; and Huston, Aletha Carol, *Child Development and Personality, Sixth Edition*, New York, Harper & Row Publishers, 1984.

Nagel, Greta, Ph.D., *The Tao of Parenting*, New York, A Plume Book, 1998.

Nelsen, Jane, Ed.D., and Lott, Lynn, *I'm on Your Side*, Rocklin, Calif., Prima Publishing, 1991.

Ornish, Dean, M.D., *Love and Survival*, New York, HarperCollins, 1998.

Peterson, Karen S., "Celebrating the Bond between Fathers and Sons," *USA Today*, April 2, 1996, quoting Hanson, Bill, *Father and Son*, New York, Bright Books, 1996.

Pipher, Mary, Ph.D., *Reviving Ophelia*, New York, Ballantine Books, 1994.

Pogrebin, Letty Cottin, *Getting Over Getting Older*, New York, Little, Brown & Company, 1996.

Powell, Douglas H., Teenagers: *When to Worry and What to Do*, New York, Doubleday, 1987.

Price, Susan Crites, and Price, Tom, *The Working Parents Help Book*, Princeton, N.J., Peterson's, 1996.

Roberts, Cokie, *We Are Our Mother's Daughters*, New York, William Morrow & Company, 1998.

Roiphe, Anne, *Fruitful*, New York, Penguin Books, 1996.

Saavedra, Beth Wilson, *Meditations for New Mothers*, New York, Workman Publishing, 1992.

St. James, Elaine, *Simplify Your Life with Kids*, Kansas City, Mo., Andrews & McMeel, 1997.

Schiff, Harriet Sarnoff, *How Did I Become My Parent's Parent?* New York, Penguin Books, 1996.

Schoen, Elin, *Reflections on Parental Development*, New York, Doubleday, 1995.

Sheehy, Gail, *Passages*, New York, E. P. Dutton & Company, 1976.

———, *New Passages*, New York, Random House, 1995.

———, *Understanding Men's Passages*, New York, Random House, 1998.

Spock, Benjamin M., M.D., *A Better World for Our Children*, Bethesda, Md., National Press Books, 1994.

Steinberg, Laurence, Ph.D., and Levine, Ann, *You & Your Adolescent*, New York, HarperPerennial, 1990.

Stevens-Long, Judith, *Adult Life*, Palo Alto, Calif., Mayfield Publishing Company, 1984.

Stoddard, Alexandra, *Mothers: A Celebration*, New York, Avon Books, 1996.

Tracy, Louise Felton, M. S., *Grounded for Life,* Seattle, Wash., Parenting Press, Inc. 1994.

Unell, Barbara C., and Wyckoff, Jerry L., Ph.D., *20 Teachable Virtues,* New York, Perigee Press, 1995.

Viorst, Judith, *Necessary Losses,* New York, Fawcett Gold Medal, 1986.

Wolf, Anthony E., Ph.D., *Get Out of My Life,* New York, Noonday Press, 1991.

Wyckoff, Jerry L., Ph.D., and Unell, Barbara C., *Discipline Without Shouting or Spanking,* Minneapolis, Minn., Meadowbrook Press, 1984.

———, *How to Discipline Your Six-to-Twelve-Year-Old . . . Without Losing Your Mind,* New York, Doubleday, 1991.

Recommended Reading

Albom, Mitch, *Tuesdays with Morrie,* New York, Doubleday, 1997.

Benedek, Therese, M.D., and Anthony E. James, M.D., eds., *Parenthood, Its Psychology and Psychopathology,* Boston, Little, Brown & Company, 1970.

Edelman, Marian Wright, *The Measure of Our Success,* Boston, Beacon Press, 1992.

Friday, Nancy, *My Mother My Self,* New York, Delta, 1977.

Kaufman, Sharon R., *The Ageless Self,* Madison, Wisc., University of Wisconsin Press, 1986.

Kelly, Marguerite, and Parsons, Elia, *The Mother's Almanac, Revised,* New York, Doubleday, 1992.

Lamott, Anne, *Operating Instructions,* New York, Fawcett Columbine, 1993.

Lerner, Harriet, Ph.D., *The Mother Dance,* New York, HarperCollins, 1998.

Lindbergh, Anne Morrow, *Gift from the Sea,* New York, Pantheon Books, 1995.

Miller, Alice, *The Drama of the Gifted Child,* New York, Basic Books, 1981.

Moore, Thomas, *Care of the Soul,* New York, HarperPerennial, 1994.

Ornish, Dean, M.D., *Love and Survival,* New York, HarperCollins, 1998.

Roberts, Cokie, *We Are Our Mother's Daughters,* New York, William Morrow & Company, 1998.

Roiphe, Anne, *Fruitful,* New York, Penguin Books, 1996.

Sheehy, Gail, *Passages,* New York, E. P. Dutton & Company, 1976.

————, *New Passages,* New York, Random House, 1995.

————, *Understanding Men's Passages,* New York, Random House, 1998.

Unell, Barbara C., and Wyckoff, Jerry L., Ph.D., *20 Teachable Virtues,* New York, Perigee Press, 1995.

Viorst, Judith, *Necessary Losses,* New York, Fawcett Gold Medal, 1986.

Wyckoff, Jerry L., Ph.D., and Unell, Barbara C., *Discipline Without Shouting or Spanking,* Minneapolis, Minn., Meadowbrook Press, 1984.

————, *How to Discipline Your Six-to-Twelve-Year-Old . . . Without Losing Your Mind,* New York, Doubleday, 1991.

Index

ABOUT THE AUTHORS

BARBARA C. UNELL is a parent educator and author who has been a columnist for the *Kansas City Star*; writer and host of the nationally syndicated parenting information and radio feature "Kid's Stuff"; and co-founder and editor of many publications, including *Twins* magazine, *Caring Parent,* and *Kansas City Parent.* In 1990, Barbara created the nationally acclaimed, school-based character education program "Kindness Is Contagious . . . Catch It!" and opened the Daniel L. Brenner Family Education Center in 1997. She lives in Leawood, Kansas, with her husband, Robert. Since their twins, Amy and Justin, left for college, Barbara and Robert have become avid Family Remodelers.

JERRY L. WYCKOFF, Ph.D., is a former university professor who is now a psychologist in private practice specializing in working with children and families. He and his wife, Millie, live in Prairie Village, Kansas, and have two grown children. They consider themselves vintage Plateau Parents.

Together, Barbara and Jerry have co-authored four books, including the bestseller *Discipline Without Shouting or Spanking, How to Discipline Your Six-to-Twelve-Year-Old . . . Without Losing Your Mind,* and *20 Teachable Virtues.* Learn more about the 8 seasons of parenthood by visiting the authors' website at www.8seasons.com